✣ Designing Dead Souls

DESIGNING
DEAD SOULS
An Anatomy of Disorder
in Gogol

Susanne Fusso

Stanford University Press   Stanford, California
1993

Stanford University Press
Stanford, California
© 1993 by the Board of Trustees of the
Leland Stanford Junior University
Printed in the United States of America

CIP data appear at the end of the book

To the memory of my parents,
Joseph and Rebecca

Acknowledgments

Robert Louis Jackson, Gary Saul Morson, and Howard Stern have provided valuable advice, criticism, and support at every stage of this project; Priscilla Meyer presided over a collegial atmosphere that made teaching and research mutually beneficial. I would also like to thank the following people for their generous assistance: Irina and Yuz Aleshkovsky, Susan Amert, Julia Bell, Sergei Bocharov, Catherine Ciepiela, Victor Erlich, Donald Fanger, John Feneron, James D. Fusso, Olga Peters Hasty, Ulf Kleven, Alexander Lehrman, Michael Levine, Iurii Mann, Olga Monina, Mary Lou Nelles, D. P. Nikolaev, Mary Pasti, Nancy Pollak, Sergei Semenov, Aleksandra Semenova, George Smalley, Edward and Florence Stankiewicz, Gail Stern, Raja Stern, Helen Tartar, Rachel Trousdale, William Trousdale, Mikhail Andreevich Trubetskoi, Judith Vowles, Duffield White, Robert Whitman, and Julia Johnson Zafferano.

Support was provided by the International Research and Exchanges Board, the National Endowment for the Humanities, and Wesleyan University.

Chapter 4 first appeared in *Slavic Review* 49 (1990): 32–47 (material copyrighted by the American Association for the Advancement of Slavic Studies); a shorter version of Chapter 5 was previously published in *Essays on Gogol: Logos and the Russian Word*, edited by Priscilla Meyer and me (Evanston, Ill.: Northwestern University Press, 1992). The illustration is reprinted from H. Steinhaus, *Mathematical Snapshots* (New York: Oxford University Press, 1969), tables 115–19. I am grateful to *Slavic Review*, Northwestern University Press, and Oxford University Press for permission to reprint this material.

S.F.

Contents

Note on Translations

As readers of Gogol in Russian know, his style is anything but smooth and elegant. He is a peculiar writer whose style abounds with inapt words and phrases, redundancies, and rhetorical excesses. Published translations of Gogol are usually smoothed out and sanitized for general consumption. The translations I have provided here are as literal as possible, so that the English reader can both follow my argument and get a sense of the originality of Gogol's style.

✖ Designing Dead Souls

Nur diejenige Verworrenheit ist ein Chaos,
aus der eine Welt entspringen kann.
                    —Friedrich Schlegel

Introduction

> Diese künstlich geordnete Verwirrung, diese reizende Symmetrie von Widersprüchen, dieser wunderbare ewige Wechsel von Enthusiasmus und Ironie, der selbst in den kleinsten Gliedern des Ganzen lebt, scheinen mir schon selbst eine indirekte Mythologie zu seyn. . . . Gewiss ist die Arabeske die älteste und ursprüngliche Form der menschlichen Fantasie.
>
> —Friedrich Schlegel

In constructing a theory of Nikolai Gogol's art in general and of *Dead Souls* in particular, I have tried as much as possible to let that theory be guided by Gogol himself. In his fiction, his nonfiction, and the complicated dialogue between the two, Gogol suggests a strategy that has proved to be productive for a reading of *Dead Souls*. Throughout his career, but especially in the years 1834–42, Gogol manifests two seemingly contradictory urges: the urge toward order, system, clarity, and wholeness and the urge toward disorder, disruption, obscurity, and fragmentation. The former tends to be expressed through explicit, bald assertion; the latter is expressed more indirectly, not so much stated as embedded in the texture and structure of Gogol's works. The present study, as its title indicates, seeks to make a system, an anatomy, of Gogol's impulses toward disorder and disruption in *Dead Souls* in all their various and distinctive aspects.[1]

To understand the nature of the system that is disrupted, I have turned to Gogol's history writings, where the striving toward order is most fully enunciated. Paradoxically, the explicit tenets of Gogol's historiography, which assert an ideal of order, immutability, fixity, clarity, and wholeness, are scattered throughout *Arabesques*, itself a tortuous, obscure, and motley patchwork of fiction and nonfiction.

To abstract Gogol's historiographical principles from the essays in *Arabesques*, as I do in Chapter 1, is to simplify and diminish one of Gogol's most original works, especially because his historiography is anything but original, borrowed mainly from Johann Gottfried Herder and August Ludwig von Schlözer. The exercise of extrapolating the major principles of Gogol's historiography, though in a sense it does violence to his achievement in *Arabesques*, is necessary to more fully understand what he accomplished in *Dead Souls*, to which those principles provide a key. For the purposes of this study, Gogol's historiographical principles are of interest not as ways of modeling history but as formal structures that are related to analogous structures in his literary works.

The explicit principles of Gogol's historiography suggest ways of defining the modes of disruption that are the source of the peculiar artistic vitality of *Dead Souls*. Gogol's history writing seeks to banish chance and randomness in its quest for the immutable order established by Providence; the plot of *Dead Souls* is generated by the chance disruptions of the plan of its hero, a con man who is most free and exalted when he is most mobile and changeable. Gogol's historical models forbid hypothesis, the filling of gaps in knowledge with guessing; in *Dead Souls* the supreme creative activity is precisely hypothesis, a kind of divination that fills the void of ignorance with graphically imagined details. Gogol's ideal of universal history encompasses the entire world in a "magnificent complete *poema*"; the *poema*, the epic poem, of *Dead Souls* is emphatically incomplete, and it embodies a particular type of Gogolian closure whose earmark is the promise of continuation. Each chapter of the present study examines in detail one of the above versions of disruption. The varieties of disorder prove to have rich ramifications, not limited to questions of imagery and style. In anatomizing Gogolian disorder I have had to explore the mythology of creativity and lying in Gogol; his (at least literary) fear of the family; the relation between the uses of obscurity in *Dead Souls* and the poetry of Russian Sentimentalism, especially Vasilii Zhukovskii's; the status of *Dead Souls* as parable; and the mutually subversive relation between fiction and nonfiction in Gogol.

The final chapter returns to *Arabesques*, this time with the goal of understanding its distinctive structure and the complex interrelations among its fictional and nonfictional components. The intricately digressive and internally fragmentary structure of *Arabesques* is specifically related to early Romantic English garden theory, which reached Russia through translations and enlightened amateurs like Zhukovskii well before the 1830's. The aesthetics of the English garden in turn leads back to the center of *Dead Souls*, to Pliushkin's picturesque garden, where the combination of man's orderly planning and nature's random disruption creates a peculiarly Gogolian "desolate beauty." One of the earliest, and still one of the best, interpreters of *Dead Souls*, P. A. Pletnev, saw in this scene Gogol's entire "theory of the fine arts": "[Here the author] in passing, but with amazing precision, has expounded . . . his entire theory of the fine arts [*teoriia iziashchnogo*]—and in doing so has prepared an answer to his critics and all their remarks on his taste, type of composition, style, ornamentation, and even, as they put it, the lack of finish of his language [*neotdelka iazyka*]. His book is like this garden" (p. 493).

The present anatomy is offered as both explanation and confirmation of Pletnev's wise but gnomically brief observation. My aim is to explore Gogol's own theory of art as expressed most succinctly in the description of Pliushkin's garden, in order to make the desolate beauty of *Dead Souls* more intelligible and more deeply felt.

I

The Comic Plot of History

Der Roman ist aus Mangel der Geschichte entstanden.

—Novalis

It is well known that Gogol failed as a historian. What is not often appreciated is that this failure lies at the heart of his artistic achievement in *Dead Souls*. S. A. Vengerov long ago noted that Gogol's studies in the field of history, carried out in the early 1830's during his tenure as teacher of history at the Patriotic Institute and at St. Petersburg University, were far from unserious or unsophisticated:

In the 1830's the vast majority of historians approached their business exclusively from an external and anecdotal point of view. . . . Gogol is interested in something entirely different. In his notebooks dedicated to "materials on medieval history," he inscribes information drawn from various sources, on superstitions, domestic life, commerce, the situation and role of the Jews, maritime trade, and industry. And when we consider that in the *Arabesques*, little valued in their day, Gogol approaches history from the standpoint of such phenomena as architecture, painting, daily life, and religion, then we must admit that Gogol's approach to history was very profound and speaks less than anything of dilettantism. (p. 152)

Yet it has appeared that the only finished results of Gogol's research are the few essays on history and historiography published in *Arabesques* (*Arabeski*, 1834–35). In fact, Gogol's work on history bore more important fruit, for there is a deep connection between the principles of his historiography and the aesthetic strategies of his fiction.

The Plan of the Creator

In the first historical essay in *Arabesques*, "On the Middle Ages" ("O srednikh vekakh"), Gogol begins by earnestly setting forth the

reasons for the importance of this apparently "barbaric" and "igno-
rant" age. At first glance, this apologia for the Middle Ages strikes a
strange note. We feel that Gogol is polemicizing with someone, but
the context of the polemic is not immediately apparent. The answer
is that he is recapitulating Johann Gottfried Herder's polemic with
Enlightenment historians, who approached historical eras with pre-
conceived notions of inherent worth or worthlessness and for whom
the medieval era was a dark slough in the upward road of progress.
One of Herder's major contributions was the historicism reflected in
Gogol's essay—the insistence on approaching each era on its own
terms without prejudice. The Middle Ages that Gogol describes here
are not Russian but European, with a Teutonic Order, Crusades, and
a cult of chivalry. This European orientation is a reflection of Gogol's
sources, for the underlying principles of his historiography are also
European, primarily Herderian.

The first five books of Herder's *Ideen zur Philosophie der Geschichte
der Menschheit* (Ideas on the Philosophy of the History of Mankind,
1784–91) set forth a conception of the universe that looks through
the chaotic, mutable surface of reality to the eternal laws that lie at
its basis. The divinely sanctioned goal of the investigator's quest is
to uncover this unchanging order:

When I open the great book of the heavens and see before me that immense
palace, which the Deity alone can fill in every part, I reason as closely as I
can from the whole to its parts and from its parts to the whole. . . . If, in
what seems to me the most limited and inconsistent, I find not only traces
of the great creative power but an evident connection of the minutest things
with the plan of the Creator in immensity, the best quality of my reason,
striving to imitate God, will be to pursue this plan and adapt itself to the
divine mind. . . . The power, which thinks and acts in me, is, from its nature,
as eternal as that which holds together the sun and the stars: its organs may
wear out, and the sphere of its action may change, as earths wear away and
stars change their places; but the laws, through which it is where it is and
will again come in other forms, never alter. (pp. 2–3, translation slightly
altered; 13: 14–15; pp. 3–5)[1]

Although Gogol nowhere presents his conception of the universe as
explicitly as Herder does, in his history writing he proceeds from a
similar sense of the rightness of the established order, of an unchanging harmony hidden beneath the motley trappings of human affairs.

In the essay on the Middle Ages, Gogol defines the historian's task as that of seeing through the chaos of temporality:

People have regarded [the history of the Middle Ages] as a pile of dissonant, heterogeneous events, as a crowd of fragmented and senseless movements that have no main thread to combine them into a single whole. In fact, its terrible, unusual complexity cannot help but seem chaotic at first; but look more attentively and deeply, and you will find a connection and a goal and a direction. However, I will not deny that to know how to find all this, you must be gifted with the kind of sensitivity that few historians possess. These few have the enviable gift of seeing and presenting everything with amazing clarity and harmony. (8: 16)[2]

In the climax of Gogol's account of the Middle Ages, the "universal chaos of revolution" is purified and clarified into the single graspable fact of national monarchies, just as the variegated mass of ornament on a Gothic cathedral culminates in the pure, heaven-piercing spire that itself provides the final word of Gogol's essay (8: 25).

What follows from the assumption that there is a divine, immutable order underlying the "temporary forms and images" (8: 27) that meet the eye is that events which seem to be misfortunes or disasters serve a secret purpose in God's plan. Herder points out that Voltaire's lament over the destruction of Lisbon is "very unlike the conduct of a philosopher," almost a blasphemy, because when the elements, "agreeably to the ever-acting laws of nature, periodically rouse and claim their own . . . , what more happens than the eternal laws of wisdom and order require?" (p. 9; 13: 24; p. 18). Gogol sees the "wisdom of Providence" in the despotic power of the popes:

In following the marvelous ways of Providence, one involuntarily bends one's knee: the power of the popes was as it were given intentionally in order that young states would become strong and mature during that time. . . . And as soon as the nations achieved the status to govern themselves, the power of the pope, as if no longer necessary, suddenly wavered and began to collapse, despite all the strong measures and all the desire to support its dying forces. (8: 17–18)

The belief in Providence allows the historian to explain events that seem to be wrong, tragic, or unjust as being "precisely what they *ought to be* as well as what they manifestly *are*."[3] The providential theory of history is not so much a theory as a narrative stance, as Hayden White has pointed out:

The *plot structure* or underlying myth which permitted Herder to bind together the themes and motifs of his story into a comprehensible story of a particular sort was that which has its archetype in Comedy, the myth of Providence, which permitted Herder to assert that, when properly understood, all the evidence of disjunctions and conflict displayed in the historical record adds up to a drama of divine, human, and natural *reconciliation* of the sort figured in the drama of redemption in the Bible. (p. 79)

In the Herderian comic mode, historians do not rest content with recounting events; they must also provide an explanation of the rightness of the events, their secret purpose, the way in which they are, in Gogol's words, "penetrated by the mysterious ways of Providence" (8: 27).

Geography as Destiny

Corollary to the idea that whatever is, is right, is the axiom that every being has its assigned place—in the chain of being from the lowest forms of life to the highest, human, level of terrestrial organization and on the face of the earth, whose landscape shapes and determines the form and character of its inhabitants.[4] Herder analyzes in detail the effect of topography on human character, the way that mountainous regions produce "the spirit of bravery and freedom, when the gentler plains are sunk beneath the yoke of laws, arts and vices" (p. 18; 13: 36; p. 38), the way the open steppes of Asia produce a uniformity of customs and prejudices while the variegated, divided topography of Europe gives birth to a variety of peoples, customs, and arts and a power of influence over other parts of the world (pp. 19–20; 13: 38, 39–40; pp. 42, 45). In the essay "On the Movement of Peoples at the End of the Fifth Century" ("O dvizhenii narodov v kontse V veka"), Gogol characterizes the difference between Central Asia and other parts of the world in terms that, if not identical to Herder's, are clearly indebted to his theory of geographical determinism:

Central Asia is completely opposite from south and southwest Asia, from the African and European shores of the Mediterranean, where the flourishing diversity of nature, of the soil, of products, the mixture of land and sea, the heaps of innumerable islands, capes, and bays, seem to have been created on purpose to quickly develop human activity and intellect. The nature of Central Asia is of a completely different sort: it is monotonous and immeasurable. Its steppes are boundless, somehow enormously flat, resembling a desert ocean nowhere interrupted by an island. The motionless lakes of boundless plains could not arouse any activity. (8: 115)

The title of the (apparently nonexistent) two-volume universal history that Gogol claims in an 1833 letter to be preparing for publication is *Land and People* (*Zemlia i liudi*; 10: 256). The title reflects the importance of place in Gogol's scheme of history: "Geography must explain much in history that is inexplicable without it" (8: 27).

From the premise that topography determines character, Gogol proceeds to a clear political conclusion:

[Geography] must show how the lie of the land influenced entire nations; how it gave them a particular character; . . . how it influenced mores, customs, governments, and laws. Here [students] must see how government is formed: that it is not established entirely by people but is imperceptibly established and developed by the very lie of the land, that therefore its forms are sacred, and a change in them must inevitably call down misfortune on a nation. (8: 28)

Teachers of universal history must not merely impart knowledge but train their students to preserve the existing political order, which in its rightness and sacredness is both modeled on and engendered by the higher, divine order: "[My goal] is to make [my students] firm and courageous in their principles; . . . to make them meek, submissive, noble, indispensable, and necessary comrades of the great sovereign, so that neither in fortune nor in misfortune will they betray their duty, their faith, their noble honor, or their vow to be faithful to their fatherland and to their sovereign" (8: 39). Although Herder does not go so far as Gogol in asserting that forms of government are sacred, for him, too, patriotism is the logical result of the providential worldview. He sees the noblest expression of free will and the human striving for self-determination in voluntary submission to limitation and law: to the bonds of marriage and friendship and the laws of society, to a national loyalty that leads people to defend their homeland with their lives (p. 94; 13: 149; p. 214). It is fitting that human freedom is expressed through submission to law, for free will and intellect are themselves limited by the Omnipotent "and happily limited," so that the stream of human passions may never escape God's restraining hands (pp. 92–93; 13: 147; p. 210).

The Banishment of Chance

Not only Herder but also the two other historians mentioned in *Arabesques*, Johann Müller (1752–1809) and August Ludwig von Schlözer (1735–1809), subscribe to a theory of history that subordinates what White calls the "heaving, tossing ocean of *apparently* casual happening" (p. 70) to the underlying providential order. In letters translated by Gogol's friend and mentor V. A. Zhukovskii and published in the journal *Herald of Europe* (*Vestnik Evropy*) in 1810, Müller exclaims: "God save me from the hateful thought that the world is the product of Chance! No, I believe, I must believe, that a Being, incomprehensible to my reason but adored in my heart, governs the immensity of these worlds."[5] In his outline of universal history, Schlözer asserts that the noblest role of history is to be a servant of religion and that its teachers must be votaries of Divine Providence: "The presentation of particular series of events will lead to the overview of universal events in all of space, the government of the world, and the connection among all things."[6] Gogol's friend the historian M. P. Pogodin (1800–1875), who helped popularize the ideas of Herder and Schlözer in his journal the *Moscow Herald* (*Moskovskii vestnik*, 1827–30), succinctly summarizes the role not just of history but of all scholarship in an 1832 essay, "On Scholarship" ("Nechto o nauke"):

> True scholarship is the depiction of nature in the intellect, the *translation of nature into intellect*. By means of such scholarship, when the intellect reflects in itself the whole world with all its phenomena, all of visible and invisible nature rises to the highest degree of its existence. Man is joined with the world by strong, unbreakable bonds; he adapts it to himself in a sense, becomes one with it. It is as though he stretches out his organs everywhere and lives in the world as in his own body, contemplating God's great laws and lost in the eternal Wisdom. (p. 131)

Like Herder, Schlözer, and Müller, Pogodin believes that the revelation of God's great laws entails the transcendence of chance phenomena: "Not every type of knowledge, even if it is true, belongs in our life and scholarship: for example, everything that pertains to petty, conditional, particular relations, that takes place almost by chance and remains without consequences, does not merit our attention and should be left to those pagans who, not understanding man's higher calling, are bogged down in the abyss of everyday vanities" (p. 132).

To avoid being bogged down in the petty and particular, the historian in the Herderian mode tidies up the messiness of the human personality by dealing not with individuals and their chance variations but with types. In his review of Pogodin's *Historical Aphorisms* (*Istoricheskie aforizmy*, 1836), Gogol refers approvingly to Pogodin's theory of the type: "He was the first among us to say that 'history must create out of the entire human race a single unit, a single person, and present that person's biography through all the stages of his growth'" (8: 191). Herder, too, "views one person as the representative of all humanity," although Gogol sees Herder's concern with types leading to excessive abstraction: "He is a sage in his knowledge of ideal man and of humanity but an infant in his knowledge of man" (8: 88).[7] With Schlözer, however, concern with the species over the individual does not, as with Herder, deprive his exposition of "perceptible forms" ("osiazatel'nye formy"; 8: 88):

He analyzed the world and all the extinct and living peoples, but he did not describe them: he cut the whole world open with an anatomical knife, he sliced it and divided it into massive parts, he arranged and divided peoples in the same way that a botanist distributes plants according to signs with which he is familiar. And from this, one would think that the outline of his history would be too skeletal and dry; but amazingly, it all sparkles . . . with vivid features. (8: 86).[8]

Schlözer himself appears to subordinate the description of vivid features to the project of generalization and assimilation. He speaks of reducing all the states of the earth to a single unit, "i.e. the human race"; he points out that although the collation of world events at first draws the attention to difference and variety, when one takes away "everything fortuitous" from the actors and examines "that which is essential in their actions," universal history "discovers everywhere a striking similarity and resemblance."[9]

In one of the aphorisms quoted by Gogol in his review, Pogodin speaks of the "slender, rotten threads" of individual biographies being woven together to form "the stony fabric of history" (8: 192). In his own essay on the Middle Ages, Gogol advances a similar idea:

> The actions of the individual in the Middle Ages seem completely unaccountable; the very greatest events contrast with each other completely and contradict each other in everything. But their combination into a whole manifests an amazing wisdom. If one may compare the life of a single person with the life of all humanity, then the Middle Ages are the same as the time of a person's education in school. His days flow by unnoticed by the world, his actions are not so strong and mature as the world requires: no one knows about them, but they are the result of passionate impulse and expose all the person's inner movements, and without them his future activity in the sphere of society would not take place. (8: 24)

Just as in Pogodin's scheme egoistic, personal plans—the rotten threads of biography—when added together serve "another higher plan" and achieve permanence and importance, as the stony fabric of history, in Gogol's conception the unaccountability and seeming absurdity of individual actions in the Middle Ages are transformed into amazing wisdom when viewed as a whole. The whole is not equal to the sum of its parts; generalization produces a qualitative change in the meaning of events.

The Expanding Point

The historian who deals in types deals in synecdoche: the whole is asserted to be essentially present in the part. The use of synecdoche is vital to the project of universal history, which must "embrace at once and in a full picture all of humanity" (8: 26), "encompass the whole world and everything living with one glance" (8: 85). In Gogol's sketch of universal history the ruling trope is synecdoche, for the succession of epochs is presented as a series of reductions of all to one: "Cyrus subjected the entire East to his rule. . . . The whole world is divided into Roman provinces. . . . Everything turned into chivalry. . . . The Jesuit order penetrated everything, traveled everywhere. . . . Paris became the capital of the whole world. . . . The Word from Nazareth finally flowed throughout the whole world" (8: 30–35). The same principle is applied synchronically in Gogol's essay on the Middle Ages, as first the pope, then the Crusades, then chivalry is made to stand as the token phenomenon of the age.[10]

The synecdochic generalization serves the intellect as the ascent to a great height serves the vision. For both Gogol and Schlözer, the panoramic view from a height is the metaphorical expression of the universal historian's essential work of generalization:

Gogol	*Schlözer*
First of all, I consider it necessary to present a sketch of the entire history of humanity to my audience in a few powerful words . . . so that they will suddenly take in everything they are to hear; otherwise, they will not grasp the whole mechanism of history so quickly or with such clarity. In the same way, one cannot come to know a city completely by walking through all its streets: for this one must ascend to an elevated place, from which it is all visible, as if on the palm of one's hand. (8: 30)	Only a universal view that takes in the whole transforms a *summa* into a system. One may know all the streets of a city individually and not be able to picture its layout without a map or a view from an elevated place. One may know the changes taking place in various German principalities, counties, sees, and imperial cities without knowing the history of Germany.[11]

The essence of the panoramic view is its power of unification and concentration. Schlözer's short but dense sketch of universal history is so concentrated that, according to Gogol, it equals "entire tomes": "One may compare it to a little window through which, when one places one's eye close to it, one can see the whole world" (8: 86).

Schlözer's book-window is only one embodiment of the central metaphor for the work of integration and unification in *Arabesques*: the expanding point, the monad of concentrated significance. It appears again in the essay on teaching geography: "While listening to [the teacher], the student should look at the place on his map and that little point should, as it were, open up before him and contain in itself all the pictures that he sees in the teacher's speeches" (8: 100). Herder employs a similar image for the understanding of nature's laws: "Everywhere we perceive that Nature must destroy in order to reconstruct, that she must separate in order to recombine. From simple laws, as from ruder forms, she proceeds to the more complex, artful, and delicate: and had we a sense, enabling us to perceive the primitive forms and first germs of things, perhaps we should discover in the smallest point the progress of all creation" (p. 27; 13: 48–49; pp. 58–59). For Gogol the mission of the teacher of universal history and geography is to devise a presentation that, like the expanding point or the panoramic view, makes possible the perception of countless details in a single flash, "so that the world amounts to a single vivid, picturesque *poema*" (8: 99).[12]

The Limits of the Known

The universal historian's ideal of wholeness, which the historian seeks to embody in the expanding point, is necessarily thwarted by a built-in deficiency of historiography: historiography must rely on recorded facts, and facts are not available for all periods of history and all peoples. As Schlözer writes, "It is true that there was history before historians existed, before the art of writing, even before the counting of years; but all this history, at least in relation to Universal History, is only a fragment and a remnant, only darkness and obscurity." Schlözer attempts to salvage the universal aspirations of his project by making the recognition of the historian's gaps in knowledge into a type of knowledge:

Where there is nothing, universal history recounts nothing; or, to put it in a better way, it instructively carries out its task by precisely indicating the limits of the known and the unknown, noting exactly in the universal overview of each period how one people and land after another slowly emerge from the night of oblivion, how for various reasons they sink back into it and in time again come to light, when their history begins to be their own full and authentic one. History does not fill the *emptiness* that necessarily proceeds from this in the chain of events with hypotheses or whimsical theses and imaginings but only indicates that emptiness. It does not authenticate the entirely *unknown* by introducing it into its narration, and still less the obviously *fabulous*. In this way is the history of the world only a collection of fragments, and does it provide precise data only about the smallest part of the globe? But who wants more than this? Just collect what is on hand, arrange it into a system, as much as the fragments can be arranged, and do not grieve over the irretrievable loss of other events of the world.

Schlözer provides an example of this transformation of the negative into the positive: in his listing of the peoples of antiquity, between number seven, the people of Asia Minor, and number nine, the Romans, is number eight, "The Unknown Peoples of the Ancient World."[13]

Schlözer's injunction to the historian not to fill the absence of facts with hypotheses is echoed in a *Moscow Herald* article on Müller: "His love for truth was pure and was not clouded by any sort of hypotheses."[14] Gogol, too, decries the type of historical scheme that is created "in the head, independent of the facts" (8: 27). Reliable sources are required to call forth the truth of history, just as the light of the sun calls forth the "invisible light" in a radiant gem (8: 16). The result of this devotion to the recorded facts is that much of the historian's activity consists of copying, an ascetic renunciation of imagination. When G. P. Georgievskii published Gogol's historical notes in 1908–10, the evidence of Gogol's patient, Akakii Akakievich–like copying out of pages and pages from secondary sources and Russian chronicles astounded those who had regarded him as a dilettante in history.[15] On the basis of Georgievskii's publication, Vengerov awarded Gogol the title Benedictine:

By "Benedictinism," which recalls the colossal folios created by the inspired industriousness of the Western European Benedictines, I mean a love or, rather, a passion for scholarly work as such, almost independent of the results to which it leads. The scholarly laborer by calling is afforded a purely physiological pleasure by the very process of working. It is pleasant to make excerpts, to copy interesting documents; it is pleasant to, as they say, "root around" in one's material, to breathe "the dust of the archives." (pp. 163–164)

The Benedictine copyist need not worry about originality; he deals in that which has already been written. While at work on his history of the Ukraine, Gogol actually claims that he would welcome the news that others were working on the same project, and would wait for them to finish so that he could use their work to make his own history more complete (10: 298).

The Desire to Be Original

Despite his Benedictinism, there are indications in *Arabesques* and in Gogol's letters of 1831–34 that he was not entirely satisfied with the historian-copyist's task. He writes to Pogodin in 1833,

I have just read the Böttiger you have published. It is indeed one of the most convenient and best histories for us. I found some ideas completely similar to mine and therefore immediately got rid of them. This is a bit stupid on my part, because in history inventions are made for the use of all, and it is legitimate to take possession of them. But what can I do—there's this cursed desire to be original! (10: 256) [16]

In the essay on Schlözer, Gogol accords the imagination an independent role that would perhaps have appalled Schlözer himself: "Reading this compressed sketch of the world, you note with amazement that your own imagination burns, expands, and fills everything according to the very same law that Schlözer defined with a single omnipotent word; sometimes it goes even further, because a bold road has been pointed out" (8: 86). In the essay on Ukrainian songs ("O malorossiiskikh pesniakh"), Gogol glorifies folk songs as a historical source that cannot be copied word for word or consulted for hard facts:

The historian must not look in them for indications of the day and date of a battle or an exact explanation of its place or for a faithful communiqué. . . . But if he wants to . . . discover [*vypytat'*] the spirit of a past age . . . , he will be completely satisfied. . . . From [the sounds of the songs] he can guess the past sufferings [of the Ukraine], just as one can find out about a past thunderstorm with hail and pouring rain from the diamantine tears that stud the refreshed trees from bottom to top. (8: 91, 97) [17]

The key word here is *guess* (*dogadyvat'sia*): it signals precisely the operation of filling gaps with hypothesis that Schlözer warns against.

It is not surprising that *Arabesques* contains indications of an antischolarly bent, for the work is not only the summation of Gogol's scholarly work but a farewell to scholarship, a final turn to fiction. Throughout *Arabesques*, the model for the historian is the poet, and the highest honor that can be offered Schlözer is to be praised in the same terms as the supreme poet, Pushkin:

"Schlözer, Müller, and Herder" ("Shletser, Miller, i Gerder")	A Few Words About Pushkin ("Neskol'ko slov o Pushkine")
His style is lightning. (8: 85)	His style is lightning. (8: 51)
He had in the highest degree the virtue of being able to squeeze everything into a small focus and with	[His virtues] consist in an extreme rapidity of description and an unusual skill in signifying an entire

two or three vivid features, often a single epithet, to suddenly signify an event and a people. (8: 85)

object with a few features. His epithets are so distinct and bold that sometimes a single one replaces an entire description. (8: 52)

He destroys [his predecessors] with a single crushing word, and in that single word is combined delight and a sardonic smile at his victim, together with the invincible truth. (8: 86)

In each word there is an infinitude of space; each word is boundless, like the poet. (8: 55)

As Donald Fanger has pointed out, this emphasis on style, which leads Gogol to offer Shakespeare and Walter Scott as the best models for the historian, is clearly meant to remind one of the virtues of his own fiction: "Style is the animating force of all Gogol's texts, the sign of his profoundest originality" (p. 61).

Although Gogol complains that his scholarly style is criticized for being "unhistorically ardent and lively" (10: 294), in the essay "On the Movement of Peoples in the Fifth Century" he admirably emulates the dry, choppy, telegraphic style of Schlözer's outline of universal history.[18] Significantly, *Arabesques* ends not with the final sober, scholarly lines of this essay but with the fictional ravings of Poprishchin, hero of "Diary of a Madman" ("Zapiski sumasshedshego"). Viewed in the context of *Arabesques*, Poprishchin is a parody of the serious historian who appears elsewhere in the work. His quest for and examination of reliable documents (in the form of dogs' letters) travesty the historian's activity; at the end of his researches he announces, "Now I see everything, as if on the palm of my hand" (3: 208; cf. 8: 30). As befits a historian gone mad, he ends by writing himself into history as a "great man," the king of Spain.

Elegant Concord and Stormy Chaos

Gogol abandoned his scholarly career with some rancor, and Poprishchin was not the last of his attempts at parodic revenge on the pretensions of historians. But although he may have abandoned his work in history, it did not abandon him: it bears an important and illuminating relation to his fiction, particularly to *Dead Souls* (*Mertvye dushi*, 1842), the work he began immediately after publishing

Arabesques. Gogol's theory of history, in accordance with that of his German models, is based on the laws of Providence that lie beneath the illusory, aleatory surface of reality; the rightness of established hierarchies, both biological and political; faithfulness to facts and the refusal to fill gaps in knowledge with unfounded hypotheses; and an ideal of universal comprehensiveness. His aesthetic practice, especially as manifested in *Dead Souls*, is based precisely on the negation of these categories of fixity and plenitude and strives toward mobility, the crossing of boundaries and the breaking of rules, fictive invention without regard to facts, and fragmentation. Whereas Gogol's Herderian historiography fixes its gaze on the immutable and incomprehensible order of Providence, *Dead Souls* deeply and multifariously explores the incompetences of experience. In the process, these incompetences are transformed from deficiencies into strategies of artistic empowerment. For Herder, the mutability, obscurity, fragmentariness, and entanglements of human life point beyond their own unsatisfactory nature, proving that clarity and fulfillment must exist beyond the grave; for Gogol the artist, these categories of deficiency become ends in themselves, richly ramified sources of narrative and aesthetic energy.

Herder's proof of the existence of the soul is based on the impossibility of incompletion and contradiction in the perfectly harmonious universe: because only human beings, of all the creatures on earth, almost always fail to complete the higher tasks to which they are assigned in the grand scheme, they must be destined to fulfill their ends in some future state of existence beyond the "exercise ground" of earthly life.[19] The Russian translator of Herder's *Ideen*, apparently afraid that his readers would fail to get the point, inserted his own summary of Herder's proof:

Such is the world as it appears to man in his present organism. Everywhere are phantoms, transmutations, contradictions, impenetrable darkness. In this stormy chaos, where much is begun and nothing finished, man perceives in the distance the dim glimmering of immortality, his sole consolation and hope. The more attentively he meditates, the more he becomes assured that his present state is not the essential and constant one, that it is only the preparatory, infantile age of the immortal. There, in the most perfect state, man will see everything in a different form; many problems will be solved, and many beginnings fulfilled. Instead of chaos, order and harmony will appear; instead of darkness, light will arise. Otherwise, man cannot reconcile God's justice with his own purpose; his innate striving toward knowledge, with the brevity of earthly life. He cannot reconcile the love for elegant concord and justice that is ingrained in him with the incessant disorders of this world, with the constant struggle between mind and feelings. Therefore, hope in immortality has been instilled in man by Nature itself, established by its eternal laws. This is confirmed by Faith and reason. There is a God, He is wise and just, He has invested the thirst for immortality in the human soul—and man is immortal. (pp. 241–42)[20]

Gogol's history writing locates itself in the realm of "elegant concord," "order and harmony," where "many problems are solved and many beginnings fulfilled." In the succeeding chapters I shall demonstrate that the creative energy of *Dead Souls* is released only in the sphere of "phantoms, transmutations, contradictions, impenetrable darkness," the "stormy chaos, where much is begun and nothing finished."

2

Plans and Accidents

Die romantische Dichtart . . . allein ist unendlich, wie sie
allein frey ist, und das als ihr erstes Gesetz anerkennt, dass
die Willkühr des Dichters kein Gesetz über sich leide.

—Friedrich Schlegel

Dead Souls is the story of a disrupted plan. It follows the adventures
of Pavel Ivanovich Chichikov, a rogue who makes the rounds of a
strange assortment of landowners, offering to buy those of their serfs
who have died since the last census. At the climax of the novel Chichikov's purchase of these "dead souls," which until this point has
been kept secret by those who know about it, is made public and
causes a riot of speculation and suspicion in the provincial town.
Chichikov is forced to flee, and as he dozes in his getaway troika we
learn of his childhood and previous life, particularly the series of
outlandish, ultimately failed swindles that has culminated in the
dead-souls scheme. The novel ends with Chichikov fleeing as the
narrator apostrophizes the flying troika, now identified with the fate
of Russia.

The providential historians on whom Gogol modeled himself
strove to overcome chance and mutability in their search for God's
unchanging laws. In *Dead Souls*, chance disruptions of Chichikov's
orderly plan generate the plot of the novel, and creative energy is
centered in those who refuse to remain fixed, who violate laws, rituals, and prescriptions.[1]

The Untypical Type

Universal historians, in seeking to avoid elements of chance and
randomness, resort to synecdoche and generalization. Schlözer

writes that historians should imitate the taxonomist Carolus Linnaeus and offer a *Systema populorum, in classes et ordines, genera et species redactorum.* In *Dead Souls*, Gogol the novelist seems to be doing just that as he introduces each of the major characters:

There is a sort [*rod*] of people who are known by the name of so-so people, neither this nor that, neither Bogdan in the city nor Selifan in the village, as the proverb says. (6: 24)

A minute later the mistress entered . . . one of those grannies, small landowners, who lament over bad harvests. (6: 45)

There are people who have a nasty little passion for playing dirty tricks on their neighbors. . . . Just such a strange passion did Nozdrev also have. (6: 71)

It is well known that there are many such personages in the world, on whose finishing touches Mother Nature didn't waste much time. (6: 94)

The narrator of *Dead Souls* presents each person not merely as an individual but also as the representative of a class or species. At first glance he appears to be employing the historian's technique of maximum generalization in the service of maximum comprehensiveness. If the truth of the generalization is maintained, no scene in *Dead Souls* takes place at a single moment and with individual participants; the scene represents instead a typical transaction that could be repeated in exactly the same way among any of the representatives of the same categories. One could not add together the accidental adventures of a random group of individuals and hope to get a picture of "all Rus'," but when the adventures represent the habitual behavior of entire classes of people, such a comprehensive picture seems much more attainable.[2]

On closer inspection, however, it becomes clear that the narrator is not offering a straightforward generalization: the "slender, rotten threads" of individual biography insistently stand out from the common fabric. The characterization of the class of grannies to which Korobochka belongs develops into a complete life story, down to the last will and testament:

A minute later the mistress entered, . . . one of those grannies, small landowners, who lament over bad harvests and losses and hold their heads cocked a little to the side and in the meantime gather a bit of money in little coarse cotton bags, stowed in their chests of drawers. Into one bag they sort all one-ruble coins, into another half-rubles, into a third, quarter-rubles, although it seems at first glance that there's nothing in the drawers but linen and bed jackets and skeins of cotton and a torn woman's coat, which is to be turned into a dress later, if the old one somehow gets a hole burned in it during the baking of holiday flat cakes and all sorts of Lenten cookies or wears out all by itself. But the dress does not burn and does not wear out; the old lady is thrifty, and the coat is destined to lie for a long time in its torn state and then be passed by last will and testament to her second cousin's niece, along with all sorts of other junk. (6: 45)

The narrator gets so caught up in idiosyncratic detail that the sense of generalization is lost: one would be surprised to find even one other individual of the taxonomic species *matushka Korobochka*.[3]

The narrator's apparent urge toward generalization moves along a temporal axis as well: he presents the given moment as representative of habit or custom, asserting that certain things are usually done or that something always looks the same. The constructions "kak obychno" (as usual), "kak voditsia" (as usual), and "po nashemu obychaiu" (according to our custom), give the impression of endlessly repeated, perfectly predictable actions. The interior and exterior landscapes that Chichikov encounters on his arrival in the town of N. are, according to the narrator, so familiar to the reader as to make description superfluous:

The room was of a familiar type [*izvestnogo roda*], for the inn was also of a familiar type, that is, precisely the kind of inn they have in provincial towns. (6: 8)

The upper story was painted the eternal yellow. (6: 8)

What these common rooms are like, every traveler knows very well. (6: 9)

The houses were of one, two, and one-and-a-half stories, with the eternal mezzanine that provincial architects consider to be so beautiful. (6: 11)

In a word, familiar sights. (6: 22)

As with the characterization of Korobochka, however, these generalized descriptions are filled with details like "a cat who just had kittens," and "a mirror that reflects four eyes instead of two and some kind of flat cake instead of a face"—items that one could hardly expect to always find in every "small wooden tavern" (6: 62).[4] In all

these cases, the narrator pretends to be a historian, banishing the
petty and particular in the service of science, but in fact he is an
artist, more interested in the rotten threads of biography than in the
stony fabric of history.

Even more disturbing than the eruption of absurdly specific detail
into an ostensibly generalized description is the confusion of verb
tenses that one of Gogol's most tenacious critics, O. I. Senkovskii,
seized upon as an indication of his execrable style (1: 226–49). The
grammatical structure of one of the passages singled out by Senkovskii is indeed disturbing:

Kakie byvaiut eti obshchie zaly—vsiakoi proezzhaiushchii znaet ochen'
khorosho: te zhe steny, vykrashennye maslianoi kraskoi . . . ta zhe kopche-
naia liustra so mnozhestvom visiashchikh steklyshek, kotorye *prygali i zveneli*
vsiakii raz, kogda polovoi *begal* po istertym kleenkam, pomakhivaia boiko
podnosom, na kotorom *sidela* takaia zhe bezdna chainykh chashek, kak ptits
na morskom beregu; . . . slovom, vsë to zhe, chto i vezde, tol'ko i raznitsy,
chto na odnoi kartine izobrazhena byla nimfa s takimi ogromnymi grudiami,
kakikh chitatel', verno, nikogda ne vidyval. (6: 9; emphasis added)

(What these common rooms are like, every traveler knows very well: the
same walls painted with oil paint . . . the same smoke-blackened chandelier
with a multitude of little hanging pieces of glass, which *would leap and tinkle*
every time the waiter *ran* along the worn-out oilcloth mats, smartly bran-
dishing a tray on which *sat* such an infinitude of teacups as there are birds
on the seashore; . . . in a word, just the same things as everywhere; the only
difference being that on one painting was depicted a nymph with breasts so
huge that the reader has probably never seen their like.)

The narrator seems unable to make up his mind whether he is describing the class of room known to every traveler, in which case one
would expect verbs in the present tense, to maintain the generalized
character of the description, or the specific room that Chichikov has
just entered, as the verbs in the imperfective past tense would indicate. If the common room were truly identical to all other common
rooms, there would be no point to the narrative project. In moving
from history to fiction, the relative importance of "general" and "particular" is reversed: only the peculiar individual specimen, made possible by chance variation, is of interest to the artist. The common
room differs from all other common rooms not only in its possession
of the buxom nymph, the "sport of nature" whose uniqueness is

immediately negated by the narrator, but in the fact that Chichikov, a character with an unusual and mysterious mission, enters it at the privileged, narrated moment, making that moment, like Korobochka's life story, unique and unrepeatable.[5] As we shall see, the same reversal, which privileges unpredictable chance over an order created by rule, is central to Chichikov's character and career.

The Plot(s) of Dead Souls

The generalized common room has been invaded by chance and randomness, the petty and particular, in the person of Chichikov, who arrives in the town of N. with a scheme in mind, "the main object of his taste and inclinations" (6: 40): he plans to buy for bargain prices, and then mortgage, serfs who have died since the last census, whose owners are still burdened by taxes on the defunct goods. From one point of view the scheme, though fraudulent, is logical and sensible, as orderly as Chichikov's compartmentalized traveling case, whose "plan and inner arrangement" are described in Chapter 3 (6: 55). But the scheme is also a conundrum, expressed through the jarring conjunction of the words *dead* and *soul*, which has a devastating effect on most of Chichikov's interlocutors.[6] The most striking feature of the scheme is its novelty:

Manilov finally heard things so strange and unusual that no human ears had ever heard the like. (6: 34)

[Korobochka] saw that the business would seem to be a profitable one, only it was just too new and unheard-of [*nebyvaloe*]. (6: 52)

"Land sakes! Those are such strange, quite unheard-of goods!" (6: 54)

We learn at the end of the novel that in conceiving the scheme Chichikov considered its strangeness a major virtue: "A glavnoe, to khorosho, chto predmet-to pokazhetsia sovsem neveroiatnym, nikto ne poverit" (And the main thing is, it's good that the object will seem so improbable—no one will believe it; 6: 240).[7]

The narrator appears to give Chichikov credit for the novel itself, as well as for his own highly original plan: "And in such a way was this strange plot [*siuzhet*] composed in our hero's head, for which I do not know if my readers will be grateful, but the author is so grateful that it's hard to express. No matter what you say, if this thought had not come into Chichikov's head, this *poema* would not have seen the light" (6: 240). Chichikov's plot is not, however, identical to the plot of the novel. Strange and unique as it is, it surprises only Chichikov's interlocutors, not Chichikov, its creator. The author-narrator goes Chichikov one better, introducing chance disruptions to the plan that are unforeseen by Chichikov himself. There is a distinct difference between the episodes involving Chichikov's intended destinations and those in which he ends up somewhere by mistake or accident. He plans to visit Manilov, Sobakevich, and Pliushkin; he transacts his business with them; and they recede into the background, not playing any further decisive role in his career. His encounters with Korobochka, Nozdrev, and the governor's daughter are accidental, and all three come to play a fatal instrumental role in Chichikov's crisis.[8]

The Interrupted Journey

According to Iurii Lotman's categorization of "artistic space" in *Dead Souls*, the road becomes the "universal form for organizing space": "All characters, ideas, and images are divided into those that belong to the road, that move and have a direction and a goal, and those that are static and lack a goal."[9] To the latter category belong the citizens of the town of N., who seek to draw Chichikov into their closed, static world. But an intermediate position is occupied by Korobochka, Nozdrev, and the governor's daughter, who belong neither to the road nor to the town: they are neither travelers nor solid citizens, and rather than seeking to fix Chichikov in place, they serve unwittingly to preserve his status as one of Lotman's "mobile characters."

In chapters 1 and 2, Chichikov proceeds according to his plan, methodically gleaning information about the town, selecting the upstanding citizens Manilov and Sobakevich as his first two marks, and making a successful visit to Manilov. Then, on the way from Manilov to Sobakevich, a "powerful clap of thunder" ("sil'nyi udar groma"; 6: 41) signals a storm that, given the coachman Selifan's drunken befuddlement, causes Chichikov to lose his way. Fumbling in the darkness and mud after the carriage is overturned, Chichikov is saved by fate—"Kazalos', kak budto sama sud'ba reshilas' nad nim szhalit'sia" (It seemed as if fate itself decided to have pity on him; 6: 43)—when he is led by the barking of dogs to the home of Korobochka.

Korobochka is not part of the social structure of the town of N.; she is a small landowner so isolated that she has never heard of Manilov or Sobakevich. Although she seems innocuous, her home is filled with what Jerzy Faryno calls the "topological features of the world of sorcery and demons" (p. 615). There is indeed an ominous tone to the description of Chichikov's unplanned visit to Korobochka's all-female realm, where he is deprived of his vision ("his eyes stuck closed as though someone had smeared them with honey"; 6: 45) and then of his protective covering, called "harness" and "armor" rather than "clothes." Against the background of the story "Vii," even the death of Korobochka's blacksmith by spontaneous combustion may be classified with the other topological features of the demonic world that appear in Korobochka's household.

The next interruption in Chichikov's itinerary is his meeting with Nozdrev, who arrives at the inn where Chichikov has stopped on his way from Korobochka to Sobakevich. Nozdrev's first words signal that Chichikov's well-planned route is again about to be inexorably detoured: "'Ba, ba, ba!' vskrichal on vdrug, rasstaviv obe ruki pri vide Chichikova. 'Kakimi sud'bami?'" ("Well, well, well!" he suddenly cried, opening his arms wide at the sight of Chichikov. "What brings you here [lit. "by what fates"]?" 6: 64). And later: "Mizhuev, smotri: vot sud'ba svela: nu chto on mne ili ia emu? on priekhal bog znaet otkuda" (Mizhuev, look, fate has brought us together. After all, what is he to me or I to him? He came from God knows where; 6: 66).

Like Korobochka, Nozdrev is an outsider, not a part of the civilized world of N. In his case, his own behavior has caused his outsider status: "Nozdrev was in a sense a historical personage. No gathering at which he was present could get by without some *histoire*. There would always be some sort of *histoire*: either the gendarmes would lead him by the arm out of the hall, or his own friends would be obliged to push him out" (6: 71). As if to emphasize that the Nozdrev episode is the second link in a fatal chain, certain parallels are drawn between it and the scene at Korobochka's. Just as Korobochka plies Chichikov with sundry esoterically named pastries of which she herself does not partake, Nozdrev provides an array of outlandish liquors but drinks little himself. At Korobochka's, Chichikov awakes to find flies assaulting mouth, nose, and ear; at Nozdrev's he is bitten all night by "some sort of small and very lively insect" (6: 82). In both instances, the host relates an unpleasant dream that Chichikov, either aloud or to himself, wishes intensified: to Korobochka's lament that the Devil appeared to her, he replies, "I'm surprised you don't dream of dozens of them" (6: 54); when Nozdrev tells of having been beaten in his dream, Chichikov thinks, "Yes, it would have been well if they'd skinned you alive" (6: 83).

Chance brings about the visit to Nozdrev, and Chichikov must deal with chance again during the visit, for Nozdrev persists in forcing Chichikov to gamble. Chichikov resists abandoning himself to luck in his dealings with Nozdrev. When Nozdrev proposes to stake the dead-souls bargain on a game of cards, Chichikov refuses to subject himself to "neizvestnost'" (the unknown; 6: 81), although what he really fears is "iskusstvo" (art, skill), the possibility that Nozdrev has marked the cards. Nozdrev's blandishments link "schast'e" (fortune) with the demonic and the feminine, a link that will recur later in Chichikov's adventures:

"Otchego zh neizvestnosti?" skazal Nozdrev. "Nikakoi neizvestnosti! Bud' tol'ko na tvoei storone *schastie*, ty mozhesh' vyigrat' *chortovu propast'*. Von *ona*! ekoe schast'e!" govoril on, nachinaia metat' dlia vozbuzhdeniia zadoru. "Ekoe schast'e! ekoe schast'e! . . . vot *ta prokliataia deviatka*, na kotoroi ia vsë prosadil! Chuvstvoval, chto prodast, da uzhe, zazhmuriv glaza, dumaiu sebe: '*chort tebia poberi*, prodavai, *prokliataia*!'" (6: 81; emphasis added)

("Why unknown?" Nozdrev said. "There's nothing unknown about it! If only *fortune* is on your side, you could win *a hell of a lot* [lit. "the Devil's abyss"]. There *she* is! What good fortune!" he said, starting to shuffle the cards to arouse eagerness. "What good fortune! what good fortune! . . . There's *that damned nine* [fem.] on which I lost everything! I felt that it would sell me out, but anyway I closed my eyes and thought to myself, 'The *Devil take you*, sell me out, *damned one* [fem.]!'")

By imparting the dead-souls secret to the liar and braggart Nozdrev, Chichikov has, despite his caution, already subjected himself to *neizvestnost'*. The ultimate outcome of this indiscretion is foreshadowed in an extended simile that compares Nozdrev, siccing his muscular serfs on Chichikov, to a desperate lieutenant leading a doomed siege on an impregnable fortress: "'Rebiata, vpered!' krichit on, pory- vaias', ne pomyshliaia, chto vredit uzhe obdumannomu planu ob- shchego pristupa" ("Forward, lads!" he cries, carried away, not thinking about how he is harming the already-thought-out [*obdu- mannyi*] plan of the general attack; 6: 86–87). Nozdrev, with similar enthusiasm and lack of malicious intent, is destined to do his part in destroying Chichikov's "obdumannyi plan."

The deus ex machina that saves Chichikov from Nozdrev's beating is both a prosaic policeman arriving to arrest Nozdrev for a previous crime and a miraculous troika descending from the clouds:

Neozhidannym obrazom zviaknuli vdrug *kak s oblakov* zadrebezzhavshie zvuki *kolokol'chika*, razdalsia iasno stuk koles *podletevshei* k kryl'tsu telegi, i otozvalis' dazhe v samoi komnate tiazhelyi khrap i tiazhkaia odyshka razgo- riachennykh *konei* ostanovivsheisia *troiki*. (6: 87; emphasis added)

(In an unexpected manner, *as if from the clouds*, the jingling sounds of *a little bell* suddenly tinkled; there clearly resounded the rumble of the wheels of a cart *that had flown up* to the porch, and even in the room itself there echoed the hard snorting and heavy panting of the overheated *steeds* of the stopped *troika*.)[10]

These panting steeds, though not the airy, incorporeal troika of the finale, also make it possible for Chichikov to escape immediate ret- ribution, to keep moving toward his next fatal encounter.

The meeting with the governor's daughter follows hard upon the escape from Nozdrev. Fleeing from his persecutor, Chichikov shud- ders at the possibility of perishing "like a bubble on the water, with- out any trace, not leaving any descendants, having obtained neither a fortune nor an honorable name for his future children" (6: 89). Again, as on the road from Manilov's, his thoughts are interrupted by a sudden noise above his head, this time the screams of the fright- ened ladies in a carriage with which Selifan collides. The harnesses are inextricably entangled, like the fates of Chichikov and the beau- tiful young lady in the other carriage, the governor's daughter: "vsë pereputalos'" (everything got entangled; 6: 90). The horses submit to the encounter willingly, in a parody of the human courtship rite that will be played out between Chichikov and the governor's daughter later, at the ball: "The dappled steed liked his new acquaintance so much that he didn't at all want to get out of the rut into which he had landed thanks to unforeseen fate; having placed his muzzle on the neck of his new friend, he seemed to be whispering something into his very ear, probably some terrible nonsense, because the new-comer was constantly twitching his ears" (6: 91). Chichikov, too, finds some pleasure in the accidental encounter; although he does not at this point forget "himself and his job and the world and everything in the world" as a twenty-year-old youth might (6: 92), he does fall into a reverie about the young lady, wondering who she is and what might become of her.

The young lady is the daughter of the governor, but like Koro-bochka and Nozdrev, she is something of an outsider. When Chi-chikov meets her, she has just returned from boarding school, a fact that lends significance to the comparison of her oval face to a freshly laid egg (6: 90). Her lack of full-fledged status as one of the town's own means that she is condemned along with Chichikov when his scheme is exposed: "prigovor ee uzhe byl podpisan" (her sentence had already been signed; 6: 171). As he meditates on her, Chichikov seems to realize, at least unconsciously, that he is again submitting to the *neizvestnost'* of chance: "Eto by moglo sostavit', tak skazat', *schast'e* poriadochnogo cheloveka" (This could constitute, so to speak, the *fortune* of a decent man; 6: 93; emphasis added).

Utterance as Event

Each of Chichikov's three chance acquaintances reappears, in re-verse order, in chapter 8, and the new encounters combine to destroy Chichikov's good standing in the town of N. The echoes between Chichikov's first meeting with the governor's daughter and the sec-ond one at the ball in his honor allude to the fateful nature of the encounter. When Chichikov sees the governor's daughter at the ball, the narrator recalls their entanglement: "[On the arm of the gover-nor's wife] was that same little blonde whom he had met on the road while driving away from Nozdrev's, when, because of the stupidity of the coachmen or the horses, their carriages so strangely collided, entangling [*pereputavshis'*] the harnesses, and Uncle Mitiai and Uncle

Miniai undertook to disentangle [*rasputyvat'*] the matter" (6: 166). The reference to the serfs who tried to undo the work of fate and separate the carriages is also to the point; for all their strenuous attempts to disentangle the matter, it was only when left to themselves that the horses began to move. Significantly, the ineffectual Mitiai is likened to "kriuchok, kotorym dostaiut vodu v kolodtsakh" (the hook they use to get [buckets of] water from wells; 6: 91); in a prophetic meditation at the ball, Chichikov avers that women's eyes are "takoe beskonechnoe gosudarstvo, v kotoroe zaekhal chelovek—i pominai kak zvali! Uzh ego ottuda *ni kriuchkom, nichem ne vytash-chish'*" (such an endless polity—just let a man drop into it, and that's an end of him! You won't be able to drag him out of there *with a hook or with anything else*; 6: 164; emphasis added). Immediately after his first meeting with the governor's daughter, he muses that she could be "the fortune of a decent man" (6: 93); his first words upon seeing her at the ball are "chto uzhe imel *schastie* nechaiannym obra-zom poznakomit'sia" (that he had already had the good *fortune* to become acquainted with her in an accidental manner; 6: 167; emphasis added).

The effect that all three of Chichikov's chance acquaintances have on his fate is of a verbal nature. At the beginning of the ball, Chichikov is an active participant in conversation with the ladies. This activity is verbal but has the same consequences as physical labor: so ingenious are the ladies' allegories and allusions that the effort of deciphering them causes sweat to break out on Chichikov's brow. In response to the greeting of the governor's wife, which is so elaborate that the narrator despairs of reproducing it exactly, Chichikov is ready to offer a speech worthy of any hero of the society tales from which her language is taken. Before he can speak, he sees the governor's daughter and immediately loses his grasp of the ladies' language: "Chichikov became so confused that he couldn't utter a single sensible word and mumbled the Devil knows what, which neither Gremin nor Zvonskii nor Lidin would have said under any circumstances" (6: 167). Having forgotten how to speak the language of those around him, he becomes a stranger, a foreigner, an outcast: "Tak i Chichikov vdrug sdelalsia chuzhdym vsemu, chto ni prois-khodilo vokrug nego" (Thus even Chichikov suddenly became alien to everything that was occurring around him; 6: 167). The ladies' attempts to interpret Chichikov's utterances reverse the process of his former efforts to understand theirs: "In certain dry and ordinary words he uttered by chance they found pointed allusions" (6: 171). From their elaborately and intentionally encoded speeches he struggled to extract a morsel of intelligible significance; in his indifferent and absentminded remarks they readily perceive hidden, pithy meanings. The narrator points out that "there are things that ladies won't forgive anyone, no matter who he is" (6: 171). The thing in question is clearly verbal: Chichikov's failure to understand and speak the ladies' language makes them eager to seize upon the hint offered by Nozdrev, the next fatal guest.[11]

The "prenepriiatneishaia neozhidannost'" (most extremely unpleasant unexpectedness; 6: 171) of Nozdrev's appearance at the ball and his utterance of the phrase "dead souls" is called a "vzdornoe proisshestvie" (stupid event; 6: 173). There is an isomorphic relation between *proizoiti* (to occur) and *proiznesti* (to utter, pronounce), which for Gogol becomes an identification. *Proiznesenie*, the utterance of the word, is equivalent to *proisshestvie*, the event. The plot of the "Story of How Ivan Ivanovich Quarreled with Ivan Nikiforovich" ("Povest' o tom, kak possorilsia Ivan Ivanovich s Ivanom Nikiforovichem"), for example, which hinges on the fatal utterance of a word (the epithet "gander," at which Ivan Ivanovich takes offense), is repeatedly labeled *proisshestvie*, beginning with the first line of the tale; the titles of parts II, III, and IV of the story include forms of the verb *proizoiti*.

As in "The Two Ivans," the essence of the *proisshestvie* at the ball is an act of *proiznesenie*: the words that Nozdrev blurts out about the dead souls provide the seeds for a negative reinterpretation of Chichikov's character, a reinterpretation to which the ladies have already become disposed owing to Chichikov's absorption in the governor's daughter and consequent loss of fluency in their verbal code. After Nozdrev's disclosure, Chichikov also loses his former fluency in one of the masculine discourses, that of card playing: "The chairman couldn't at all understand how Pavel Ivanovich, who had so well and, one might say, subtly understood the game, could make such mistakes" (6: 173). The chapter ends with yet another fatal *proisshestvie*:

"V eto vremia na drugom kontse goroda *proiskhodilo* sobytie, kotoroe gotovilos' uvelichit' nepriiatnost' polozheniia nashego geroia" (At the same time, at the other end of town an event *was occurring* that was about to increase the unpleasantness of our hero's position; 6: 176; emphasis added). This event is the arrival of Korobochka, who provides her own narrative, expanding Nozdrev's fragmentary and unreliable disclosure of "dead souls" and making Chichikov's expulsion from town inevitable.

The Realm of Pre-scription

To understand the significance of Chichikov's ostracism, one must understand the world from which he is expelled. By the time Chichikov emerges from his room after three days of illness, the rumors about him have spread throughout the town, and he finds to his dismay that he is no longer welcome in the homes of the social leaders. At the governor's house the porter replies to his demand for an explanation with the words "Takoi prikaz, tak uzh, vidno, sleduet" (That's the order, so obviously that's the way it's supposed to be; 6: 212). It is appropriate that Chichikov's expulsion is marked by the words "tak sleduet" (that's the way it's supposed to be), for the phrase encapsulates the moral system of the town of N. Formed from the verb *sledovat'* (to follow), it is the motto of a town in which behavior is valued only to the degree that it follows the prescriptions of fashion, the laws and rituals of polite society. If we look more closely at the social system of the town, we find that Chichikov's downfall is less an expulsion from paradise than an escape from a sterile realm of slavish adherence to ritual.

The ladies of the town are strict in their observance of their own code: "As far as knowing how to conduct oneself is concerned, to keep a certain tone, to maintain etiquette and a multitude of the most subtle proprieties, and, especially, to observe fashion to its last, smallest details—in this they outstripped even Petersburg and Moscow ladies. They dressed with great taste and drove around town in carriages in the way that the latest fashion prescribed" (6: 158). So extreme is their reverence for fashion and etiquette that a visiting card becomes a "sacred object" for them (6: 158). Chichikov is not long in realizing that within the social structure of the town of N. the men follow the lead of the women, and he sets himself the task of ingratiating himself with the latter. Helped by the rumor that he is a millionaire, he succeeds so well that he receives their highest form of praise: "V mnogikh gostinykh stali govorit' iasno, chto, ko-nechno, Chichikov ne pervyi krasavets, no zato takov, *kak sleduet* byt' muzhchine" (In many drawing rooms they began to say openly that although of course Chichikov was not the handsomest of men, then again he was just what a man *is supposed to be*; 6: 159; emphasis added).

The Russian *predpisanie*, like its English equivalent, *prescription*, is formed from the verb "to write" and the prefix "before." The people of N. act and speak according to prescription, to what has been "written before," and as a result, their conversations have a familiar, repetitive, predictable quality. A typical example is their greeting of Chichikov at the ball: "Pavel Ivanovich! Oh, my God, Pavel Ivano-vich! Most kind Pavel Ivanovich! Most respected Pavel Ivanovich! My dear Pavel Ivanovich! Here you are, Pavel Ivanovich! Here he is, our Pavel Ivanovich! Allow me to embrace you, Pavel Ivanovich! Give him here, let me kiss him a little more firmly, my dear Pavel Ivanovich!" (6: 162). Chichikov himself has mastered the art of re-peating polite and empty phrases, as his conversation with Manilov illustrates (6: 26–28).[12] On his first meeting with the governor's daughter, however, he seems for a moment to recognize the sterility of the prescriptions of society as he meditates on the young girl's fate:

Now she is like a child; everything in her is simple: she'll say whatever comes into her head, laugh whenever she feels like laughing. One could make any-thing of her, she could be a marvel, but she could also turn out to be trash, and she will turn out to be trash! Just let the mammas and aunties get to work on her now. . . . She'll start twirling around according to instructions learned by heart, she'll start racking her brains and trying to figure out with whom and how and how much she should talk, how she should look at whom; every minute she'll be afraid of saying more than she should. (6: 93)

The young, unformed creature of infinite, unpredictable possibilities is doomed to limitation: "She could be a marvel, but she could also turn out to be trash, and she will turn out to be trash."

The Man of Metis

Although he at times recognizes the danger of submitting to the town's "instructions learned by heart," in chapter 7 Chichikov comes close to being initiated, accepted, and fixed in his proper place by the town of N. In this chapter, in which he obtains official bureaucratic sanction for his dead-souls purchases, he displays his intimate knowledge of the administrative code:

He was completely familiar with the rules for filling out forms [*formennyi poriadok*]. (6: 135)

Listen, my good fellows . . . I know very well that all deeds of purchase, no matter what the price, are located in one place, and therefore I beg you to show us the desk. (6: 142)

Chichikov's visit to the administrative offices in chapter 7 is the fulfillment of his promise to Manilov to carry out the dead-souls agreement with punctilious attention to the law: "Ia privyk ni v chem ne otstupat' ot grazhdanskikh zakonov. . . . Ia nemeiu pered zakonom" (I am in the habit of never deviating from the civil laws. . . . I grow dumb before the law; 6: 35).

Chapter 7, in which Chichikov makes his obeisance to law, is saturated with classical allusions—to Zeus, to Vergil, and, repeatedly, to Themis, second wife of Zeus and mother of Order, Justice, Peace, and the Fates.[13] Because of the filthy state of the administrative offices and the seediness of the clerks, the deity is presented in an unflattering way:

Themis received her guests simply, just as she was, in negligée and dressing gown. (6: 141)

One of the rite performers who was right there, who had made sacrifices to Themis with such zeal that both his sleeves had split at the elbows and the lining had long ago come sticking out . . . waited upon our friends as once Vergil had waited upon Dante, and led them to the reception room. (6: 144)

The depiction of Themis as a slattern, whose threadbare devotees are skilled at taking bribes, is an obvious comment on the status of Justice and Order in the town of N.[14] The implicit message is that the eclipse of Themis means the ascendancy of Zeus's first wife, Metis, goddess of cunning intelligence (to which she lends her name)—the kind of intelligence that is the primary quality of the god Hermes, of the *pícaro*, and of the con man Chichikov.

The person of *metis*, whose hypostases include Hermes, Odysseus, the trickster, and Chichikov's closest relative, the *pícaro*, copes with the changeable world by making himself "even more multiple, more mobile, more polyvalent than his adversary." [15] His major tool is a verbal ingenuity that can make the power of language serve his own purposes, whether in commerce or in seduction. Chichikov's ability to adapt his discourse to the style of his interlocutor is a brilliant demonstration of such skill. The duplicity of the man of *metis* is given figurative expression through his association with the crossing of borders, an association that originates in the derivation of the name Hermes from the name for an ithyphallic stone heap used as a boundary marker.

A trace of this ancient link may be found in Chichikov's crowning achievement, securing a job at the border as a customs inspector: "This job had long formed the secret object of his designs. . . . It seemed that fate itself had determined for him to be a customs official" (6: 234–35). [16] The position fate has assigned him is at the edge of the Russian world, within grasping distance of Holland linen and French soap. The verbs in the sentence that immediately precedes the announcement of his triumph emphasize the action of crossing, expressed by the prefix *pere-*: "No perenosíl vsë geroí nash, perenosíl síl'no, terpelívo perenosíl, i—pereshël nakoníets v sluzhbu po tamozhne" (But our hero endured everything, endured strongly, patiently endured, and—finally—passed into a job in the customs; 6: 234).

By Gogol's time the characteristics of the person of *metis* had been appropriated by the *pícaro*, the hero who refuses to remain fixed in the place fate has assigned him. The provenience is clear. Quarreling with his mother in their cave home, Hermes offers his rationale for his roguish behavior: "Better to live in fellowship with the deathless gods continually, rich, wealthy, and enjoying stores of grain, than to sit always in a gloomy cave: and as regards honour, I too will enter upon the rite that Apollo has. If my father will not give it me, I will seek—and I am able—to be a prince of robbers." [17] These words could serve as the motto for the *pícaro*, the robber-prince Captain Kopeikin, or for Pavel Ivanovich Chichikov. The person of *metis* refuses to accept the poverty and obscurity that is his patrimony; if the world will not give him the wealth and honor he feels he deserves, he resolves to seize it by wielding the only weapons he has: his wily intelligence and his verbal virtuosity.

Playing for Peanuts or Breaking the Bank

Themis is the patron of a world of fixity and order that offers no opportunities for people unhappy with their assigned status. Metis is the deity of upward mobility:

The omniscience of Themis relates to an order conceived as already inaugurated and henceforth definitively fixed and stable. Her pronouncements have the force of assertoric or categorical propositions. She spells out the future as if it was already written, and since she expresses what will be as if it were what is, she gives no advice but rather pronounces sentence: she commands or she forbids. Metis, by contrast, relates to the future considered in its aleatory aspect: her pronouncements are hypothetical or problematical statements. She advises what should be done so that things may turn out one way rather than another; she tells of the future not as something already fixed but as holding possible good or evil fortunes; and her crafty knowledge reveals the means of making things turn out for the better rather than for the worse. Themis represents the aspects of stability, continuity, and regularity in the world of the gods: the permanence of order, the cyclical return of the seasons . . . , the fixity of destiny. . . . Her role is to indicate what is forbidden, what boundaries must not be crossed and the hierarchy that must be respected for each individual to be kept forever within the limits of his own domain and status.[18]

The Russia depicted in *Dead Souls* is a society with a rigid, well-defined hierarchy extending from the subhuman serfs up to the tsar, a society so stratified that one speaks differently to a person who owns 300 serfs than to one who owns 500 (6: 49). It is only with the help of Metis, who gives advice on how to take advantage of the unforeseen opportunity, that Chichikov, born to poverty, can hope to make his way up the social ladder.

In his essay "On Khlestakov" ("O Khlestakove"), Iurii Lotman discusses the two possible routes open to the ambitious person in post-Petrine Russia, symbolized by two different ways of playing games of chance:

Service was assimilated to card playing: one could play respectable and placid mercantile games—ombre or Boston—and advance in the service with the help of "moderation and exactness," or one could choose the path of venturesomeness [*azart*] (the career term *sluchái* is a simple translation of the card term *azart*—"*hasard*"), making the risk commensurate with ambition: one could play for peanuts or double the stakes and try to break the bank. (p. 301)

Chichikov's biography, as recounted in the final chapter of *Dead Souls*, consists of an oscillation between these two methods—between a preference for safely, predictably carefully following rules and prescriptions and daringly crossing boundaries and gambling with fate.

Elements of both daring mobility and cautious fixity are present in Chichikov from the beginning. Like the classic *pícaro*, Chichikov is of obscure origin: "Temno i skromno proiskhozhdenie nashego geroia" (Obscure and humble is our hero's origin; 6: 224). The proverb with which one of Chichikov's relatives greets his birth implies not only that he is illegitimate but that he is the son of a wanderer: "Ni v mat', ni v ottsa, a v proezzhego molodtsa" (He resembles neither father nor mother but a passing lad; 6: 224). His early education, however, is oriented toward immobility and obedience, toward following prescription and avoiding the slightest creative departure from expected behavior:

vechnoe siden'e na lavke, s perom v rukakh, chernilami na pal'tsakh i dazhe na gubakh, vechnaia propis' pered glazami: "Ne lgi, poslushestvui starshim i nosi dobrodetel' v serdtse"; vechnyi shark i shlepan'e po komnate khlopantsev, znakomyi, no vsegda surovyi golos: "opiat' zaduril!," otzyvavshiisia v to vremia, kogda rebenok, naskucha odnoobraziem truda, pridelyval k bukve kakuiu-nibud' kavyku ili khvost. (6: 224)

(the eternal sitting on a bench with a pen in his hands and ink on his fingers and even his lips, an eternal copybook phrase before his eyes, "Do not lie, obey your elders, and carry virtue in your heart"; the eternal scraping and shuffling of [his father's] slippers about the room, the familiar but always stern voice saying, "He's started playing the fool again," responding to that moment when the child, bored by the monotony of the labor, would attach some sort of hook or tail to a letter.

The eternal sitting of Chichikov's childhood is ended by a journey, to school in another town, that is the first of his wanderings.

Chichikov's adult career follows a well-defined pattern: he begins by strictly limiting his needs and desires, following rules to the letter, and doing everything *kak sleduet*—as it is supposed to be done. As he becomes established, he begins to relax his self-control and allows himself to break rules in the hope of making a quicker profit than can be gained by playing Boston for peanuts. His daring ventures into illegality are always discovered, however, leading to disgrace, loss of worldly goods, and the necessity of starting again, carefully, in some new career. The movement of his career is expressed as a series of expansions and contractions:

He displayed unheard-of selflessness and patience and the limitation of his needs [*ogranichenie nuzhd*]. (6: 228)

Only here and only now did Chichikov begin to extricate himself [*vyputyvat'sia*] little by little from the severe laws of abstinence and his implacable selflessness. . . . A few excesses began to appear. (6: 232)

And now he decided to begin his career anew, to again rearm himself with patience, to again limit himself [*ogranichit'sia*] in everything, no matter how freely and well he had formerly expanded [*razvernulsia*]. (6: 233)

He was immediately entrusted with a detachment [of guards] and an unlimited right [*neogranichennoe pravo*] to carry out any kind of search. (6: 236)

In a word, he displayed a kind of patience beside which the wooden patience of a German is nothing, for it is already contained in the slow, lazy circulation of his blood. Chichikov's blood, on the contrary, ran high, and he needed a great deal of rational will to throw a bridle on everything that wanted to spring out and have a spree at liberty. . . . Again he shrank [*s"ezhilsia*] . . . again he limited himself [*ogranichil sebia*] in everything. (6: 238–39)

This last self-limitation immediately precedes Chichikov's concoction of the dead-souls scheme. In chapters 1 through 9 of *Dead Souls*, the reader has witnessed Chichikov's gradual reexpansion, which passes its lawful boundaries when he casts his eye on the governor's daughter.

In his analysis of Gogol's artistic space, Lotman recognizes Chichikov's duality, but relegates him to the category of "mobile" heroes: even though his goals are petty and thus the trajectory of his movements is short, he does have goals, he is not hopelessly stationary. "He has not yet congealed, and the author has hopes of turning temporary, egotistical movement into constant, organic movement."[19] In chapter 7 the people of N. strive to encourage Chichikov's impulses toward congealing, toward fixity and limitation; their main hope of doing so is by furnishing him with family ties.

The Tyranny of the Family

Chichikov's obeisance to law in chapter 7 is acknowledged to be a momentous act. When the townspeople congratulate him on acquiring serfs, he responds, "Whatever you may say, a person's goal is not yet defined until he has finally stood with a firm tread on a stable foundation and not on some sort of freethinking chimera of youth" (6: 146). The townspeople, who consider it their "obligation and duty" to solemnize the deal with Chichikov with a drunken celebration at the home of the police chief, encourage his yearnings toward a stable foundation (6: 148). In hopes that he will remain in the town, they promise to marry him off, by force if need be: "'We'll get you married, we'll get you married!' the chairman caught up the cry. 'No matter whether you resist hand and foot, we'll get you married!'" (6: 151). Even when they reconcile themselves to the fact that Chichikov plans to resettle his serfs in Kherson province, they plan a family role for him there: "Pochtmeister zametil, chto Chichikovu predstoit sviashchennaia obiazannost', chto on mozhet sdelat'sia sredi svoikh krest'ian nekotorogo roda ottsom" (The postmaster noted that a sacred obligation lay ahead for Chichikov, that he could become a sort of father among his peasants; 6: 156). Just before the ball where his ostracism is rendered inevitable, Chichikov begins to feel himself in serious danger of getting stuck: "They had come to love him so much that he couldn't see any way of tearing himself out of the town" (6: 157).

Although the townspeople represent the role of husband and father as entirely positive and desirable, elsewhere in *Dead Souls* family obligations are depicted in a less favorable light. The financial demands of wives and children are what lead officials to take bribes (6: 174, 198); throughout his career Chichikov is able to bounce back from each disaster only because "neschastnogo semeistva . . . , k schast'iu, u nego ne bylo" (fortunately, his unfortunate family did not exist; 6: 233); the paterfamilias Kifa Mokievich, who appears in a brief parable at the end of *Dead Souls*, is distracted from his philosophical activity by the need to defend his strongman son Mokii Kifovich (6: 244). Most important, the man with a family, who can count on unquestioning affection and support, is compared to the writer who takes the easy way, buying the affection of the public with prettified depictions of reality; only the "bessemeinyi putnik" (familyless traveler; 6: 134), the writer in the mold of Gogol, has the courage to expose "the whole terrible, staggering mire of petty things that entangle our life" (6: 134). Family ties encumber movement, cloud the moral sense, smother creative freedom.

The work in which Gogol most brilliantly explores the relation between family ties and limitation (creative and otherwise) is *Getting Married* (*Zhenit'ba*, written 1833–35, published 1842). Each of the major characters in the play is attempting to escape the role fate has assigned him or her. Agaf'ia Tikhonovna is determined to escape her class and marry a member of the gentry, rather than the merchant for whom her late father had destined her. The matchmaker Fekla Ivanovna has greater success in the male activity of storytelling than in her own sphere; the hero Podkolesin invites her to his house day after day merely to hear her talk about his possible brides. ("Ia polezhu, a ty rasskazhesh'" (I'll lie down for a while, and you tell me stories; 5: 13). When the suitor Iaichnitsa is told that Fekla has lied to him about the house owned by Agaf'ia, even in his anger he praises her narrative skill: "Zhivopisets, vot sovershennyi zhivopisets! . . . slovom, v romane redko vyberetsia takaia stranitsa" (A painter, a true painter! . . . In short, such a page can rarely be found in a novel; 5: 43). And Podkolesin's friend Kochkarev takes over Fekla's role as matchmaker, despite her warning that "eto ne muzhskoe delo" (it's not a man's business; 5: 16). Later in the play he makes explicit his usurpation of a female role: "Skazhite, chto on mne? rodnia chto li? I chto ia emu takoe—nian'ka, tetka, svekrukha, kuma chto li?" (Tell me, what is he to me—a relative or something? And what am I to him—a nanny, an aunt, a mother-in-law, a godmother or something? 5: 54–55). Although the subject of the play is the attempted betrothal of Podkolesin to Agaf'ia Tikhonovna, the only true betrothal scene takes place between Podkolesin and Kochkarev:

Now, listen, Ivan Kuz'mich [Podkolesin], don't be stubborn, darling. Get married now. . . . Ivan Kuz'mich, now, I'm begging you. If you don't want to for your sake, then at least for my sake. . . . Now, please, don't be capricious, darling! . . . I'm saying this to you not to flatter you, not because you're a head clerk, but simply out of love. . . . Well, do you want me to get down on my knees to you? . . . Well, here I am on my knees! (5: 53)

To the roles of nanny, aunt, mother-in-law, and godmother, must be added fiancée.[20]

The central mystery of the play is Kochkarev's motive for trying to make Podkolesin marry. A clue is contained in Kochkarev's first conversation with Fekla, in which he reproaches her for having found him a wife. She replies, "A chto zh durnogo? *Zakon ispolnil*" (And what's so bad about it? *You carried out the law*; 5: 14; emphasis added).[21] Podkolesin, in his passive but obstinate way, is determined to escape the bonds of this unspecified law to which Kochkarev hopes to subject him. At his moment of triumph, when it seems as if Podkolesin and Agaf'ia are truly betrothed, Kochkarev reveals his joy in Podkolesin's subjection to necessity: "Nu, Ivan Kuz'mich, potselui svoiu nevestu. Ty teper' mozhesh' eto sdelat'. Ty teper' dolzhen eto sdelat'" (Well, Ivan Kuz'mich, kiss your fiancée. You may do it now. You must do it now; 5: 57). Podkolesin himself, in his final monologue, expresses the desire to continue the chain of coercion: "Esli by ia byl gde-nibud' gosudar', ia by dal povelenie zhenit'sia vsem, reshitel'no vsem, chtoby u menia v gosudarstve ne bylo ne odnogo kholostogo cheloveka" (If I were the sovereign somewhere, I would give a command that everyone, absolutely everyone, get married, so that there would not be a single bachelor in my kingdom; 5: 58).

Immediately after saying this, however, Podkolesin realizes the enormity of what he is about to do: "Na vsiu zhizn', na ves' vek, kak by to ni bylo, sviazat' sebia i uzh posle ni otgovorki, ni raskaian'ia, nichego, nichego—vsë koncheno, vsë sdelano" (For your whole life, for all eternity, no matter what, to bind yourself, and then there are no excuses, no repentance, nothing, nothing—everything's finished, everything's done; 5: 58). At the beginning of the play, the word *ekhat'* (to go by vehicle) is used by Kochkarev as a synonym for the decision to marry: his entreaties to Podkolesin to see Agaf'ia take the repeated form *edem* (let's go; 5: 16, 18, 19). At the end of the play,

Podkolesin has the vision to reinterpret the word *ekhat'* as the key to his escape from the eternal bondage of the *zakon* of matrimony: he leaps from the window, leaving the servant Duniashka to announce, "One-s vyprygnuli v okoshko . . . a potom kak vyskochili, vziali iz-vozchika i *uekhali*" (His honor jumped out the window . . . and after he hopped out, he hired a cabbie and *left*; 5: 61; emphasis added). At the moment of Podkolesin's betrothal, Kochkarev has already antici-pated Duniashka's words, as if the male matchmaker had a premo-nition that Podkolesin would be the only character in the play to succeed in escaping the law: "Brak eto est' takoe delo . . . Eto ne to, chto vzial izvozchika, da i poekhal kudy-nibud', eto obiazannost' sovershenno drugogo roda, eto obiazannost'" (Marriage is the kind of thing . . . it's not the same thing as hiring a cab and leaving for somewhere. It's an obligation of a completely different kind; it's an obligation . . . ; 5: 57).[22]

Although Korobochka, the governor's daughter, and Nozdrev cause Chichikov's expulsion from the town of N., thus helping him escape, like Podkolesin, from fixity, binding prescription, and family ties, each of them is presented at various times as a possible family member for him. Korobochka attempts to cast him in the role of her late husband, offering to scratch his feet before bed: "Pokoinik moi bez etogo nikak ne zasypal" (My late husband couldn't go to sleep without it; 6: 47). The governor's daughter, according to town ru-mor, is to be his abducted bride. And Nozdrev places Chichikov in the role of father:

Vy ne poverite, vashe prevoskhoditel'stvo, kak my drug k drugu priviazany, to-est', prosto, esli by vy skazali, vot, ia tut stoiu, a vy by skazali: "Nozdrev! skazhi po sovesti, kto tebe dorozhe, otets rodnoi ili Chichikov?" skazhu: "Chichikov," ei-bogu. (6: 172)

(You wouldn't believe, Your Excellency, how we're attached to each other [lit. "tied to each other"]; that is, simply, if you were to say—here, I'm standing here, and if you were to say, "Nozdrev, be honest now, who is dearer to you, your own father or Chichikov?" I would say, "Chichikov," I swear to God.)[23]

Although Chichikov is horrified by Nozdrev's attempt to cast him in the role of father, he later realizes their closeness: "We all have some inclination to spare ourselves a little bit, and we'd rather try to find some neighbor on whom to vent our spite. . . . Thus Chichikov soon found a neighbor who carried on his shoulders everything that spite could suggest. This neighbor [*blizhnii*] was Nozdrev" (6: 175–76). The word *blizhnii* means "neighbor," but it retains here the connotation "close" (*blizkii*), for Nozdrev serves as an alter ego for Chichikov. Nozdrev expresses Chichikov's daring, mobile side in an exaggerated form. He provides a counterweight to the congealing influence of the town—a model for creatively crossing boundaries and disregarding the rules of society.

Lying as a Type of Inspiration

When Chichikov meets Nozdrev at the inn, Nozdrev is accompanied by his brother-in-law Mizhuev, who provides a striking contrast to Nozdrev—a schematic opposition of tall to short, light to dark, neat to disheveled. The opposition extends to their personalities as well: Mizhuev's phlegmatic politeness versus Nozdrev's brusque familiarity, his steadfast refusal to bet even on a sure thing versus Nozdrev's compulsive gambling, and his pedantic insistence on verisimilitude in the face of Nozdrev's wild fictions. This slavery to verifiable fact is reflected in the pedestrian conversation Mizhuev has with Chichikov, the eternal verbal chameleon: "The two of them at almost the same time expressed satisfaction that the dust on the road had been completely laid by yesterday's rain and that now it was both cool and pleasant to drive" (6: 63–64). Significantly, the predictably truthful Mizhuev is described as "worn-out," whereas the creatively lying Nozdrev is endowed with health and a prodigious "vegetative force" (6: 63, 70).[24]

Nozdrev's disregard for referentiality and rules is what makes him a richer, more surprising character than Mizhuev; his role is assimilated in a number of ways to that of creative artist. When he and Chichikov accuse each other of cheating at checkers, their choice of epithet is ambiguous: "'Da ty, brat, kak ia vizhu, sochinitel'!' 'Net, brat, eto, kazhetsia, ty sochinitel', da tol'ko neudachno'" ("So I see that you, brother, are a storyteller [also "writer"]." "No, brother, it seems that you are the storyteller, but an unsuccessful one"; 6: 85). It is Nozdrev's efforts as a storyteller that interrupt the monotony of the prescribed moves of the game, introducing novel and illicit ways of moving his pieces. Similarly, his absurd lies provide the only varying element in his dialogues with Mizhuev, which follow a conventional format of assertion, denial, and reaffirmation. The rules of the game and the rules of Mizhuev's discourse provide the rigid norm to which Nozdrev's deviations lend flexibility and surprise.

Nozdrev's chronic lying is governed not by any practical aim but by an irrepressible life force: "neugomonnaia iurkost' i boikost' kharaktera" (indefatigable briskness and boldness of character; 6: 71).[25] His compulsive fabrication of absurdities, such as a horse with a pink coat, could hardly serve any calculated purpose. It can be said of Nozdrev, as Gogol says of Khlestakov, the hero of *The Inspector General* (*Revizor*, 1836), that he is "not a liar by trade" (ne lgun po remeslu; 4: 99). In the same discussion of Khlestakov's character, it emerges that lying is not just an "art for art's sake" activity but even a kind of honesty:

On razvernulsia, on v dukhe, vidit, chto vsë idet khorosho, ego slushaiut—i po tomu odnomu on govorit plavnee, razviaznee, govorit ot dushi, govorit sovershenno otkrovenno i, govoria lozh', vykazyvaet imenno v nei sebia takim, kak est'. (4: 99)

(He has become expansive, he's in high spirits, he sees that everything is going well, that people are listening to him—and for that reason alone he speaks more fluently, more freely, he speaks from the heart, he speaks with complete frankness, and when telling a lie, he displays himself precisely in that lie just as he is.)

The paradoxicality of this statement also applies to Nozdrev; despite his constant mendacity he gives an impression of straightforwardness and openness. Unlike Chichikov, he is perceived by everyone "just as he is."[26] His stories about Chichikov are widely accepted not because he deceives the townspeople into trusting him; on the contrary, everyone regards him as an inveterate liar. The rumors are accepted and repeated *as lies*, achieving veracity through repetition.

Despite the exaggerated opposition between the liar Nozdrev and the truth teller Mizhuev, the men are still relatives: a connecting center is provided for the ends of the polarity.[27] Truth and lies are not the exclusive province of Mizhuev and Nozdrev, respectively. When Mizhuev speaks of his wife, he adopts Nozdrev's characteristic expressions "pravo," "poverish," and "kak chestnyi chelovek" (truly, believe me, on my honor), and they give the same impression of protesting too much; one wonders if the reason for his haste to return home is truly the sweetness of his wife and not some more formidable quality of hers. Significantly, Nozdrev's taunt "Rasska-zyvai ei chepukhu" (Tell her some nonsense; 6: 382) was changed to "Vri ei chepukhu" (Tell her some nonsensical lies; 6: 77) in the final version. In fact, every character in chapter 4 lies at one time or another: the landlady lies about the price of the vodka, Porfirii lies about brushing the pup, and Chichikov tries out a succession of lies to allay Nozdrev's suspicions. By the same token, Nozdrev occasion-ally speaks the truth, evoking a mildly surprised confirmation by the narrator: "Osmotreli i suku—suka, tochno, byla slepaia" (They in-spected the bitch, too—the bitch, sure enough, was blind; 6: 73). Nozdrev's most dramatic disclosure, his story about Chichikov and the dead souls, is entirely true. Thus the narrator's cluckings about the willingness of the townspeople to repeat the words of a liar like Nozdrev are not entirely straightforward, for the liar in this case is a prophet leading them to the truth. In general, the condemnation of Nozdrev as a liar cannot be taken seriously against the background of dishonesty established immediately upon Chichikov's entrance into the town, when he encounters the pitiful saplings, no bigger than reeds, described by the town fathers as "shady, wide-branching trees" (6: 11). The narrator who points a finger at Nozdrev in a world such as this seems no better than Pliushkin, who threatens his tor-mented housekeeper with demons' pitchforks for "lying" about a scrap of paper.

Nozdrev is pointedly supplied with virile physical attributes and masculine pursuits and belongings, yet in the fatal trio (Koro-bochka–Nozdrev–governor's daughter) he occupies a central place between two females. Simon Karlinsky's explanation for this seem-ing anomaly is not entirely convincing: "Nozdryov's womanizing is seen as an integral component of his volatile and dangerously violent character. His violence and his involvement with women, perceived as alien and threatening by the peaceable and asexual Chichikov, are what make Nozdryov an unwitting member of the otherwise all-female coalition that causes Chichikov's fall from grace and precipitates his hasty escape."[28] Why should it be precisely his masculine characteristics that make Nozdrev a part of the all-female coalition? On the contrary, his inclusion in that coalition endows him with a metonymic androgyny that is borne out in at least one other important particular. In the townspeople's interpretation of "dead souls" after the ball, the narrator characterizes two opposing parties, the masculine and the feminine. The masculine is marked by indecisiveness and doubt: "Everywhere there appeared the male's shallow nature, a coarse, heavy nature with no talent for housekeeping or for heartfelt convictions, a nature of little faith, lazy, filled with constant doubts and eternal fear" (6: 192). Lacking the imagination to invent an explanation of "dead souls," the men associate the phrase with two recent events concerning covered-up deaths; the details have already been supplied for them by history itself. The connection between Chichikov and the events remains doubtful and obscure. The women, in contrast, quickly and confidently concoct a finished picture, which derives its details from the clichés of Gothic and Sentimentalist fiction. The men concentrate on "dead souls," the women on the abduction of the governor's daughter. In the townspeople's minds the two components of the mystery are irreconcilable:

> I na kakoi konets, k kakomu delu mozhno pritknut' eti mertvye dushi? i zachem vmeshalas' siuda gubernatorskaia dochka? Esli zhe on khotel uvezti ee, tak zachem dlia etogo pokupat' mertvye dushi? Esli zhe pokupat' mertvye dushi, tak zachem uvozit' gubernatorskuiu dochku? (6: 190)

> (And for what end, to what matter, can you attach these dead souls? And why has the governor's daughter gotten mixed up with this? If he wants to carry her off, then why buy dead souls for it? But if he wants to buy dead souls, then why carry off the governor's daughter?)

Only Nozdrev incorporates both dead souls and the abduction into his story, which evinces none of the tentativeness peculiar to the masculine party: "This was decidedly a person for whom there existed no doubts at all: and, noticeably, there was as much firmness and self-confidence in his assumptions as there was instability and timidity in theirs" (6: 208). Nozdrev's union of the main concerns of the male and female parties is especially fertile: while the divided parties must borrow their details from history and pre-scribed fiction, respectively, his arise spontaneously:

Tut on i spokhvatilsia bylo, vidia, chto solgal vovse naprasno i mog takim obrazom naklikat' na sebia bedu, no iazyka nikak uzhe ne mog priderzhat'. Vprochem, i trudno bylo, potomu chto predstavilis' sami soboiu takie interesnye podrobnosti, ot kotorykh nikak nel'zia bylo otkazat'sia. . . . Podrobnosti doshli do togo, chto uzhe nachinal nazyvat' po imenam iamshchikov. (6: 209)

(Here he was about to catch himself, seeing that he had lied completely in vain and might in this way bring disaster on himself, but he could no longer hold his tongue at all. It was difficult anyway, because such interesting details arose all by themselves and were quite impossible to refuse utterance to. . . . The lies were so detailed that he had already begun to call the coachmen by name.)

Nozdrev's interrogators allude to his uniting of male and female in the proverb with which they dismiss him: "I vse soglasilis' v tom, chto kak s bykom ni bit'sia, a vsë moloka ot nego ne dobit'sia" (And everyone agreed that no matter how you struggle with a bull, you still won't get milk out of him; 6: 209). Nozdrev's appropriation of both male and female peculiarities is yet another manifestation of his imperialistic disregard for boundaries and rules. As he says when showing Chichikov the edge of his property: "Vsë, chto ni vidish' po etu storonu, vsë eto moe, i dazhe po tu storonu . . . vsë eto moe" (Everything you see on this side, all that is mine, and even on that side ... all *that* is mine; 6: 74).[29]

For Nozdrev, the kernel of truth contained in the phrase "dead souls" blossoms into a full-blown invention, whose details proliferate "sami soboiu" (all by themselves). This impulse is the same one that caused the narrator in his youth to imagine the details of the home life of every passerby and that inspires his runaway similes. In all these cases the imagination conjures a world of vivid details that are impossible to refuse, although they could not possibly be verified by the senses. Nozdrev's irrepressible invention recalls the "divinatory power" exalted by Friedrich Schlegel in the *Dialogue on Poetry* (*Gespräch über die Poesie*, 1800) as one of the poet's most important dormant faculties: "Alles Denken ist ein Diviniren, aber der Mensch fängt erst eben an, sich seiner divinatorischen Kraft bewusst zu werden" (All thinking is a divination, but man is only now beginning to realize his divinatory power; 2: 363).[30] In *Dead Souls* the boundary between liar and artist is nearly as meaningless as the boundary

marking the edge of Nozdrev's property. As Gogol says of Khlestakov's lying, "Eto voobshche luchshaia i samaia poeticheskaia minuta
v ego zhizni—pochti rod vdokhnoveniia" (This is in general the best
and most poetic moment in his life—almost a type of inspiration;
4: 100).

The Cheater's Sure Thing

There is a moment in *Dead Souls* when even the blooming, vital
Nozdrev appears to be tired and spent: "Dazhe iskhudal i pozelenel"
(He had even become gaunt, and his skin had turned greenish; 6:
208). The moment is important, for it illustrates a central ambivalence in the psychology of the Gogolian cheater. Nozdrev has sacri-
ficed his health temporarily to the task of preparing a marked deck
of cards: "The business required great attentiveness: it consisted in
choosing a single deck out of several tens of dozens of cards, the
most precise deck, on which one might rely as on the most faithful
friend" (6: 208). The cheater, who disrupts the prescribed rules of
the game, seeks to establish his own rigid, predictable order in its
place. It is no coincidence that Nozdrev loses his vitality at this moment, for in seeking to control the vagaries of chance he is forsaking
his own realm of surprise and creative unpredictability.

The most important text for the psychology of cheating in Gogol
is the play *The Gamblers* (*Igroki*, written 1836–42, published 1842).
Nozdrev's reliable deck of cards makes its appearance here as the
"zapovednaia kolodishka" (precious little pack; 5: 66) in the possession of Ikharev, whom fate brings together at an inn with a gang of
even more skilled cheaters. So valuable is his deck, obtained "by
sweat and labor" (5: 66), that he has given it a name, Adelaida
Ivanovna.

In encouraging the young would-be hussar Glov to gamble with
his father's money, Ikharev's new companions exalt risk taking as the
highest virtue:

Natural'no, odno iz dvukh: libo vyigraesh', libo proigraesh'. Da v etom-to i
delo, v riske-to i est' glavnaia dobrodetel'. A ne risknut', pozhalui, vsiakii
mozhet. Naverniaka i prikaznaia stroka otvazhitsia, i zhid polezet na kre-
post'. (5: 87)

(Naturally, it's one or the other: either you'll win or you'll lose. And that's the point: the main virtue consists precisely in risk. Of course, anybody can *not* take a risk. When there's no risk, even a petty clerk will get daring, and a Yid will attack a fortress.)

Despite this stirring speech (which is part of a masquerade designed to con Ikharev), the gamblers themselves refuse to submit to *neiz-vestnost'*—the unknown. Their cheating is based on hard-earned skill ("iskusstvo"), the product of assiduous practice "ot let gibkogo iu-noshestva" (from the years of pliant adolescence; 5: 73), and is designed to ensure a predetermined, intended result.

Throughout the play the joys of gambling are set against family responsibilities, as first the elder Glov is urged to play ("Otecheskie chuvstva sami po sebe, a karty tozhe" [Fatherly feelings are one thing, and cards another]; 5: 82), and then the younger is encouraged to abandon his father for the risk-loving hussars ("Da zachem tebe ekhat' k ottsu? ne nuzhno!" [Why do you have to go to your father? There's no need!]; 5: 91). But the success of the gamblers' scheme is itself dependent on the concept of duty and responsibility, on the ties that bind: it hinges in the end on Ikharev's being constrained by the "ties of comradeship" ("uzy tovarishchestva"; 5: 96). With an amazing naïveté that equals Chichikov's ill-advised confidence in Nozdrev, he allows his newfound friends to abscond with his capital, leaving him holding a worthless promissory note.

When Ikharev realizes that he has been deceived, his reaction seems paradoxical at first—the con man calls upon the protection of the law:

Ikharev. . . . K pravosud'iu! k pravosud'iu!
Glov. Pomilui, ne imeesh' nikakogo prava.
Ikharev. Kak! ne imeiu prava? Obvorovat', ukrast' den'gi sredi dnia, moshen-
    nicheskom obrazom! Ne imeiu prava? Deistvovat' plutovskimi
    sredstvami! Ne imeiu prava? . . . Budete vy znat', kak obmany-
    vat' doverie i chestnost' dobrodushnykh liudei. Zakon! zakon!
    zakon prizovu! (5: 100)

(*Ikharev.* . . . To justice! To justice!
Glov. Excuse me, but you don't have any right.
Ikharev. What! I don't have the right? They can rob me and steal my money
    in broad daylight by means of a swindle! I don't have the right?

They can operate with knavish methods! I don't have the right? . . . I'll teach you to deceive the trust and honesty of good-hearted people. The law! the law! I will call upon the law!)

In fact, this reaction is fully consonant with Ikharev's character: he is not a risk taker but an artisan, who relies on his skill and his precious deck as on a crutch. Before the swindle is revealed, Ikharev deceives himself as to his true character, aligning himself with those who play *azartom* (in a venturesome way), who either break the bank or themselves in one day:

Eshche poutru bylo tol'ko 80 tysiach, a k vecheru uzhe dvesti. A? Ved' eto dlia inogo vek sluzhby, trudov, tsena vechnykh sidenii, lishenii, zdorov'ia. A tut v neskol'ko chasov, v neskol'ko minut—vladetel'nyi prints! (5: 97)

(This morning I had only 80,000, and in the evening I've already got 200,000. Eh? For someone else this would represent an age of service and labors, the price of eternal sitting, deprivations, loss of health. But here in a few hours, a few minutes—I'm a sovereign prince!)

If one takes this speech at face value, then in his disillusioned monologue at the end of the play Ikharev seems to be revising and reversing his life's philosophy:

Tol'ko i lezet tomu schast'e, kto glup, kak brevno, nichego ne smyslit, ni o chem ne dumaet, nichego ne delaet, a igraet tol'ko po groshu v boston poderzhannymi kartami! (5: 101)

(The only person who has good luck is the one who's dumb as a post, doesn't understand anything, doesn't think about anything, doesn't do anything, and only plays Boston for pennies with secondhand cards!)

This revelation is not a reversal but a recognition of Ikharev's true character: his life of sweat and labor in pursuit of the cheater's sure thing has in fact been not *azart*—venturesomeness—but playing Boston for pennies.[31]

Chichikov, like his "neighbor" Nozdrev, combines elements of both the daredevil and the Boston player. He is the schoolboy forced to eternally copy his father's *propis'* (model phrase) and the inventor of the original, unheard-of *sujet* of *Dead Souls*. The realm of Themis—where, as in Herder's cosmology, everything is fixed in its proper place—is a reassuring and safe one; no wonder even cheaters attempt to establish their own mirror image of it. But it is less attractive to people who have been fixed at the level of a petty clerk rather than at the level of a sovereign prince; for them, the mobility and change fostered by Metis offer a more attractive, if more dangerous, field of activity. Disruption attains its highest expression, however, only when, as in Nozdrev's best moments, it is divorced from the desire for personal profit and becomes pure creativity, "a type of inspiration." Chichikov's dead-souls plan transcends its egotistical purpose only when it is itself disrupted for the higher purposes of the author. The entwining of the slender threads of Chichikov's biography with those of Korobochka, Nozdrev, and the governor's daughter turns out to be less an entanglement than a liberation, setting him free from the binding, limiting power of prescription and family ties.

3

The Uses of Obscurity

Пора [Жуковскому] иметь собственное воображенье и крепостные вымыслы.

— A. S. Pushkin to P. A. Viazemskii

Здесь только в первый раз видишь поэзию крепостного человека.

— N. V. Gogol to V. A. Zhukovskii

In his outline of universal history, Schlözer warns the historian against filling gaps in knowledge with hypothesis. In *Dead Souls*, such gaps become the space in which imagination comes into its own, unfettered by facts. The world of the Russian muzhik and the world of the dead, both realms of the mysterious and the unknown, are united in *Dead Souls*. The result is not only a liberation of the faculty of creative hypothesis in the characters and readers of the novel but also an opportunity for Gogol to revise the project of early Romanticism in a highly original manner.

Fashion and Aphasia

When the lady pleasant in all respects and the simply pleasant lady meet to discuss the dead-souls mystery, their first topic of conversation is the latest fashions. Their rhetoric recalls the unique status accorded Chichikov's dead-souls *siuzhet* (plot) itself:

It's so enchanting that you simply can't express it in words. Just imagine, little stripes so narrow—*as narrow as the human imagination can conceive.* . . . In a word, *incomparable!* One may decidedly say that *there never was anything like it on earth.* . . . Well, now, be amazed. Just imagine, bodices have gotten even longer, there's a little protruberance in front, and the front rib *com-*

pletely passes all bounds. . . . Truly, when you imagine what lengths fashion sometimes goes to . . . *it's like nothing on earth* [*ni na chto ne pokhozhe*]! (6: 180–81; emphasis added)

This rhetoric of originality and boundary crossing is, however, a mask, for fashion belongs squarely in the ladies' realm of prescription and predictability. It represents not the creation of something new but the cyclical repetition of old forms ("iubka vsia sobiraetsia vo-krug, kak byvalo v starinu fizhmy" [the skirt is gathered all around, like the farthingales of olden times]; 6: 181); it is a matter not of individual inspiration but of mass adherence to certain patterns (*vykroiki*) passed from hand to hand and copied. Fashion leaves no latitude for individual taste: one who knows the code can predict its realization, as the narrator predicts the color of the parlor walls: "Obe damy otpravilis' v gostinuiu, razumeetsia, golubuiu" (The two ladies proceeded into the parlor, which was, of course, light blue; 6: 180).

In the conversation of the two pleasant ladies, which initiates the flood of rumors, a strict hierarchy of creative skills (with Nozdrev as an absent member) is established. Sof'ia Ivanovna (the simply pleas-ant lady) is at the mercy of her friend for a possible explanation of "dead souls," because "ona umela tol'ko trevozhit'sia" (she knew only how to become alarmed; 6: 184). Anna Grigor'evna (the lady pleasant in all respects) provides the story of the abduction of the governor's daughter, but beyond that her imagination cannot carry her, and she fails to provide the "further details" demanded by her friend: "Ona ne umela lgat': predpolozhit' chto-nibud'—eto drugoe delo, no i to v takom sluchae, kogda predpolozhenie osnovyvalos' na vnutrennem ubezhdenii" (She didn't know how to lie. To suppose something—that's a different matter, but then only if the supposi-tion was based on an inner conviction; 6: 188). Her failure to lie is a failure of divinatory power; deprived of that "type of inspiration," she cannot provide the details that it would be beyond Nozdrev to withhold.

There is a continuum in *Dead Souls* that extends from the world of the Russian muzhik "up" to the world of upper-class ladies. In general, the higher one goes on this scale, the more limited become the creative possibilities of language. The language of the serf is powerfully illustrated by Chichikov's encounter with a muzhik who responds to his inquiry about Pliushkin with a concise characterization:

"Oh! the patched, the patched!" the muzhik exclaimed. A noun was also added to the word *patched*, and a very felicitous one, but one that cannot be used in genteel conversation, and therefore we will omit it. One may, however, guess that it was very aptly put, because Chichikov, although the muzhik had long been lost from sight and they had traveled very far ahead, was sitting in his carriage, still grinning. (6: 108)

The language of the muzhik is marked by terseness, a high concentration of meaning per word, no flinching from impropriety, and a characteristic Russianness. The language of the ladies of the town of N. is the direct opposite: for them, the demands of propriety make it virtually impossible to assign a precise and pithy name to anything.[1]

The ladies' moral code is based on the preservation of an appearance of propriety, while adultery itself is acceptable as long as it is not named. Without *proiznesenie*—utterance—the *proisshestvie*, or event, carries no weight:

Esli zhe mezhdu nimi i proiskhodilo kakoe-nibud' to, chto nazyvaiut *drugoe-tret'e*, to ono proiskhodilo vtaine, tak chto ne bylo podavaemo nikakogo vida, chto proiskhodilo. (6: 158)

(If, however, something did happen of the kind that is called "a thing or two," then it happened in secret, so that it did not appear that it had happened among them at all.)

Their demand for propriety in language leads to elaborate periphrasis and euphemism, such as "etot stakan nekhorosho vedet sebia" (this glass is behaving itself badly; 6: 159), for "etot stakan voniaet" (this glass stinks).[2] They "improve" the Russian language by replacing half of its words with French ones, which may be obscene as long as they are French.

The ladies' language is oriented toward the avoidance of direct naming through the use of euphemism. One reason for this is the supposedly ineffable subtlety of the phenomena of high society. The ladies' dresses at the ball are "takikh blednykh, blednykh modnykh tsvetov, kakim dazhe i nazvan'ia nel'zia bylo pribrat' (do takoi stepeni doshla tonkost' vkusa)" (of such very pale fashionable colors that one could not even choose names for them [such a level had subtlety of taste reached]; 6: 163); Chichikov despairs of capturing the delicacy of the ladies in words ("nichego ne peredash'" [you won't be able to convey anything]; 6: 164); and perhaps the supreme symbol of the false cleansing action of Western civilization, Chichikov's French soap, cannot be named—"kak ono nazyvalos', bog vedaet" (God knows what it was called; 6: 234).

The impotence of the ladies' language is infectious; the narrator, in particular, is overcome by aphasia when he approaches their realm:

> It would not be out of place to make the further remark that Mrs. Manilov . . . but I admit, I'm very afraid of speaking about ladies. (6: 26)

> The ladies of the town of N. were . . . no, I can't do it at all; indeed I feel a certain timidity. (6: 157)

The narrator's fear of speaking about women is expressed in a metaphor of impotence, which somehow escaped the notice of Karlinsky: "Dazhe stranno, sovsem ne podymaetsia pero, tochno budto svinets kakoi-nibud' sidit v nem" (It's rather strange—my pen won't rise at all, as though there were some sort of lead in it; 6: 158).[3] As much a linguistic chameleon as Chichikov, the narrator couches his description of the ladies' discourse *in* that discourse, lacing his account with such macaronisms as "prezentabel'ny" and "mankirovka" (6: 158; French *présentable* and *manquer* with Russian suffixes).

The Marvelous Expression of the Russian Muzhik

The language of the muzhik contrasts vividly with the ladies' language of euphemism and macaronism: here the resources of the Russian language are expanded to the utmost in finding names for a staggering variety of phenomena. From 1841 to 1844, Gogol kept a notebook in which he jotted information on peasant life, usually lists of names and terms, most of it provided by P. M. Iazykov.[4] This notebook fills 41 pages in volume 7 of the Academy edition of Gogol's works, but aside from a few scattered expressions, only two of these lists made their way into part I of *Dead Souls*. These lists, of dog types and dog nicknames, were incorporated into chapter 4, which describes Nozdrev's estate. This chapter has as a basic motif the "natural" language invention of the Russian peasant, in tacit contrast to the "artificial," macaronic invention of upper-class ladies. The central figure of the chapter, Nozdrev, is an adept at both types (yet another manifestation of his disregard for boundaries, here the boundaries of class and gender).

In a previous version, the sentence introducing Nozdrev's dogs is a rather simple one:

Voshedshi v etot dvor, uvideli tam Razboia, Razora, Naletku, Krasotku, Ptitsu, Zmeiku, kotorye, pustivshi mel'nitsami khvosty, pobezhali vo ves' galop k nim na vstrechu. (6: 378)

(On entering this yard, they saw Robbery, Destruction, Raider, Beauty, Bird, and Snakelet, who, having set their tails going like windmills, were running at full gallop to meet them.)

Supplemented by the information from Gogol's notebook, this sentence expands into a series of lists: types of dogs, types of colors of dogs, and dog nicknames.[5] The list of nicknames illuminates Gogol's method of using data like those in his notebooks. Very seldom does he copy the data verbatim; instead, he deduces the morphological patterns used in the coinages and constructs his own words on their analogy, in imitation of the "natural" process of language growth. In this case, he realized that his initial conjecture about the predominant pattern of dog nicknames (feminine diminutives of nouns) did not ring true and that a more characteristic form is the imperative verb. This realization is noted in the text: "Tut byli vse klichki, vse povelitel'nye nakloneniia" (There were all the nicknames, all the imperative moods; 6: 73). Also added to the final version of the passage is the esoteric word for tails "zovomye u sobacheev pravílami" (called rudders by dog fanciers; 6: 73). Another dialect term is introduced to name a part missing from Nozdrev's mill: "verkhnii kamen', bystro vrashchaiushchiisia na veretene, porkhaiushchii, po chudnomu vyrazheniiu russkogo muzhika" (the upper stone that turns rapidly on the spindle, the "flutterer," according to the marvelous expression of the Russian muzhik; 6: 73–74). The use of the adjective *marvelous* here is instructive, for in Gogol's works it is the frequent attribute of natural light, usually in opposition to the "magical" action of artificial light. As with natural and artificial light, natural and artificial language invention are associated with native Russian and foreign influences, respectively.

It is appropriate that unfamiliar, technical, and dialect terms form an integral part of this novel, because Gogol's first major work, *Evenings on a Farm near Dikan'ka* (*Vechera na khutore bliz Dikan'ki*, 1831–32), began with a list of such words ("slova, kotorye v knizhke etoi ne vsiakomu poniatny" [words in this little book that are not intelligible to everyone]).[6] The lists of words in *Evenings*, however, were provided with definitions in a facing column and thus fulfilled their stated function. In *Dead Souls*, even when the lists are scrupulously copied from the notebooks, the definitions are omitted, so that readers are forced either to imagine their own definitions or to concentrate on the phonological aspects of the words. In one instance, Gogol includes the word *skaldyrnik* and a modified form of its definition ("chelovek, kotoryi so vsego khochet vygodu skhvatit'; plevu s g[...] sodrat'" [a man who wants to seize a profit from everything; to scrape the coating off shit]; 7: 326) but separates the two, never making the connection explicit.

Only twice does Gogol offer footnotes defining unfamiliar words, specifically invented words, in the text (in a way reminiscent of "Vii," that "colossal creation of the common people's imagination"; 2: 175). The first instance glosses Nozdrev's epithet "fetiuk," one of his many untranslatable but vivid coinages (6: 77). The second explains the muzhiks' cry in chapter 5, "On koriachitsia, kak koramora!" (He's bucking like a koramora! 6: 91).[7] Thus the two footnotes honor Nozdrev, whose vocabulary, as Karlinsky notes, "shows the greatest verbal invention and variety," and the common people, whose verbal ingenuity is celebrated at the end of chapter 5 of *Dead Souls*.[8] Yet Nozdrev's conversation is also laced with macaronic French expressions, such as "samaia subtil'naia siuperfliu" (the most subteel superfliu; 6: 75). On his lips even the effete French phonemes seem to partake of his "neugomonnaia iurkost' i boikost' kharaktera" (indefatigable briskness and boldness of character; 6: 71).

The paean to the Russian word at the end of chapter 5 is inspired by the apt but unprintable epithet assigned to Pliushkin by the laboring serf. In its published version, the passage celebrates the power of the muzhik's coinage to withstand upper-class efforts at "ennobling" it:

Vyrazhaetsia sil'no rossiiskii narod! i esli nagradit kogo slovtsom, to poidet emu v rod i potomstvo, utashchit on ego s soboiu i na sluzhbu, i v otstavku, i v Peterburg, i na krai sveta. I kak uzh potom ni khitri i ni oblagorazhivai svoe prozvishche, khot' zastav' pishushchikh liudishek vyvodit' ego za naem-nuiu platu ot drevnekniazheskogo roda, nichto ne pomozhet: karknet samo za sebia prozvishche vo vsë svoe voron'e gorlo i skazhet iasno, otkuda vyle-tela ptitsa. (6: 109)

(The Russian nation expresses itself powerfully! and if it rewards someone with an apt word, then that word will accompany him within his family and among his posterity; he will drag it with him throughout his career and into retirement, to St. Petersburg and to the ends of the earth. And no matter how he schemes and tries to ennoble his nickname, even forcing little scribblers for hire to trace it from an ancient princely family, nothing will help: the nickname will of its own accord caw at the top of its corvine lungs and state clearly where the bird has flown from.)

The creative history of this passage, which in its initial form conveys precisely the opposite message, reveals a vacillation in Gogol's conception. The passage appears in an unusually wide variety of forms in the existing drafts and thus was apparently still being reworked at a late stage of composition. In the earliest surviving version (1836–39), the power of the serf's coinage is denied. Although the common people may assign names and nicknames "sovershenno protivopolozhnye tem, kotorye daet pri kreshchenii pop" (completely opposite of those that the priest gives at christening; 6: 301), and these names cannot be used in polite society, they eventually undergo a process of ennobling so that their original indecency is imperceptible: "*Some*, for instance, *might not know* that there are people among us who have risen to the first ranks and who bear such names that at first one was ashamed to utter them in the company of ladies. Now, however, even ladies utter them—and it's all right" (6: 301; emphasis added). This process is subsumed under a universal process to which everything is eventually subjected: "Tak vsë na svete nakonets oblagorazhivaetsia!" (Thus everything on earth is finally ennobled! 6: 303).

In the next version (1840–41) Gogol offers a dramatization of the ennobling process. In a drawing room "of a subtle pearly color," a newly created statesman takes every opportunity to mention his ancient and noble lineage and even produces a genealogy for his guests' perusal. By force of this repeated assertion of the antiquity of his name, his guests take up the same refrain and even go a step further, finding intrinsic beauty in the name itself. The narrator then reveals the secret of its origin: "A mezhdu prochim etoi familiei, takoi priiatnoi dlia proiznosheniia, podarili roditelia Petra Nikolaevicha krepostnye muzhiki okruzhnykh dereven'" (And by the way, this name, so pleasing in the pronunciation, was bestowed upon Petr Nikolaevich's sire by the serfs in the neighboring villages; 6: 413–14).

This passage was replaced in the same manuscript by a passage very close to the final version, in which the efforts at ennobling the given epithet are to no avail:

I kak uzh potom ni khitri i ni oblagorazhivai etu svoiu familiiu, kak ni vstavliai v seredinu erchiki bol'shie i malye, kak ni pribavliai okonchaniia na *v* i *n*—nichto ne pomozhet. . . . rokovaia familiia postoit sama za sebia i skazhet iasno, iz kakogo gnezda vyletela ptitsa. (6: 412)

(And no matter how you later scheme and try to ennoble this name of yours, no matter how you stick large and small *iers* [Cyrillic letters] into the middle of it, no matter how you add endings with *v* and *n*—nothing will help. . . . The fatal name will stand up for itself and state clearly from which nest the bird has flown.

One could see this as a duel between the common people and the upper classes, in which the weapon is the power of language. In Gogol's earlier conception, the manipulation of public opinion by the presumptive nobility is just as powerful as the christening power of the people. The later conception is more in keeping with the rest of the novel: the further one moves from polite urban society, the more original, apt, and powerful is the coinage of names.[9]

The Divinatory Power

Just as the narrator is infected with the sterility and euphemism of the ladies' discourse, so, too, may those who come in contact with the Russian serf be temporarily endowed with linguistic potency. The laconic Sobakevich becomes a poet when expounding the qualities of his dead muzhiks:

Chichikov otkryl rot s tem, chtoby zametit', chto [karetnika] Mikheeva, odnako zhe, davno net na svete; no Sobakevich voshel, kak govoritsia, v samuiu silu rechi, otkuda vzialas' rys' i dar slova. (6: 102)

(Chichikov opened his mouth to note that [the coachmaker] Mikheev had nevertheless long left this earth; but Sobakevich had, as they say, been empowered in his speech and thus was endowed with liveliness and the gift of language.)

Chichikov, in turn, is inspired soon after this to perform a feat of imagination, meditating on Sobakevich's previous life and on how he might have turned out had he been raised in St. Petersburg "according to fashion" (6: 106).

It is only later, at the beginning of chapter 7, that contiguity with the world of the serfs inspires Chichikov's most visionary and creative moment. Having written up the deeds of purchase with the lists of names of the serfs he has bought, Chichikov begins to see the human beings behind their graphic representation:

When he then looked at these little sheets—at the muzhiks, who had indeed once been muzhiks, had worked, plowed, gotten drunk, driven carriages, deceived their masters, or perhaps had simply been good muzhiks—a strange feeling, incomprehensible to himself, overcame him. Each of the little entries seemed to have its own particular character, and it was as if the muzhiks themselves took on their own character thereby. . . . All these details lent an appearance of freshness [svezhesti]: it seemed as if the muzhiks had still been alive just yesterday. (6: 135–36) [10]

Prompted by details given in the lists or remembered from his conversations with the owners, Chichikov begins to guess at the lives and deaths of the serfs he has bought, spinning miniature biographies and, in one case, an entire dramatic dialogue. The fate of Maksim Teliatnikov is determined in Chichikov's mind not by given data but by the proverb associated with his occupation: "drunk as a cobbler" (6: 136). The gnomic statement provides Chichikov with all the authority he needs, and he embroiders the story boldly, without the disclaimers ("chai," "mozhet byt'" [methinks, perhaps]) that accompany his other hypotheses: "I know you, I know you, my lad; if you like, I'll tell your whole story" (6: 136). Sometimes the graphic shape of the name is used as an emblem of the serf's physical nature and ultimate fate, as in the case of Petr Savel'ev Neuvazhai-Koryto ("Ekh kakoi dlinnyi, vo vsiu stroku raz"ekhalsia" [Oh, what a long (also "tall") one; he's stretched over the whole line]; 6: 136), bisected in the middle of the road by a passing wagon train.[11]

Despite Chichikov's refusal to buy female serfs ("V zhenskom pole ne nuzhdaius'" [I have no need of the female sex]; 6: 107), Sobakevich has slipped in Elizaveta Vorobei, "disguised" as a man through a change of desinence: "Elizaveta" becomes "Elizavet"." The narrator speaks of this disguised graphic representation as if it were a disguised human being: "Kak ona zabralas' tuda, neizvestno, no tak iskusno byla propisana, chto izdali mozhno bylo priniat' ee za muzhika" (How she had gotten in there he didn't know, but she was so skillfully inscribed that from a distance one could take her for a muzhik; 6: 137). As if to emphasize that all women, even female serfs, are excluded from the linguistically creative world of the Russian muzhik, Elizaveta Vorobei is denied a hypothesized biography; possessing only a graphic manhood, she is given only a graphic death: "He disregarded it and crossed her out right then and there" (6: 137).

Finally, in a double act of imagination, the narrator takes over: he imagines what Chichikov must be imagining about the runaway serf Abakum Fyrov on the basis of what "any Russian" must think under the circumstances. He poses two alternatives: "What was he pondering? Was he pondering the fate of Abakum Fyrov, or was he just pondering for its own sake, as any Russian must ponder, no matter what his age, rank, and circumstances, when he begins to think about the revelry of a free life [*shirokoi zhizni*]" (6: 139). The two alternatives merge into one as the narrator describes Fyrov's free life on the barges in the present indicative without disclaimer. The move from the hypothetical to the declarative, from Chichikov's voice to the narrator's, transforms Fyrov from a name into as "authentic" a character as any other.

Chichikov's meditation on the hypothetical lives of the dead and runaway serfs is immediately preceded by a moment of regression to youth: "Having forgotten his staidness and his proper middle age, he executed two little leaps about the room and very adroitly smacked his own backside with the heel of his foot" (6: 135). Throughout this novel, which is centered on the middle-aged, the phantom of youth appears periodically with varying symbolic weight. At times characters who make foolish mistakes are compared to children (6: 82, 210); youth is associated with political freethinking (6: 146, 151); the schoolboy is the paradigm for the sinner surprised by retribution (6: 189, 235); and the recurrently appearing "twenty-year-old youth" is a spectral character who, unlike Chichikov, is capable of forgetting himself and his petty interests when smitten by female beauty (6: 92, 94, 131). Youth, in short, is associated with the mobile, flexible, changeable, incautious, visionary aspects of the world of *Dead Souls*. The narrator's admonition to the reader to avoid the fate of the hardened miser Pliushkin makes it clear that whatever the disadvantages of youthful ardor, it is more human than elderly caution: "Even today's fiery youth would recoil in horror if one showed him a portrait of himself in old age. When you emerge from your soft young years into stern embittering manhood, take all your human impulses [lit. "movements"] with you on your journey. Do not leave them on the road: you will not be able to pick them up again!" (6: 127). When Chichikov is finally struck dumb by the beauty of the governor's daughter, herself compared to a "toy" (6: 169), he is likened to a man "who has remembered that he has forgotten something" (6: 167): he has recovered the twenty-year-old youth's capacity to forget—not a handkerchief or money but his own egotistic aims. It is not surprising that on leaving the town where he was temporarily carried away by this "toy precisely carved out of ivory" (6: 169), Chichikov looks back as on a childhood memory: "Gorod N. kak budto ne byval v ego pamiati, kak budto proezzhal on ego kogda-nibud' davno, v detstve" (The town of N. seemed never to have been in his memory, as if he had passed through it long ago, in childhood; 6: 222).

Toward the end of *Dead Souls*, the narrator desires to deny in himself the capacity for self-forgetfulness:

Neprilichno avtoru, buduchi davno uzhe muzhem, vospitannomu surovoi vnutrennei zhizn'iu i svezhitel'noi trezvost'iu uedineniia, zabyvat'sia podobno iunoshe. (6: 223)

(It is unseemly for the author, who has long been a grown man, educated by a rigorous inner life and the refreshing sobriety of solitude, to forget himself like a youth.)

At the beginning of chapter 6, however, the sobriety of the adult narrator is shown to be the opposite of refreshing. Here the capacity of youth to forget itself and open itself to the world leads to the kind of visionary hypothesis that the muzhiks inspired in Chichikov. The narrator laments his loss with the words "O moia iunost'! O moia svezhest'!" (Oh, my youth! Oh, my freshness! 6: 111).[12] What he has lost is the capacity and inclination for divination and hypothesis. When he was young, the sight of people on the street used to lead to an attempt to guess their lives based on the scanty evidence available:

If a district clerk passed by, I would fall to pondering: Where is he going, to a party at the home of one of his colleagues or straight home? (6: 110)

I would wait impatiently for the gardens that were blocking the view [of the manor house] to part and for it to appear with its entire exterior—then, alas, far from vulgar—and from the house I would try to divine what the landowner himself was like. (6: 111)

In both cases the process of divination leads to precise little scenes full of detail and color. The narrator claims to have irrevocably lost this curiosity and vision: "Now I approach every unfamiliar village with indifference, and I look with indifference at its vulgar exterior; . . . and my motionless lips preserve an apathetic silence" (6: 111). At the end of the novel, however, it emerges that *Dead Souls* itself is the product of a similar operation of divination, carried out not even from the vantage point of a passing carriage but from miles away, in a different country: "Rus'! Rus'! vizhu tebia, iz moego chudnogo, prekrasnogo daleka tebia vizhu" (Rus'! Rus'! I see you; from my marvelous, beautiful faraway place I see you; 6: 220).[13] The obsessive questions addressed to Rus' in the ensuing passage are more characteristic of the wildly hypothesizing, curious youth than of the sober, indifferent, silent man.

Chichikov's reverie about Sobakevich, his fantasies about the dead and runaway serfs, and the narrator's youthful conjectures all share a peculiar grammatical and rhetorical structure, which might be called the rhetoric of forking paths. It consists of the presentation of two or more possibilities, couched in the form of questions, some of them brief and some of them expanded into whole narratives. Some examples:

Were you already born a bear [*rodilsia li ty uzh tak medvedem*], or were you made into a bear by life in the backwoods, by grain sowing and petty bother with the muzhiks, and through all this did you become what they call a fist-person [*chelovek-kulak*]? (6: 106)

Grigorii Try-to-get-there-you-won't-get-there! What kind of person were you? . . . Did you give up the ghost on the road [*na doroge li*], or did your own friends knock you off because of some fat red-cheeked soldier's wife, or did the gauntlets stuck in your belt and your troika of squat but strong little steeds catch the fancy of a forest tramp, or, maybe, did you yourself, lying on the sleeping bench, start thinking and thinking and all of a sudden drop in to a tavern, then right into an ice hole, and vanish into thin air? (6: 137)

I would try to divine [*ugadat'*] what the landowner himself was like: Was he fat [*tolst li on*], and did he have sons [*synov'ia li u nego*] or a whole sextet of daughters, with their ringing maidenly laughter, their games, and the eternal little sister, the beauty, and were they dark eyed [*chernoglazy li oni*], and was he himself a jolly fellow [*vesel'chak li on sam*] or as gloomy as the last days of September, and did he look at the calendar and talk about rye and wheat, so boring for young people? (6: 111)

The same rhetoric of forking paths appears in an impassioned apostrophe to the year 1834, which Gogol wrote at the end of 1833, when he was still undecided about his true vocation. Here the two paths are represented by St. Petersburg, the site of his debut as a fiction writer, and Kiev, where he hoped to become a professor of history:

Tainstvennyi neiz"iasnimyi 1834 god! Gde oznachu ia tebia velikimi trudami? Sredi li etoi kuchi nabrosannykh odin na drugoi domov, gremiashchikh ulits, kipiashchei merkantil'nosti, etoi bezobraznoi kuchi mod, paradov, chinovnikov, dikikh severnykh nochei, blesku i nizkoi bestsvetnosti? V moem li prekrasnom, drevnem, obetovannom Kieve, uvenchannom mnogoplodnymi sadami, opoiasannom moim iuzhnym prekrasnym, chudnym nebom, upoitel'nymi nochami, gde gora obsypana kustarnikami s svoimi kak by garmonicheskimi obryvami i podmyvaiushchii ee moi chistyi i bystryi moi Dnepr. (9: 17)

(Mysterious ineffable 1834! Where will I mark you with great works? Among this pile [*sredi li etoi kuchi*] of houses thrown one on another, of roaring streets, seething commerce, this hideous pile of fashions, parades, clerks, savage northern nights, glitter, and base insipidity? In my [*v moem li*] beautiful, ancient, promised Kiev, crowned with many-fruited gardens, engirdled by my southern, beautiful, marvelous sky, by intoxicating nights, where the mountain is bestrewn with bushes and harmonious precipices, washed by my pure and rapid Dnieper.)

Reading this passage, one has no trouble in choosing the more attractive prospect. The tipping of the semantic scales toward Kiev and historical scholarship was an unsuccessful attempt to influence fate, however, for the university position did not come through, and Gogol soon abandoned the writing and teaching of history. Beneath the apparent favor shown to Kiev in this fragment, moreover, is a deep ambivalence, because by using the rhetoric of forking paths—the rhetorical structure in which Chichikov and the narrator of *Dead Souls* couch their most creative flights of divination—Gogol in a sense demonstrates that he has already made his choice in favor of imaginative literature.

An enigmatic but provocative notebook jotting by Novalis addresses the relation between the divinatory power and history writing. It begins: "Good fortune is talent for history, or fate. The feeling for events is the *prophetic*—and good fortune is the *divinatory*—instinct. There is such a thing as a divinatory inclination. The novel arose out of a deficiency of history [*Der Roman ist aus Mangel der Geschichte entstanden*]. It presupposes, for poet and reader, a divinatory, or historical, feeling and inclination" (3: 667–68). According to Novalis, the deficiency of history resides in its inherent incompleteness—history must be incomplete unless it is narrowly defined as the history of a specific science, art, human life, or national constitution. Histories of broader, more indefinite entities like nations or eras cannot be complete because there can never be enough sources to make an exhaustive account possible. The breach caused by the impossibility of achieving wholeness in a historical account is filled by art: "The novel is, as it were, *free history*—as it were, the mythology of history. (Mythology here in my sense, as free poetic invention, which symbolizes reality in multifarious ways, etc.)" (3: 668).

In *Dead Souls* Gogol illustrates what happens when the divinatory inclination is freely exercised by the scholar, offering a wicked lampoon of "learned dissertations":

First the scholar sidles up like an uncommon groveler, he begins timidly, moderately, he begins with the humblest inquiry: Could it have been from here [*ne ottuda li*]? Could this country have gotten its name from this corner of the globe [*ne iz togo li ugla*]? Or: Might this document belong [*ne prinadlezhit li etot dokument*] to another, later period? Or: Might we understand this nation as being this other nation [*ne nuzhno li pod etim narodom razumet' vot kakoi narod*]? He immediately cites ancient authors right and left, and as soon as he sees some allusion or something that just seems to him to be an allusion, he gets bolder and picks up speed, he converses intimately with the ancient authors, asks them questions and answers them himself, completely forgetting that he began with a timid supposition; it already seems to him that he can see it, that it's clear—and the dissertation is concluded with the words: "So this is how it was, this is the nation that is meant, this is the viewpoint from which one must look at the subject!" Then it is proclaimed from the lectern, and the newly discovered truth goes tripping off into the world, picking up followers and admirers along the way. (6: 188)

This passage is not just an expression of Gogol's bitterness at his failure as a historian; it points to one of the reasons for the failure. When applied to historical documents, the exercise of the divinatory power can, as in this case, become a fraudulent activity. Gogol had the divinatory inclination but was constrained by the necessity of making his imagined details correspond to reality as it had been recorded. He could not settle for the necessary incompleteness of history; it became clear that his divinatory power could only be used in "free history." To paraphrase Novalis, the novelist arose out of the deficiency of the historian.

The Unknowable Souls

For Gogol the novelist, gaps in knowledge offer a liberating and productive space for divination. He, as well as his hero Chichikov, might well join in Kifa Mokievich's cry "Glasnost'-to—vot beda!" (Public knowledge—that's the trouble! 6: 244). For both Gogol and Chichikov, withholding information is what preserves the validity and interest of their respective plots. Chichikov, himself an obsessive gatherer of information, is safe only as long as he remains essentially unknown to the townspeople. The author, too, needs for Chichikov to keep the secret of his character as long as possible. The narrator periodically drops mysterious hints not only about Chichikov's coming actions within the novel but also about the projected continuation of the novel beyond its published version, thus keeping the reader guessing, forcing the reader to divine what might follow.

The title *Dead Souls* accords with the author's need for mystery and obscurity. From all angles the title remains an enigma: as metaphysical paradox, as promise of a ghost story, but perhaps most powerfully in its literal sense, as "dead serfs." Near the beginning of the novel the narrator proposes to acquaint the reader with Chichikov's two serfs, Petrushka and Selifan, "although, of course, they are not such outstanding characters but are what are called secondary or even tertiary characters and even though the chief events and mainsprings of the *poema* are not fixed on them and actually just touch and lightly hook on them here and there" (6: 19). The statement is disingenuous, for serfs are central to the novel: they figure in the title, they form the core of Chichikov's scheme, and by the end of the work they have achieved a prominent position in the narrator's conception of the mission of Russia. Thus it is all the more striking that the narrator really possesses no information about their inner life:

What was he thinking when he was silent. . . . God knows, it's hard to know what a house serf thinks while the master gives him an admonition. (6: 20)

Selifan . . . scratched the back of his head for a long time. What did this scratching signify? . . . God knows, you won't be able to divine it [*ne ugadaesh'*]. Scratching the back of the head means a lot of different things to the Russian people. (6: 215)

In each instance the narrator does make an attempt to divine the answer to his question, reminding us that divination flourishes in those spaces where "only God knows."

For Gogol's narrator, characters, and readers, the inner life of the serfs is unknown and unknowable for a number of reasons, the most compelling of which is that their subhuman status as commodities makes them as much a different species as the horses, dogs, and poultry that surround them. Moreover, the serfs with whom the novel is most centrally concerned are dead, hence doubly unknowable. To the degree that *Dead Souls* derives narrative energy from the hypotheses that proliferate around the unknowable dead, it might be regarded as a relative to the murder mystery. Murder mysteries are concerned with divination and forking paths: in the best of them, the reader is given a chance to participate, not only in the most obvious and perhaps least satisfying sense of discovering who the murderer is. More important is the reader's composition of phantom plots: on the one hand, the reader may be allowed to resurrect the victim, reconstructing his or her character on the basis of information disclosed during the investigation; on the other, with each new suspect the reader involuntarily imagines how and why the murder might have happened if this person was the murderer. The endings of mysteries are always disappointing because the reader's phantom forking paths are closed off, leaving only the author's path, inevitably less rich and surprising than the individual's flights of divination.

The Heavenly Language of Premonition

Gogol's decision to make "dead souls" the mysterious core of his novel does not arise in a vacuum but bears a complex relation to the aesthetics of early Russian Romanticism, particularly as embodied in the work of Gogol's friend and mentor V. A. Zhukovskii. In 1840 Gogol signed a letter to Zhukovskii with these words: "Vash i do groba, i za grobom, i po etu storonu, i po tu storonu zhizni Gogol'" (Yours to the grave and beyond the grave, on this side and on the other side of life, Gogol; 11: 283). This closing is rather a literary than a personal homage, for Zhukovskii's major theme is the theme of this world and that world, "zdes' i tam" (here and there), the boundary between and interpenetration of the worlds of the living and the dead.

Zhukovskii signaled his taste for the thematics of the grave early in his career, in an 1807 epistle to A. I. Turgenev:

> Во всем внимаю я знакомый смерти глас.
> Зовет меня … зовет … куда зовет? … Не знаю;

Но я зовущему с волнением внимаю;
Я сердцем сопряжен с сей тайною страной,
Куда нас всех влачит судьба неодолима;
Томящейся душе невидимая зрима—
Повсюду вестники могилы предо мной.

(1: 82)

(In everything I hearken to the familiar voice of death.
It calls me, calls . . . whither does it call? I know not;
But I hearken to the caller with emotion;
My heart is linked to that secret land
To which inexorable fate pulls us;
The invisible is visible to my languishing soul—
Everywhere the harbingers of the grave are before me.)

This *dvoemirie* (system of two worlds), borrowed from early German and English Romanticism, permeates Zhukovskii's work from beginning to end, dictating both the themes of his original works and his choice of material to be translated from Western European literature. The motif of the revenant, the lover who returns from beyond the grave, is obsessively repeated, not only in his three versions of Gottfried August Bürger's *Lenore* (*Liudmila*, 1808; *Svetlana*, 1811; and *Lenora*, 1829), but in such other ballads as "Alonzo" (1829) and "St. John's Eve" ("Zamok Smal'gol'm ili Ivanov vecher," 1822). Even trivial ceremonial poems written for girls'-school graduations employ the rhetoric of *dvoemirie*:

> *Here* we together entrusted ourselves to happiness;
> But *there*, under the mysterious power of fate,
> We will all acquire something different.
>
> "Farewell Song of the Students of
the Society of Ladies of the Nobility,
on the Graduation of 1824"
(2: 399)

We ourselves have in the past parted
From our friends more than once;
Our tears have accompanied them
Into a world unknown to us,
And we have sent prayers
To follow the departing ones.

    Ah, now our time has come
To hear the sad farewell—

To take on the burden of life's care,
To go into an unknown world [*v svet neznaemyi*].

"Farewell Song of the Students
of the Society of Ladies of the
Nobility, on the Graduation of 1827"
(2: 401–2)

Although here the border between *zdes'* and *tam*, between here and there, is not the border between life and death, the structure—crossing a boundary from a known into an unknown world—remains the same.

Essential to Zhukovskii's *dvoemirie* is the quality of mystery and obscurity, the unknown that beckons the mind across the boundary. In a fragment excised from the text of "Detailed Report on the Moon: Epistle to Her Majesty the Empress Mariia Fedorovna" ("Podrobnyi otchet o lune. Poslanie k gosudaryne imp. Marii Fedorovne," 1819), he asserts that the other world is authentic, even if unknowable:

И всё то ложно, что чудесно?
Не то одно, что нам известно,
Что внемлет ухо, видит глаз,
Уму доступное, земное
Имеет бытие прямое!
Есть и незримое для нас.
Ужель земля всё истощила
И вне ее созданий нет,
И темного стремленья сила
Влечет нас в небывалый свет?
О нет! он есть сей свет чудесной!
Язык предчувствия небесной
С душой нежданно говорит!
Душа невидимое зрит![14]

(Is all that is miraculous also false?
Not only that which we know,
Which the ear hears, the eye sees,
Which is earthly and accessible to the mind,
Is endowed with true existence!
We also have an unseen world.
Has the earth really exhausted everything,
And is there nothing beyond its creations,

And does the power of dark striving
Draw us to a nonexistent world?
Oh, no! It exists, this miraculous world!
The heavenly language of premonition
Speaks unexpectedly with the soul!
The soul sees the invisible!)

For Zhukovskii, as for Herder, the human longing for the world beyond is a proof of the existence of the immortal soul. In explicating Jean-Jacques Rousseau's statement "Il n'y a de beau que ce qui n'est pas," Zhukovskii elaborates a theory of the perception of beauty based on an eternal sense of the deficiency of what meets the eye. The apprehension of earthly beauty is always mixed with sorrow and striving:

In these moments of vivid feeling you strive not toward that which produces it and which is before you but toward something better, something mysterious and distant, something that is united with it and is absent from it and that exists for you somewhere. And this striving is one of the inexpressible [*nevyrazimykh*] proofs of immortality: otherwise, why, at the moment of enjoyment, would one not experience the fullness and clarity of enjoyment! (2: 327–28)

Zhukovskii's oeuvre is an illustration of this model of beauty; his is a poetics of absence and longing, written in the "heavenly language of premonition."

Translation and Transformation

Zhukovskii was only one of a number of writers preoccupied with the themes of *zdes'* and *tam*, but his special relationship with Gogol bears closer examination. There is no question that Gogol was intimately familiar with Zhukovskii's art and philosophy. For him, Zhukovskii was friend, teacher, colleague, and intercessor with the imperial family. But most important for Gogol, as for countless other Russians, was Zhukovskii's role as transmitter and translator of Western European culture, particularly the literature of Romanticism. The influence of Zhukovskii can clearly be seen in Gogol's historical researches. Zhukovskii, like Gogol, did extensive work in history, although he never considered making a career of it: for Zhukovskii, work in history was always subordinated to a poetic project, such as his planned epic poem "Vladimir."[15] Like Gogol, but years earlier, Zhukovskii studied the historical works of Schlözer, Müller, and Herder; like him, he evolved a theory of history based on the fixed laws of Providence.[16] In "Outlines of the History of the Russian State" ("Cherty istorii Gosudarstva Rossiiskogo," 1834), Zhukovskii speaks of the lessons of history, which teaches people to remain in their proper place:

History preaches to us consolingly about this *necessary*, early or late *sprouting of good* from the soil of misfortunes, fertilized by vigilant Providence. . . . [History] says to *the nations*: "Be submissive to order; bear with dignity and firmness the burden of the present. To throw it off by force is to willfully open the crater of a volcano: its lava may be fertile, but only in distant times. To ruin the present for the benefit of the future is the crime of insanity, which capriciously sets fire to its own house in the hope that something better will arise from the ashes." Finally, it says to *each person*: "Preserve the sacredness of oath and law; know *your own* place on the earth and stand on it firmly; . . . where each person in his own place is submissive to law, there for everyone in common nothing other than law is sovereign."[17]

This comic Herderian philosophy enables the reactionary monarchist Zhukovskii to find something good even in the Decembrist Rebellion: "What can one say in conclusion about this entire terrible event? The same thing a historian says when describing times of terror that produced beneficial results. It is good that they took place. The present good is their fruit."[18] A favorite and often-repeated aphorism of Zhukovskii's could serve as the motto for both his and Gogol's philosophy of history: "A certain wise man was asked: 'What is chance?' He responded: '*The incognito of Providence*. There is no such thing as chance. Everything we encounter in life, joyful or sorrowful, expected or unexpected, is God in various forms.'"[19] Unlike Gogol, however, Zhukovskii transferred his philosophy of history into his art virtually unchanged, making "vera v providen'e" (faith in Providence; 1: 218) the hero of his poetry, neither challenged, distorted, nor ironized.[20]

On his pilgrimage to Western Europe in 1836, Gogol speaks of literally following in Zhukovskii's footsteps. Writing to Zhukovskii from Paris, Gogol claims to have reread Molière, Shakespeare, and Scott, and then he describes his stay in Vevey:

Snachala bylo mne neskol'ko skuchno, potom ia privyk i sdelalsia sovershenno vashim naslednikom: zavladel mestami vashikh progulok, meril rasstoianie po naznachennym vami verstam, kolotia palkoiu begavshikh po stenam ia-shcherits, natsarapal dazhe svoe imia russkimi bukvami v Shil'onskom podze-mel'e, ne posmel podpisat' ego pod dvumia slavnymi imenami tvortsa i pere-vodchika "Shil'onskogo Uznika"; vprochem, dazhe ne bylo i mesta. Pod nimi raspisalsia kakoi-to Burnashev,—vnizu poslednei kolonny, kotoraia v teni, kogda-nibud' russkoi puteshestvennik razberet moe ptich'e imia, esli ne siadet na nego anglichanin. (II: 73)

(At first I was a bit bored, then I got used to it and became entirely your successor: I appropriated the sites of your walks, measured the distance ac-cording to the milestones you had marked, thrashing with my walking stick the lizards running along the walls. I even scratched my name in Russian letters in the dungeon at Chillon but did not dare to sign it under the two famous names of the creator and the translator of "The Prisoner of Chillon"; besides, there wasn't any room. A certain Burnashev had signed his name under them. At the bottom of the last column, the one that is in darkness, a Russian traveler will one day make out my birdlike name, if an Englishman doesn't sit on it.)

This passage may be taken as a model for Gogol's relationship to Zhukovskii: he acknowledges him as elder and predecessor and ac-cepts the role of disciple ("sdelalsia sovershenno vashim nasledni-kom," I became entirely your successor) but shies from signing his name directly beneath Zhukovskii's, itself inscribed beneath Byron's, undoubtedly in Roman characters. Gogol's apparent modesty is also a form of pride; rather than allow himself to be subsumed under Byron and Byron's translator, he finds his own column, in the dark-ness, on which to inscribe his name in Russian letters, where it must be sought out and deciphered by a compatriot (assuming it has not been obscured by a foreign backside). The place beneath Byron and Zhukovskii is the place for imitative anonymity ("kakoi-to Bur-nashev," a certain Burnashev); Gogol finds his own space in which to inscribe his Russian name, birdlike only to those who speak his language (*gogol'* means "golden-eye duck"). As we shall see, in cre-ating *Dead Souls*, Gogol obeys analogous impulses: he pays homage to Zhukovskii and the literature of early German, English, and Rus-sian Romanticism but rejects the role of translator for that of trans-former, finding his own idiosyncratic and peculiarly Russian version of Zhukovskii's literature of the soul.

The Taste for Zhukovskii

Chichikov's dead-souls scheme is referred to as "glavnyi predmet ego vkusa i sklonnostei" (the main object of his taste and inclinations; 6: 40). The word *taste* is important, for Chichikov's *siuzhet* is related to the literary taste of the town of N. As William Mills Todd III and E. S. Smirnova-Chikina have pointed out, the dating of the action of the novel is problematic, for the narrator gives contradictory indications.[21] In the realm of literary taste, however, the action is unequivocally placed "soon after the glorious expulsion of the French" (6: 206)—that is, soon after 1812. In Todd's words, "Whenever these characters choose something to read, which happens rarely, it is inevitably a sentimentalist text of the late eighteenth or early nineteenth century" (p. 182). *Dead Souls* is saturated with explicit and implicit references to the literature of Sentimentalism and early Romanticism, both Western (Edward Young, Madame de Genlis) and Russian (Nikolai Karamzin, Zhukovskii). While placing the action of the novel at the height of the popularity of this literature, the narrator manages to distance himself from that period: "The chairman of the administrative offices knew by heart Zhukovskii's *Liudmila*, which was still a novelty hot off the presses" (6: 156).[22]

Chichikov himself seems to have been modeled on a character outlined by Zhukovskii in his famous essay "The Writer in Society" ("Pisatel' v obshchestve," 1808).[23] Zhukovskii defines two types of success in society, one represented by the "chelovek tol'ko liubeznyi" (merely amiable person), a precursor of the "prosto priiatnaia dama" (simply pleasant lady) in *Dead Souls*, and the other the more enduring success of the highly principled person of firm character.[24] The merely amiable person shares Chichikov's flexibility, mobility, and adaptability:

Imagine a person who directs all his thoughts solely toward the goal of always pleasing everybody everywhere: in appearance, dress, eloquence of language, countenance, and movement. With amazing presence of mind he turns every circumstance to his advantage; in his conversation he knows how to be both amusing and serious; he is inimitable in petty things—in the art of recounting an anecdote or tale quickly and attractively, enlivening social amusements with his inventiveness, presenting the serious as ridiculous or the ridiculous as serious, uttering a flattering word in a pleasant manner. He flits from one society to another, animates each one with his momentary presence, disappears from one in order to appear in another and again disappear. (p. 169)

As with Chichikov, the charm of his address causes his interlocutors to postpone asking essential questions about his character: "No one thinks about his moral character; they are grateful to him for the pleasure he affords others when he is with them" (p. 169). Zhukovskii even seems to foretell Chichikov's downfall: "Ideas about the merely amiable person must change with the circumstances in which he presents himself to society: there is no consensus about him; attachment [*priviazannost'*] to him either lessens or disappears at the moment when he himself is hidden from your gaze" (p. 170). The lightness and changeability of the amiable man's character work against him; having established no constant, deep connection with society, he loses its favor as soon as he is unable to directly manipulate its responses, just as Chichikov is decisively ostracized by the town of N. during his three days of illness and seclusion.

Chichikov, in a sense a creation of Zhukovskii's, pays homage to him in his rhetoric and tastes. Chichikov compares himself to "some sort of wooden bark amid the ferocious waves" (6: 37), an allusion to Zhukovskii's hymn to Providence, "The Swimmer" ("Plovets," 1811):

> Вихрем бедствия гонимый,
> Без кормила и весла,
> В океан неисходимый
> Буря челн мой занесла
>
> (1: 219)
>
> (Driven by a whirlwind of misfortunes,
> Without helm or oar,
> Into the inescapable ocean
> A storm has carried my boat.)

The governor's daughter, the woman who becomes Chichikov's ideal and destroyer, is also described in Zhukovskian terms: "with a charmingly rounded oval face, of the kind an artist would take as a model for a madonna" (6: 166). For Gogol's contemporaries, the word *madonna* inevitably recalled Raphael's Sistine Madonna, which

Zhukovskii, following Wilhelm Heinrich Wackenroder and Ludwig
Tieck, held up as the ideal of feminine and artistic beauty.[25] But the
character who most insistently recalls Zhukovskii's art and character
is Manilov.

It has often been noted that chapter 2, in which Chichikov visits
Manilov, is permeated by the language and aesthetics of Sentimentalism.[26] Both Chichikov and Manilov speak in a parody of the ur-
bane, amiable language of Karamzin and Zhukovskii. Manilov's philosophy is one of Horatian rural seclusion and the cult of friendship:
"If the neighborhood society were good, if, for example, there were
the kind of person with whom one might in a certain sense speak
about amiability [*liubeznosti*], about good address, with whom one
might follow some sort of science or other, in order to sort of stir
up the soul, to give it, so to speak, a chance to soar . . . , then, of
course, the country and solitude would afford very many pleasant-
nesses" (6: 29). Manilov may be trying to earn the right to the obitu-
ary offered the narrator in Zhukovskii's 1803 translation ("Sel'skoe
kladbishche") of Thomas Gray's "Elegy Written in a Country Churchyard" (ca. 1742–50):

> Он кроток сердцем был, чувствителен душою—
> Чувствительным творец награду положил.
> Дарил несчастных он—чем только мог—слезою;
> В награду от творца он друга получил.
>
> (1: 34)

> (He was meek in heart, sensitive in soul—
> The Creator has prepared a reward for the sensitive.
> He endowed the unfortunate with all he had—a tear;
> In reward he received from the Creator a friend.[27]

Most striking, however, is Manilov's resemblance to Zhukovskii
himself as perceived by his contemporaries: "His quiet, meek, pen-
sive character, his bright soul and tender heart, drew him into solitude, and he resolved not to seek distinction in the service but to
dedicate himself to friendship, family life, and solitary converse with
the Muses."[28] When read as a parody of Zhukovskii, the characterization of Manilov, with his "not only sweet but cloying expression,
like a mixture that a cunning society doctor has unmercifully sweet-

ened, imagining that this will make the patient happy" (6: 29), betrays more than a touch of hostility.

In the light of this parody, one can read yet another reference to Zhukovskii's biography in the hint of incest that arises in the rumors about Chichikov and the governor's daughter: it was said that Chichikov, "in undertaking to obtain the daughter's hand, started the business with the mother and had a secret affair of the heart with her and that later he made a declaration for the daughter's hand; but the mother, afraid that a crime against religion would be committed, refused outright, and that is why Chichikov resolved on an abduction" (6: 191). This is a not-very-subtle echo of the central tragedy of Zhukovskii's life, his love for Mariia Andreevna Protasova (1793–1823), the daughter of his natural sister, E. A. Protasova.[29] The mother refused to countenance a marriage between such close relatives on the grounds that it was forbidden by the church. When Mariia Protasova, exhausted by family intrigues and persecution, agreed to marry I. F. Moier, Zhukovskii's reaction focused on the hypocrisy of his sister's interference in his fate: "My God! Religion forbade her to agree to our happiness; but the same religion cannot forbid her to force you into the violation of everything sacred: of sacrament and vow! After this, can I think that religion, and not the mere desire to carry out her own will, guides her acts?"[30]

In Chichikov's case, even if the planned abduction were real, the mother's fears of incest would be illusory, for no blood relationship exists between Chichikov and the governor's daughter, only his "serdechnaia tainaia sviaz'" (secret affair [lit. "tie"] of the heart) with her mother.[31] According to Zhukovskii, E. A. Protasova's fears are equally absurd, for the Bible countenances marriage between close relatives ("Abraham married his own sister, and he is an ancestor of the Messiah") and civil law does not concern the illegitimate Zhukovskii because it does not recognize him: "The law has not called me her relative, therefore I fall only under the law of nature, and it is not against me."[32] The echoes between Zhukovskii's situation and Chichikov's are clear: the disparity in the ages of the lovers, the negotiations carried out with a mother who uses religion as a screen for perhaps more egotistical motives, and the possibility that the crime is not a crime at all.

The Discourse of Ineffability

More important than references to Zhukovskii's biography in *Dead Souls* is the discrediting of his poetic language, the identification of his discourse of ineffability with the sterile, powerless discourse of society ladies. One of Zhukovskii's most famous and beautiful poems, a precursor to Fedor Tiutchev's "Silentium," is "The Inexpressible (A Fragment)" ("Nevyrazimoe [Otryvok]," 1819), in which the poet sets limits to the power of language to convey the beauties of nature.[33] Language is adequate to one category of phenomena—the vivid, the well-defined, the obvious—but cannot find words for the more subtle effects of nature:

> Сии столь яркие черты,
> Легко их ловит мысль крылата,
> И есть слова для их *блестящей* красоты.
> Но то, что слито с сей блестящей красотою—
> Сие столь смутное, волнующее нас,
> Сей внемлемый одной душою
> Обворожающего глас,
> Сие к далекому стремленье, . . .
> Сие шепнувшее душе воспоминанье
> О милом радостном и скорбном старины,
> Сия сходящая святыня с вышины,
> Сие присутствие Создателя в созданье—
> Какой для них язык? ... Горе душа летит,
> Всё необъятное в единый вздох теснится
> И лишь молчание понятно говорит.

(2: 76–77)

(These so vivid features
Are easily captured by winged thought,
And there are words for their *brilliant* beauty;
But that which is merged with this brilliant beauty—
This vagueness that agitates us,
This voice of enchantment
Heard only by the soul,
This striving toward the faraway . . .
This memory whispering to the soul
About the dear joyful and sorrowful things of old,
This sacred thing descending from the heights,

This presence of the Creator in the creation—
What language is there for them? The soul flies on high,
All that is immeasurable crowds into a single sigh,
And only silence speaks intelligibly.)

In the description of Manilov, Gogol's narrator reprises the structure of "The Inexpressible," and the result is a trivializing of Zhukovskii's opposition between the vivid, brilliant, describable features of nature and its subtle, indescribable nuances:

Here the author must confess that [to say something about the master of the house] is very difficult. It is much easier to depict large-scale characters: there you simply throw the paints on the canvas with all your might—black burning eyes, beetling brows, a forehead creased with a wrinkle, a black or crimson-as-fire cloak thrown over the shoulder—and the portrait is finished. But all these gentlemen, of whom there are many in the world, who at first glance resemble each other very much, but in whom meanwhile, the closer you look, the more you see many of the most elusive peculiarities [*neulovimykh osobennostei*]—these gentlemen are terribly difficult to make portraits of. Here you must strain your attention to the utmost until you force all the subtle, almost invisible features [*vse tonkie, pochti nevidimye cherty*] to appear before you, and in general you must greatly deepen your glance, already refined in the science of discovery. (6: 23–24)

Chichikov suffers the same difficulty in trying to capture the ineffable features of the ladies at the ball: "Noticeable everywhere was something just barely disclosed, so elusively subtle [*neulovimo-tonkoe*], ooh, how subtle! . . . 'No!' Chichikov said to himself. 'Women are such a subject . . .' Here he waved his hand. 'There's simply nothing to be said! Just try to recount or convey everything that runs across their faces, all those twists and hints, and you simply won't be able to convey anything'" (6: 164).

For Zhukovskii the failure of language to convey the ineffable is a noble failure, and the impotence of language becomes the very stuff of poetic language. In *Dead Souls* the realm of the ineffable is the realm of Manilov and society ladies, that is, Zhukovskii's audience, and in the hands of Gogol's narrator it is thoroughly debased. The failure to capture the nuances of dress fabrics or an insipid person is placed in invidious opposition to the power and efficacy of the muzhik's "metko skazannoe russkoe slovo" (aptly spoken Russian word; 6: 109). In *Dead Souls* the literature of early Romanticism is identified with and implicated in the ladies' language of euphemism and periphrasis. As Todd points out, "Nothing by Pushkin, Griboedov, Viazemsky, or Fonvizin interrupts the flow of works which offered models of ameliorated manners, periphrastic expression, and pious resignation" (p. 183). Of course, the language of Karamzin and Zhukovskii was itself modeled on the language of polite society, dominated by women. Early Russian Romanticism consulted feminine taste not only in style but in subject matter, making romantic love its primary plot. When in attempting to interpret "dead souls" the town of N. divides into male and female camps, the men seize on the phrase "dead souls" while the women concentrate on the plot to abduct the governor's daughter. The women's suppositions, unlike the men's untidy, fragmentary, enigmatic hypotheses, are quickly composed into a "finished picture" ("okonchennaia kartina"; 6: 191). This ease of composition is due not to the ladies' superiority as housekeepers, as the narrator supposes, but to the fact that early Romantic fiction had already supplied them with the building blocks for their story, in the form of the clichéd plot moves of the romantic love story.[34]

Zhukovskii shares the ladies' tendency to see the world in terms of romantic love; his *dvoemirie*—his system of two worlds—is most often expressed as a reunion of lovers separated by the grave. Even in his most "masculine" work, the hymn to the warriors of 1812 titled "The Bard in the Camp of the Russian Warriors" ("Pevets vo stane russkikh voinov," 1812), love is accorded a preeminent place:

> Ах! мысль о той, кто всё для нас,
>   Нам спутник неизменный;
> Везде знакомый слышим глас,
>   Зрим образ незабвенный!
> *Она* на бранных знаменах,
>   *Она* в пылу сраженья;
> И в шуме стана, и в мечтах
>   Веселых сновиденья.
> Отведай, враг, исторгнуть щит,
>   Рукою данный милой;
> Святой обет на нем горит:
>   *Твоя и за могилой!*

(1: 264)

(Ah! The thought of her, who is everything to us,
    Is our constant companion;
Everywhere we hear a familiar voice,
    We see an unforgettable image.
She is on the martial banners,
    She is in the heat of battle
And in the noise of the camp and in the gay
    Reveries of dreaming.
Just try, O enemy, to wrest away the shield
    Given by the hand of the dear one.
A holy vow shines on it:
    Yours even beyond the grave!)

A contemporary of Zhukovskii's went so far as to assert that only one who has employed Zhukovskii's verse in the service of love can truly understand it:

If you did not read this poem of Zhukovskii's ["To Philaletus," 1807] in the days of your youth, not daring to glance at her from whom your gaze would never wish to tear itself, afraid that the people around you would divine your secret from your voice, and if at the same time you were not afraid that in concealing your soul you would deprive Zhukovskii's creation of poetic enchantment, if you did not wish then to utter through his verse your whole heart, your whole soul to her, *to her alone*—you cannot understand this poem! [35]

The Zhukovskian warrior goes into battle with "her" on his banner and shield; Zhukovskii's verse has "her, her alone" as its audience.

The feminine principle occupies a very different place in Zhukovskii's world than it does in the world of the three bachelors—Chichikov, the narrator of *Dead Souls*, and Gogol. Women are the model, subject, and audience for Zhukovskii's work. They offer not the danger of entrapment but inspiration and consolation. A clear indication of the difference between his attitude and Gogol's is his belief that family ties are not destructive but indispensable for the writer:

The other—narrow—circle is the one in which he is happy, loved, and loving, where he is successful without making any effort, without resorting to refined and crafty skill. . . . This, finally, is where his family is. For the writer, more than for anyone, family ties are necessary; tied [*priviazannyi*] to one place by his work, he must find around him those pleasures that nature has rendered indispensable for the human soul. In his secluded dwelling, after prolonged mental labor he must hear the touching voices of his dear ones. In their circle he must rest; in their circle he must find new strength for new work. Having nothing far away worth searching for, he must unite everything most precious to his heart close at hand, around him; the universe and all its joys must be contained in that peaceful abode where he thinks and where he loves.[36]

This image of the writer—fixed in one place by family ties, basking in the easy approval of his loved ones, achieving success without making any effort, renouncing journey and quest for a narrow, peaceful home—is explicitly rejected at the beginning of chapter 7 by the narrator of *Dead Souls*. The family man–writer is characterized in terms of his choice of subject: "Happy is the writer who passes up boring, repulsive characters that strike one with their sad reality, who is drawn toward characters that manifest man's high dignity . . . and who, not touching the earth, has plunged completely into his elevated images, torn far away from that earth" (6: 133). The writer without a family, in contrast, daringly plunges into the grime and detail of earthly life, exposing "the entire terrible, staggering mire of petty things that entangle our lives." Although the narrator of *Dead Souls* asserts that the writer with a family receives the unquestioning acclaim of his audience, Zhukovskii himself was criticized by contemporaries for "not touching the earth" and for "plunging into elevated images torn far away from that earth." The problem of Zhukovskii's "failure," as perceived by his contemporaries, is intimately related to the conception of *Dead Souls*.[37]

Elegant Images of the Cemetery

The day before the fatal ball, Chichikov receives an anonymous note from a female admirer containing a quatrain "napisano v dukhe togdashnego vremeni" (written in the spirit of that time; 6: 160). The poem, a travesty of Karamzin's "I am content with my fate" ("Dovolen ia sud'boiu," 1794), has death as its subject:[38]

> Две горлицы покажут
> Тебе мой хладный прах,

Воркуя, томно скажут,
Что она умерла во слезах.

(6: 160)

(Two turtledoves will show
You my cold ashes;
Cooing, they will languidly say
That she died in tears.)

Also "in the spirit of that time" is the simply pleasant lady's version of Chichikov's visit to Korobochka:

Just imagine, he appears armed from head to foot like Rinaldo Rinaldini and demands: "Sell me," he says, "all the souls that have died." Korobochka answers very reasonably, and says, "I cannot sell them, because they are dead." "No," says Chichikov, "they are not dead. It's my business," he says, "to know whether they're dead or not. They are not dead, not dead," he cries, "not dead!" (6: 183)

In these two exercises in literary epigonism, the ladies have captured the two sides of the Zhukovskian poetics of death: on the one hand, the melancholy, elegiac longing for the departed lover; on the other, the frightening, eerie midnight encounter with a threatening hero transplanted from Western Europe, who calls into question the apparently clear-cut boundary between the living and the dead.[39] In his 1831 essay summarizing Zhukovskii's career, N. Polevoi elucidates the relation between the two strains:

Complete dissatisfaction with oneself, with the world, with people, a quiet, doleful dissatisfaction, and hence a striving beyond the bounds of the world, a touching hope of finding happiness *there*, which has deceived *here*; the prayer of a loving heart, wearied by the struggle but not bloody, not lacerated; a striving toward sadness about the past, toward hopeless despondency in the future; a tender, friendly sympathy for the sorrow of one's neighbor; the cemetery as the favorite spot for walks, like a field sown with hearts calmed in their hopes, consoled by death; the idea of elevating the horrors of the cemetery and death into ideals, of clothing them in elegant images, of showing in man's demise not a terrible apparition but the quiet angel of peace and calmness—from all this, on the one hand, *being accustomed* [*privychka*] to superstitious legend, like being accustomed to the terrifying stories that we heard in childhood, and, on the other hand, *being unaccustomed* [*otvychka*], so to speak, to everything earthly that surrounds us, being alienated from everything that interests and fascinates others, transferring one's sole thought, one's sole idea to all objects, a quiet, calming, dreamy thought, delightful in its very sadness, gladdening the soul with a sort of forgiveness of unjust Fate, all this is the basis for the poetry of *Zhukovskii*. (no. 20, pp. 524–25)

The emphasis here is on the "turtledove" aspect of Zhukovskii's poetry, but his audience was more struck by the "horrors of the cemetery and death." A contemporary diarist offers a summary catalogue of the themes of Zhukovskii's ballads of supernatural retribution: "Mertvetsy, privideniia, chertovshchina, ubiistva, osveshchaemye lunoiu" (Corpses, apparitions, devils, murders illuminated by the moon).[40]

In the early-nineteenth-century context, Gogol's ladies are not alone in their epigonism—Zhukovskii's poetry of mystery and death inspired countless imitations. By the 1820's critics had begun to complain about the monotony of the thematics of death: "Look at our Parnassus: it is a cemetery where skulls, bones, half-crumbled coffins, and grave crosses lie about; where spirits, apparitions, corpses in shrouds and without shrouds, wander; where one hears the cries of ravens, the hissing of snakes, the howl of wolves."[41] Even Zhukovskii's friend Prince Viazemskii began in 1819 to worry about his habit of writing about death:

A poet should pour out his soul into varied vessels. Zhukovskii more than others must beware of monotony: he is terribly apt to fall into habits. There was a time when he seized upon the thought of death and would end every poem with his own funeral. The premonition of death is striking when it bursts forth; but when we see that a person awaits death every day but continues to thrive nonetheless, then his premonitions end by making us laugh.[42]

Vacancy Absorbing Space

The ladies of the town of N. share not only Zhukovskii's obsession with death but another of his habits as well, alluded to in the description of their rumormongering: "Damy umely napustit' takogo *tumana* v glaza vsem, chto vse, a osobenno chinovniki, neskol'ko vremeni ostavalis' oshelomlennymi" (The ladies knew how to send such a *mist* into everyone's eyes that everyone, and especially the civil servants, remained stunned; 6: 189; emphasis added). The word *tuman* (mist), as a shorthand for the vagueness, dreaminess, and mysticism of Zhukovskii's poetry, became such a staple of the critical vocabulary of the 1810's and 1820's that it would be virtually impossible to find a discussion of Zhukovskii that omits it. As with the thematics of the grave, however, contemporary criticism perceives Zhukovskii's *tuman* first as an artistic signature, then as an artistic tic, and finally as a ridiculous self-parody.

At the beginning of his career, in notes on the history of literature and criticism, Zhukovskii speaks of the aesthetic uses of obscurity: "For an epic poem in our time one must choose a subject from a distant time: the distance and the difference between that time and ours contain something sublime in themselves. There is always a sort of sublimity connected with the gloom [*mrak*] in which a person, seeing nothing, imagines everything."[43] Throughout his career, as in his manifesto "The Inexpressible," Zhukovskii displays a preference for the vague, misty, and formless over the vividly outlined and obviously shaped, for "the gloom in which a person, seeing nothing, imagines everything." This preference is beautifully expressed in the description of a waterfall in his "Fragments from a Letter About Switzerland" ("Otryvki iz pis'ma o Shveitsarii," written 1833, published 1849):

If you look at it as at a waterfall, if you see the whole scene of its descent, then it is not particularly striking. . . . But a striking, indescribable spectacle is presented to the eyes when you look at the fall close up, from the gallery built on the bank right next to the waterfall. Here there is no longer any waterfall, any scene; you stand in a chaos of foam, thunder, and waves that have no shape [*nikakogo obraza*]. And this spectacle is even more sublime without the sun than when the sun is shining: the sunbeams illuminating the waves give them a certain visible, familiar form; but without sunbeams everything loses shape [*vsë teriaet obraz*]. Thundering, hissing, and roaring, some immense phantoms fly by you, phantoms that rush forward, swirl, writhe, rise in a cloud of smoke, fly up in a sheaf of hissing watery rockets, cross each other's paths and, meeting, smash to pieces—in a word, an indescribable scene.[44]

It is no accident that in praising Zhukovskii's translation of "The Prisoner of Chillon," Pushkin singles out the passage in which "the first signs of madness" are described, for it is here that Byron's original offers Zhukovskii an opportunity to indulge his taste for vague outline, gloom, and formlessness: [45]

Byron
What next befell me then and there
    I know not well—I never knew—
First came the loss of light, and air,
    And then of darkness too:
I had no thought, no feeling—none—
Among the stones I stood a stone,
And was, scarce conscious what I wist,
As shrubless crags within the mist;
For all was blank, and bleak, and grey;
It was not night, it was not day;
It was not even the dungeon-light,
So hateful to my heavy sight,
But vacancy absorbing space,
And fixedness without a place;
There were no stars, no earth, no time,
No check, no change, no good, no crime,
But silence, and a stirless breath
Which neither was of life nor death;
A sea of stagnant idleness,
Blind, boundless, mute, and motionless!

(3: 278)

Zhukovskii
Но что потом сбылось со мной,
Не помню ... свет казался тьмой,
Тьма светом; воздух исчезал;
В оцепенении стоял,
Без памяти, без бытия,
Меж камней хладным камнем я;
И виделось, как в тяжком сне,
Всё бледным, темным, тусклым мне;
Всё в мутную слилося тень;
То не было не ночь, ни день,
Ни тяжкий свет тюрьмы моей,
Столь ненавистный для очей:

То было тьма без темноты;
То было бездна пустоты
Без протяженья и границ;
То были образы без лиц;
То страшный мир какой-то был,
Без неба, света и светил,
Без времени, без дней и лет,
Без промысла, без благ н бед,
Ни жизнь, ни смерть—как сон гробов,
Как океан без берегов,
Задавленный тяжелой мглой,
Недвижный, темный и немой.

(2: 338–39)

(*Literal translation of Zhukovskii's translation*
But then what happened to me
I do not remember . . . light seemed to be darkness,
Darkness light; air disappeared;
I stood benumbed,
Without memory, without existence;
Amid stones I stood a cold stone;
And as in a heavy dream everything appeared
Pale, dark, and dim to me;
Everything merged into turbid shadow;
It was neither night nor day,
Nor the heavy light of my prison,
So hateful to my eyes:
It was darkness without obscurity;
It was an abyss of emptiness
Without expanse or boundaries;
It was images without faces;
It was a terrible sort of world,
Without sky, light, or planets,
Without time, without days and years,
Without Providence, without blessings or misfortunes,
With neither life nor death—like the sleep of graves,
Like an ocean without shores,
Oppressed by a heavy mist,
Immobile, dark, and mute.)

Pushkin speaks of Zhukovskii's "re-expressing" ("perevyrazit'")
Byron's thought, and in fact his translation, though accurate, is far

from literal.[46] Zhukovskii expands on and emphasizes precisely those of Byron's images that suit his aesthetic of vagueness and formlessness. Byron's concise "vacancy absorbing space, / And fixedness without a place" becomes "To bylo t'ma bez temnoty; / To bylo bezdna pustoty / Bez protiazhen'ia i granits; / To byli obrazy bez lits" (It was darkness without obscurity; / It was an abyss of emptiness / Without expanse or boundaries; / It was images without faces). In the final lines of the stanza Zhukovskii transforms Byron's conventional epithets for the sea, "boundless" and "stagnant," into a frightening image of formlessness and haze: "Kak okean bez beregov, / Zadavlennyi tiazheloi mgloi, / Nedvizhnyi, temnyi i nemoi."

As late as 1824, Bestuzhev praised Zhukovskii for introducing "nerazgadannaia poeziia" (undeciphered poetry) into Russian literature.[47] In reacting to Bestuzhev, an anonymous critic more accurately expressed the prevailing mood: "I cannot, however, conceal my desire that the fashion for that type of poetry which A. A. Bestuzhev justly called *undeciphered* would finally pass and that we could finally read beautiful poems without a *mysterious* lexicon."[48] The word *tuman* lent itself beautifully to being turned against Zhukovskii and his epigones:

Before, Zhukovskii's poetry appeared to us in a transparent, bright mist; but there is a time for everything, and now this mist [*tuman*] has thickened.[49]

Zhukovskii spends too much time in mysticism; that is, one should not deceive oneself too often. Under that mist no light of thought is hidden [*pod etim tumanom ne taitsia svet mysli*].[50]

Most devastating, however, is V. K. Kiukhel'beker's famous 1825 summation of the elegiac early Romantic school of poetry:

Strength? Where can we find it in most of our turbid, undefined, effeminate, colorless works? With us everything is *dream* and *phantom*, everything *seems* and *appears*, everything is only *as if, as though, something* [*budto by, kak by, nechto, chto-to*]. Richness and variety? If you read any one elegy by Zhukovskii, Pushkin, or Baratynskii, you know them all. For a long while, we have had no feelings left: the feeling of dejection [*unynie*] has swallowed all the others. . . . The scenes are always the same: the moon, which is, of course, *dejected* and *pale*, cliffs and leafy groves where there never were any before, a forest beyond which the setting of the sun and the evening glow are depicted a hundred times, now and then long shadows and apparitions, something invisible, something unknown, banal allegories . . . but especially mist [*tuman*]—mist over the water, mist over the forest, mist over the fields, mist in the writer's head.[51]

Zhukovskii's preoccupation with the misty and vague, like his obsession with corpses and cemeteries, begins as a logical and effective part of a distinctive poetic program but through repetition and imitation becomes a cliché, a convenient pretext for audience rebellion and reaction.

Everything for the Soul

If any single phrase could characterize Zhukovskii's aesthetics, it would be the one uttered by Karamzin in an 1818 speech to the Russian Academy: "Zdes' vsë dlia dushi" (Here everything is for the soul).[52] In Zhukovskii's hands, the phrase is transformed from an interpretation of historical change into a program for living:

> Всё для души, сказал отец твой несравненный;
>   В сих двух словах открыл нам ясно он
> И тайну бытия, и наших дел закон ...
>   Они тебе на жизнь завет священный.[53]

(Everything is for the soul, said your incomparable father;
   In these two words he clearly uncovered for us
Both the secret of existence, and the law of our actions:
   They are the sacred behest for your life.)

Zhukovskii's preoccupation with the soul—the unseen, unearthly world of the dead—comes to be seen by Viazemskii as the chief danger threatening his poetic career with sterile failure: "Zhukovskii is also a Don Quixote in his way. He has become mad about the soul and converses with souls in the Anichkov Palace, where a soul has never been found. It is essential that he have a Sancho near him, me for example, who could sometimes return him to the earth and stick his nose into everyday life." When A. I. Turgenev attempts to defend Zhukovskii by reminding Viazemskii that Zhukovskii is not a civic poet, that for him "vsë dlia dushi" (everything is for the soul), Viazemskii is unmoved: "Of course, for Zhukovskii everything is the soul and everything is for the soul. But a soul that is the witness of real events, that sees scaffolds piled up for the murder of people, for cutting the throat of liberty, must not and cannot lose itself in the ideal realm of Arcadia."⁵⁴ By the mid-1820's, Zhukovskii's friends and audience were refusing to allow him to continue the poetic program he had followed for over a decade; "everything for the soul" was the motto of a bygone age.⁵⁵

In the discussions of Zhukovskii's poetic impasse can be discerned a number of alternative strategies proposed by the poet's critics and friends, which have as their common feature a desire for Zhukovskii to turn away from the soul and back to earth, away from translation of Western European literature and back to Russian reality. Zhukovskii's "Sancho" Viazemskii prescribes the use of current affairs as a source of inspiration: "There is nothing to be done now. A poet must sometimes seek inspiration in the newspapers. Before, poets lost themselves in metaphysics; now the *marvelous* [*chudesnoe*], that great helpmeet of poetry, is on earth. Parnassus is in Laibach."⁵⁶ Viazemskii's desire that Zhukovskii turn to the newspapers for inspiration and become a civic poet is not without rational grounds, for in his "Bard in the Camp of the Russian Warriors," Zhukovskii had given promise of becoming Russia's Homer: "Zhukovskii's friends were expecting from him an original *poema* on an important historical theme."⁵⁷ Zhukovskii never made a serious attempt to "seek inspiration in the newspapers," and his plans for an original epic on a Russian historical theme ("Vladimir") remained just plans. One former admirer, N. M. Konshin, later recalled his bitter disappointment at Zhukovskii's failure to keep what many regarded as his promise: "I loved him, despite his *silly reports on the moon, which are not at all suited to the dignity of a poet, a priest*; I loved that Zhukovskii who sang of 1812 and who—in my opinion—had died; and he should have died then in order to live eternally as the representative of a great epoch." Konshin's indignation at Zhukovskii's reports on the moon, made to the imperial family, was shared by many who believed that he was squandering his poetic gifts on ladies-in-waiting.⁵⁸ As Viazemskii wrote to Zhukovskii himself in 1821, "Providence ignited your fire of talent to honor the people [*v chest' narodu*], not to amuse the court."⁵⁹

Yet another possible remedy for the impasse perceived by Zhu-kovskii's audience arose in the polemics surrounding the ballads of P. A. Katenin (1792–1853). Katenin's 1815 "The Murderer" ("Ubiitsa") is heavily reminiscent of Zhukovskii's ballads of murder and super-natural retribution, but it is set in a Russian peasant milieu and em-ploys a folk lexicon. One critic sees in this distinction an essential superiority over Zhukovskii's Western borrowings:

> The message of this song recalls Zhukovskii's ballad "The Cranes of Ibycus," translated by him from Schiller. There it is cranes, here it is the moon, that serves to expose the murderer, but the latter is closer to us; we see in "The Murderer" the entire peasant way of life [*ves' byt krest'ianskii*] and do not doubt that everything happened the way that the writer recounted it.[60]

Zhukovskii's response to this controversy was not to plunge into the *Russian* peasant way of life but to translate the rural idylls of Johann Peter Hebel (1760–1826), beginning with "Oat Porridge" ("Ovsianyi kisel'," 1816 translation of "Das Habermus," which was written in 1803).[61] Zhukovskii's headnote to the translation is telling: it consists almost entirely of a quotation from Goethe, who commends Hebel for his faithful portrait of the life of the Basel peasantry and their Alemannic dialect (2: 18–19). Thus Zhukovskii offered his public, thirsty for a Russian national epos and Russian folk color, a transla-tion of a Western European peasant idyll, complete with a recom-mendation from a great German poet. It is as though Zhukovskii, the poet of the soul, refused to recognize the earthly difference be-tween an Alemannic peasant and a Russian one. As Polevoi wrote, "Do not seek *nationality* [*narodnost'*] in Zhukovskii. His spirit does not live on earth, and what are positive earthly forms to him!" (no. 20, p. 542). The idylls of Hebel failed to find an enthusiastic audience in Russia; as I. I. Dmitriev wrote to A. I. Turgenev, "It seems that the poet is gradually turning into a courtier . . . , and meanwhile we must live on 'Oat porridge.'"[62]

Zhukovskii, who eventually redeemed his career through yet an-other translation, of Homer's *Odyssey*, adopted none of the proposals advanced by his critics and friends in the 1810's and 1820's, becoming neither the newspaper poet desired by Viazemskii nor the author of a truly Russian *poema*, nor yet the recorder of the peasant way of life.

In the conception of *Dead Souls*, however, Gogol managed to do all three. It is as if Gogol took the motto "everything for the soul" and brought it "back to earth," assigning the word *soul* a specific, peculiarly Russian referent—the muzhik, whose world is the locus and inspirer of linguistic invention and creative hypothesis.

In view of the prominence accorded the literature of early Romanticism in *Dead Souls*, as well as the repeated references to the glorious campaign of 1812—the occasion for Zhukovskii's unfulfilled promise to deliver the great Russian *poema*—the novel is perhaps meant to be read against the background, and measured against the "failure," of the work of Zhukovskii and his school. Gogol's literary apprenticeship to Zhukovskii is an illustration of Tynianov's and Shklovskii's (and Harold Bloom's) model of literary evolution, which proceeds not by peaceful inheritance but by rebellion and revision.

Karlinsky and others have pointed out that the plot of Gogol's "Vii" is borrowed from Zhukovskii's 1814 version of Robert Southey's ballad "The Old Woman of Berkeley" (1798), but the borrowing is not a simple one. In reworking Southey's tale of a dying witch who attempts unsuccessfully to buy salvation through the prayers of "the Monk my son, and my daughter the Nun," Zhukovskii adds a few purely Russian notes to the church decor and intensifies the resemblance of the old woman's ride with the Devil to Lenore's journey with her dead lover (1: 367–74).[63] Gogol, however, goes much further, swamping the central vigil scene with naturalistic depictions of Ukrainian student and farmyard life, making the witch's ride into a fantasy of sexual perversity, and transforming the vigil itself from a scene of mass prayer into a lone man's duel with the powers of darkness. Southey's ballad, a rather conventional exercise in Gothic horror, becomes a weird and idiosyncratic psychological drama with an unmistakeable "narodnyi" (national) coloration. It could be argued that the plot of *Dead Souls* is an analogous reworking of "Sel'skoe kladbishche," Zhukovskii's translation of Gray's "Elegy Written in a Country Churchyard."[64] This elegy, a meditation on the graves of "the rude Forefathers of the hamlet," is a tissue of hypothesis, exploring the unfulfilled possibilities of the uneducated peasantry, whose deaths, and the hopelessness of their lives, have closed off all forking paths:

> Perhaps in this neglected spot is laid
> Some heart once pregnant with celestial fire;
> Hands, that the rod of empire might have sway'd,
> Or wak'd to extasy the living lyre.
>
> .   .   .
>
> Some village-Hampden, that with dauntless breast
> The little Tyrant of his fields withstood;
> Some mute inglorious Milton here may rest,
> Some Cromwell guiltless of his country's blood.[65]

The imagined lives of dead peasants are placed at the heart of *Dead Souls* as well, but no longer in the patronizing spirit of "Country Churchyard" or Southey's *Lives and Works of the Uneducated Poets* (1831).[66] In *Dead Souls* the Russian peasant does not have alien accomplishments thrust upon him to almost grotesque effect (village-Hampden, mute inglorious Milton) but is celebrated for his own plebeian realm of creativity—language and work. The narrator and the hero of *Dead Souls* may regard the muzhik as an unknown, but they hypothesize about him in terms of peasant culture, not high culture.

The Endless Song

Despite the narrator's assurance that "the chief events and mainsprings of the *poema* are not fixed" on Selifan and Petrushka (6: 19), the life of the Russian serf is a constant undercurrent in *Dead Souls*. The idea that the novel is an indignant satire on slave-owning Russia may have been discredited by Vladimir Nabokov and others, but the pathos and misery of the serfs' lives is glimpsed at every turn: begging orphans (6: 21); deaths through fire, epidemic illness, and starvation (6: 33, 99, 108, 121, 240); persecution of the poorest serfs by an unscrupulous steward (6: 33); serfs being forced by a sadistic, miserly master to walk barefoot on frosty ground (6: 124); the rape of peasant women by a police inspector (6: 194).[67] Yet the negative side of Russian peasant life is subordinated in *Dead Souls* to the higher mission of the muzhik, which by the end of the novel is synonymous with the mission of Russia. This more grandiose aspect of the muzhik's existence is embodied in the motif of the song.

The song makes its first appearance in chapter 3, when Selifan gets lost in the dark on the way to Sobakevich's village. This first description is also the most detailed, but its amplitude notwithstanding, it still has the character of a generalization: "Selifan, swinging his whip, struck up [*zatianul*] a song-not-a-song [*pesniu ne pesniu*], something so long that it had no end. Everything went into it: all the encouraging and impelling cries with which horses are regaled in all Russia from one end to the other, indiscriminate adjectives of all genders and qualities, whatever popped out of his mouth first" (6: 42). The song is without a specific form, for it has no end; it is not specific to the singer, for its material is used all over Russia; it is not even specific to its addressees, for the adjectives are indiscriminate. In earlier redactions the song is significantly more particularized. Instead of summarizing its contents, the narrator actually quotes Selifan at length, thus ascribing a definite content to the song despite the disclaimer "It began *almost* this way" (6: 268; emphasis added). In a subsequent version the quotations are removed, but a few of the adjectives are listed by the narrator, this time without a disclaimer (6: 363).

The next appearance of the song is at the home of Nozdrev: "Poseredine stolovoi stoiali dereviannye kozly, i dva muzhika, stoia na nikh, belili steny, zatiagivaia kakuiu-to beskonechnuiu pesniu" (In the middle of the dining room stood a scaffolding, and the two muzhiks standing on it were whitewashing the walls, striking up some sort of endless song; 6: 72). This song is linked to Selifan's song both by the verb *zatiagivat'* (to strike up) and by its endlessness. In this case as well, earlier versions characterize the song more specifically: "beskonechnuiu pesniu, sostoiavshuiu iz dvukh glasnykh: *a* i *o*" (an endless song, consisting of two vowels: *a* and *o*; 6: 376–77). There seems to be a conscious effort to remove all distinguishing marks, to encourage the perception of the song as essentially the same one (hence, endless) in all its manifestations.

In the central chapter Chichikov strikes up a song in his elation over buying Pliushkin's sizable lot of dead souls. *A* song, but not *the* song, or at best a perverted version of it: "I nakonets zatianul kakuiu-to pesniu, do takoi stepeni neobyknovennuiu, chto sam Selifan slushal, slushal i potom, pokachav slegka golovoi, skazal: 'Vish' ty, kak barin poet!'" (And finally he struck up some sort of song, such an unusual one that Selifan himself listened, listened and then, slightly shaking his head, said, "Just hear how the master is singing!" 6: 130). Not only does this song lack the quality of endlessness but it is incomprehensible to Selifan, the original and final singer of *the* song. The last adjective that could be applied to the true song is *unusual*, for its cardinal qualities are familiarity and universality. Moreover, the true song could not arise as an expression of greedy elation; it is above and beyond such earthly motivation.

The universal song recurs in chapter 7, but this time it arises in the shadow world of the imagined lives of the runaway serfs. The narrator's vivid picture of the grain wharf on which Abakum Fyrov works is concluded by the universal refrain, the endless song: "I druzhno, kak prezhde guliali i besilis', primetes' za trud i pot, tashcha liamku pod odnu beskonechnuiu, kak Rus', pesniu" (And, in unison, as you formerly caroused and raised hell, you will set about toiling and sweating, towing the barge to the accompaniment of a single song, endless as Rus'; 6: 139). The song, though imaginary, is clearly the continuation of the one begun by Selifan while driving his master's carriage and taken up by the muzhiks while whitewashing the walls; again it accompanies the toil of the lower classes. Chichikov's frivolous and incomprehensible aria in chapter 6 is now more obviously an anomaly.

In the final chapter the song achieves its broadest symbolic expression. On Chichikov's way out of town, the sights along the road are enumerated in a list that typifies the zoom lens of Gogol's vision: the items are placed in an undistinguished sequence, but they vary in size and particularity from the sign on a box carried by a soldier, to "polia neogliadnye, i po tu storonu, i po druguiu" (immeasurable fields, both on this side and on the other; 6: 220). Although the list is introduced as a set of visual phenomena—"poshli vnov' pisat' . . ." (there again began to be seen . . .)—aural sensations enter in as well, most notably "zatianutaia vdali pesnia" (a song struck up in the distance). This song, emblem of the "nepostizhimaia, tainaia sila" (incomprehensible secret force; 6: 220) of Russia, like all secret things, urges the narrator into compulsive questioning and hypothesis, interrupted only by Chichikov's abrupt cry to his serf, "Derzhi, derzhi, durak!" (Hold on, hold on, you fool! 6: 221).

The final appearance of the song, on the final page of *Dead Souls*, brings the motifs of work, mystery, and the fate of Russia together in the image of the bird troika. Earlier in his career Gogol had proposed that a true folk opera could be composed from the work songs of Russia:

Along the Volga, from the upper reaches to the sea, along the whole line of barges being pulled, the boatmen's songs pour out. To the accompaniment of songs, bricks are thrown from hand to hand, and cities spring up like mushrooms. To the accompaniment of the songs of peasant women the Russian man is swaddled, married, and buried. Everything of the road— nobility and commonness—flies to the accompaniment of coachmen's songs. By the Black Sea a beardless swarthy Cossack with a tarred mustache who is loading his arquebus sings an old song; and there, at the other end of the country, astride on a floating ice floe, a Russian whaler harpoons a whale and strikes up a song. Do not we have the material for our own opera? (8: 184)

By the time of *Dead Souls*, Gogol is no longer concerned with composing an opera; he has a loftier role in mind for the song that accompanies work. In the final two paragraphs of the novel, both the song and the troika are presented in a double light, as the earthly creation of the Russian muzhik and as the mysterious, hypothesis-inducing symbol of Russia. The credit for inventing the troika is given unequivocally to the muzhik:

Ekh, troika! ptitsa troika, kto tebia vydumal? znat', u boikogo naroda ty mogla tol'ko rodit'sia, . . . I ne khitryi, kazhis', dorozhnyi snariad, ne zhelez-nym skhvachen vintom, a naskoro zhivym, s odnym toporom da dolotom, snariadil i sobral tebia iaroslavskii rastoropnyi muzhik. Ne v nemetskikh bot-fortakh iamshchik: boroda da rukavitsy, i sidit chort znaet na chem; a priv-stal, da zamakhnulsia, da zatianul pesniu. (6: 246–47)

(Ah, troika! bird troika, who invented you? You, it seems, could only be born among a bold people. . . . It seems that the traveling gear is not complicated, not clamped with an iron screw, but fitted out by an efficient Yaroslavl muzhik, equipped hastily, in rough and ready fashion with just an ax and a chisel. The coachman is not wearing German jackboots but a beard and gauntlets, and he's sitting on the Devil knows what; and he has stood up, raised his arm, and struck up a song.)

In the next paragraph, this specific, earthly troika is transformed into a symbol of the nation: "Ne tak li i ty, Rus', chto boikaia neobgoni-maia troika, nesesh'sia?" (Do not you, too, O Rus', fly like a bold troika, impossible to overtake? 6: 247). Created by the hands of the efficient muzhik, this troika shares his mystery and unknowability, and, like the dead serfs, it inspires questioning and hypothesis:

Ostanovilsia porazhennyi bozh'im chudom sozertsatel': ne molniia li eto, sbroshennaia s neba? Chto znachit eto navodiashchee uzhas dvizhenie? i chto za nevedomaia sila zakliuchena v sikh nevedomykh svetom koniakh? Ekh, koni, koni, chto za koni! Vikhri li sidiat v vashikh grivakh? Chutkoe li ukho gorit vo vsiakoi vashei zhilke? Zaslyshali s vyshiny znakomuiu pesniu, druzhno i razom napriagli mednye grudi i, pochti ne tronuv kopytami zemli, prevratilis' v odni vytianutye linii, letiashchie po vozdukhu, i mchitsia, vsia vdokhnovennaia bogom! (6: 247)

(The observer has stopped, struck by a divine miracle: Is it not lightning [*ne molniia li eto*], cast down from the sky? What does this terror-inspiring movement mean? What unknown force is contained in these steeds, un-known to the world? Ah, steeds, steeds, what steeds! Are there whirlwinds [*Vikhri li sidiat*] in your manes? Does a sensitive ear burn [*Chutkoe li ukho gorit*] in each of your fibers? They have caught the sound of the familiar song from on high; they have tensed their brazen breasts in unison and all at once, and, not touching the earth with their hooves, have turned into sheer stretched-out lines, flying through the air, and the troika rushes on inspired by God!)

This symbol, powerful and provocative as it is, retains its unknow-ability: "Rus', kuda zh nesesh'sia ty, dai otvet? Ne daet otveta" (Rus', whither are you flying, answer me? It gives no answer; 6: 247).[68]

The Light of Thought

In *Dead Souls*, Gogol brilliantly overcomes the obstacle standing in the way of his creation of the Russian *poema*, the same obstacle that faced Zhukovskii: the (disputable) fact that he "had absolutely no knowledge of real Russian life." By casting the life of the Russian muzhik in the mode of mystery and hypothesis, Gogol made irrele-

vant the question of his objective knowledge of that life. He was able
to make the muzhik central to the fate of Russia without having to
speak *for* the muzhik by making both the serf and the nation an
unknowable Other, subject to endless questioning ("dai otvet") but
not obligated to answer ("ne daet otveta").

Both Gogol and Zhukovskii are preoccupied with the mysterious,
the obscure, and the unknown, the world of the "dead soul." But
Gogol manages to escape the accusation leveled at Zhukovskii: "Pod
etim tumanom ne taitsia svet mysli" (Under that mist no light of
thought is hidden). Zhukovskii himself offers a clue to the difference
between himself and Gogol in his meditation (ca. 1809–10) on a
statement by Chateaubriand: "Il n'est rien de beau, de doux, de
grand dans la vie que les choses mysterieuses."[69] First Zhukovskii
characterizes the mysterious in terms consonant with his own aesthetic practice:

I do not know why only the mysterious should be beautiful, sweet, and
sublime. Is this not stated too *generally*? Of course, everything mysterious
causes the soul more exertion: it is natural to see a thing and wish to pene-
trate everything unclear and hidden within it! Perhaps *the mysterious* is also
pleasing because a person would rather *imagine* than *know* and see. Why are
distant views so pleasing? Because they appear unclearly! Because the eye,
seeing objects, nevertheless leaves imagination (which never likes to rest) its
freedom to ornament them. Mysteriousness is always associated with the
idea of gloom. The darkness of forests always inspires a certain horror,
which is very pleasing to the heart; this horror is nothing other than the
unfamiliarity [*neizvestnost'*] of the objects that surround you; you can imagine *everything* around you, because you see *nothing*.[70]

But then Zhukovskii reveals an uncharacteristic appreciation of the
bright, clear, and vivid:

Can one believe that in life only the mysterious can be sublime, sweet, and
beautiful? I agree that it can be both pleasing and lofty. But many things in
the moral and physical world besides the mysterious produce these impressions. What is mysterious about sunrise and sunset, a starry sky, a seascape,
Alpine meadows, and so forth? What is mysterious about the patriotism of
Brutus, the charity and passionate philanthropy of Jean Paul, the character
of Henry the Great [Henry IV of France], the death of Socrates, the demise
of Jesus Christ, which in itself, apart from religion, is majestic and raptur-

ous? Obscure, unclear feelings are delightful. . . . But vivid [*iasnye*] feelings, those with which some clear [*iasnyi*], complete idea is associated, must of course be more pleasing; some sort of disquiet is always associated with unclearness or obscurity [*neizvestnost'*] to a greater or lesser degree. At the same time, everything *clear* [*iasnoe*] leaves us calm. We take *full* pleasure all by ourselves. *Unclear* ideas afford the soul sweet melancholy pleasures (for melancholy is in a certain sense a *deficiency*). *Clear* ideas afford more vivid pleasures, for they are more complete, more perceptible. The pleasures brought by unclear ideas may be prolonged, for the unknown is always new and *exciting*; the pleasures brought by clear ideas must be briefer, because that which is known becomes boring.[71]

In *Dead Souls*, Gogol manages to combine the "sweet melancholy" pleasures associated with the unknown with the fuller, more vivid pleasures of the known: the mysterious dead do not remain hidden by the mist of ignorance but are accorded vivid, specific features through the operation of hypothesis and divination. The rhetoric of forking paths, with its graphically imagined alternatives, provides the "light of thought" in Gogol's *tuman*; the lack of answers to the questions posed by the imagination keeps those proliferating alternatives from congealing into certainty, "because that which is known becomes boring."

Zhukovskii's literature of the soul is an undeniable presence in and inspiration for *Dead Souls*, but by the end of the novel Zhukovskii's poetic language, with its cult of the ineffable and inexpressible, has been rejected as a vehicle for Russian self-expression. In *Dead Souls* the language of the Russian muzhik, maximally precise, straightforward, and expressive, achieves ascendancy over the ladies' language of vagueness and indirection, inspired by the "inexpressible" ideal of early Romanticism. At the end of the novel, the narrator alludes once again to the author's difficult calling, so different from that of the family man–writer, whose lofty images never touch the earth. The bachelor-writer must accept responsibility for the message-bearing powers of language:

K chemu tait' slovo? Kto zhe, kak ne avtor, dolzhen skazat' sviatuiu pravdu? Vy boites' gluboko-ustremlennogo vzora, vy strashites' sami ustremit' na chto-nibud' glubokii vzor, vy liubite skol'znut' po vsemu nedumaiushchimi glazami. (6: 245)

(Why hide the word? Who, if not the author, must utter the holy truth? You are afraid of a deeply directed gaze, you are yourselves afraid to direct a deep gaze at anything; you love to skim along everything with unthinking eyes.)

This passage provides the key to the enigmatic words uttered by Selifan immediately afterward. The sleeping muzhik is awakened by Chichikov, who for one final time poses the question posed by the entire novel, "Ekhe-khe! chto zh ty?" (Hey! What are you—? 6: 246); the omission of the understood verb *doing* makes the statement ambiguous. Once fully awake, Selifan calls out, ostensibly to his team but conceivably to all Rus', "Ne boisia!" (Do not be afraid! 6: 246). In the light of the immediately preceding reproach, "You are afraid of a deeply directed gaze," Selifan, representative of the Russian muzhik, seems to be enjoining Gogol's audience not to fear the potency and expressivity of language.

4

Fragment, Parable, Promise

Viele Werke der Alten sind Fragmente geworden. Viele
Werke der Neuern sind es gleich bey der Entstehung.

—Friedrich Schlegel

В глазах людей весьма умных, но не имеющих
поэтического чутья, [сочинения Пушкина]—отрывки
недосказанные, легкие, мгновенные; в глазах людей,
одаренных поэтическим чутьем, они—полные поэмы,
обдуманные, оконченные, всё заключающие в себе,
что им нужно.

—N. V. Gogol

Novalis saw the deficiency of history in its built-in incompleteness,
in the impossibility of finding enough sources to make any account
universal and comprehensive. Literary history has pinpointed a similar deficiency in *Dead Souls*, to some extent spoiling our apprehension of that work. Thanks to Gogol's letters, his friends' memoirs,
and the carefully assembled fragments of his projected sequel, we
cannot escape the awareness that the novel is incomplete, unachieved.[1] In fact, when viewed in the context of Gogol's other works,
this "unfinished" novel is marked by a special type of closure and
formal unity. The text is modeled on the riddle, particularly the type
of riddle known as parable, and the illusion of open-endedness is
designed to mock the thirst for an answer awakened by the enigma.

Dead Souls ends with the flight of Chichikov in the bird troika,
itself transformed into a symbol of Russia. But this is not where
Gogol's involvement with writing *Dead Souls* ended. After the publication of the novel in 1842, he spent much of the rest of his life
trying to write a sequel, sometimes envisioned as a purgatory and

paradise to redeem the provincial inferno depicted in the first part. One of Gogol's last acts was to burn most of this sequel, a loss that literary critics and historians have mourned ever since. Gogol's intention to add something essential to *Dead Souls* continues to haunt the novel, a specter that, like Chichikov's "dead souls," is insubstantial but powerfully disturbing. It is my purpose in this chapter to demonstrate that *Dead Souls* is a finished work by the laws of Gogolian form. The unfulfilled promise of completion, when read not in biographical but in literary terms, is a device that guards the text against neat solutions and fixed interpretations. It is not only Chichikov who escapes at the end of *Dead Souls*; the novel itself escapes its readers' (and author's) desire for the last word.

The *Poema* Within the *Poema*

Near the end of *Dead Souls* the townspeople speculate on the origins and character of Chichikov, the man who has appeared out of nowhere to create turmoil in their midst. The most elaborate hypothesis is offered by the postmaster, who spins the complicated "Story of Captain Kopeikin." This interpolated narrative is a seemingly detachable exercise in *skaz*. But when the censors threatened to cut the story, disturbed by what they interpreted as slights to the tsar, Gogol reacted strongly, insisting that tearing it from the tissue of the novel would leave a gaping hole, impossible to repair. Indeed, the episode is closely related in form to the narrative in which it is set. The hero of the tale is a pathetic veteran of 1812 who has lost an arm and a leg in the service of his country but whose petitions for a pension are repeatedly rebuffed. Finally, on the point of starvation, he becomes the leader of a gang of bandits, and the story is broken off. The postmaster introduces his narrative by announcing its genre: "Da ved' eto, vprochem, esli rasskazat', budet prezanimatel'naia dlia kakogo-nibud' pisatelia, v nekotorom rode, tselaia poema" (For you know, [this story], if it's told, will turn out to be for some writer a most interesting, in a certain sense, entire *poema*; 6: 199). *Poema* is, of course, the generic designation Gogol himself appended to the title of *Dead Souls*, and the question of what he meant by it has remained largely unanswered.[2]

The postmaster claims not only the same genre but also the same hero, for he asserts that Chichikov is Kopeikin in disguise. Although the identification of Kopeikin with Chichikov is an absurd red herring, the two careers have an underlying parallelism: in both cases a rootless man, rejected by his father, travels to another city to make his fortune and is constantly led on by the vision of Western European luxury, as symbolized by Holland linen. Both receive the same message from the outside world—"Find yourself some means of subsistence"—and both heed the message by turning to a life of crime. Although the postmaster's hearers are at a loss to understand how he could have confused Chichikov with the maimed Kopeikin, both Chichikov and Kopeikin are engaged in a monomaniacal quest to obtain compensation for a perceived handicap—in Chichikov's case, the poverty of his background.

The postmaster himself aspires to the role of artist and begins his narration as the result of a sudden burst of inspiration. His speech is "garnished" with meaningless particles and phatic expressions in an exaggerated version of Gogol's characteristic narrative voice. The postmaster's eccentric manner of expression, so suitable for dramatic reading, amounts to a self-parody on Gogol's part. The two narrator-authors could even be said to share a common source. The postmaster is fond of reading Edward Young's *Night Thoughts* (1741–45), and the germ of the Kopeikin story can be found in "Night the First: On Life, Death, and Immortality," among a catalogue of the miseries of mankind:

> Some, for hard masters, broken under arms,
> In battle lopt away, with half their limbs,
> Beg bitter bread through realms their valour saved,
> If so the tyrant, or his minion, doom.
>
> (p. 19)

One is tempted to imagine the postmaster spinning his complicated tale from this meager thread just as Gogol, according to the legend that he himself promoted, spun his finest creations from trivial anecdotes. The narrator of *Dead Souls* might also conceivably have found inspiration here, for the same "Night" includes a passage that is philosophically close to both Zhukovskii's *dvoemirie* and the central conceit of *Dead Souls*. Thinking of the dear departed, the poet exclaims:

> They live! they greatly live a life on earth
> Unkindled, unconceiv'd; and from an eye
> Of tenderness let heavenly pity fall
> On me, more justly number'd with the dead.
> This is the desert, this the solitude:
> How populous, how vital, is the grave!
> This is creation's melancholy vault,
> The vale funereal, the sad cypress gloom;
> The land of apparitions, empty shades!
> All, all on earth is shadow; all beyond
> Is substance; the reverse is Folly's creed:
> How solid all, where change shall be no more!
>
> (p. 15)[3]

The dead serfs that Chichikov buys do inhabit a "populous and vital grave": conjured by the memories of their owners and the fertile imagination of Chichikov, they take on a colorful life of their own in the narrative. Chichikov has to remind the landowner Sobakevich that the serfs he has been extolling are deceased: "'Yes, of course they're dead,' said Sobakevich, as though he had thought better of it and recollected that they were in fact dead, and then added, 'But after all, even then, what about these people who are reckoned among the living these days? What kind of people are they? Flies, not people'" (6: 103).

The parallelism between the heroes and the narrators of the two stories is matched by a parallelism of structure. This "entire *poema*" not only concerns a fragmentary hero but is itself a fragment, at least in terms of plot. At the end, the narrator asserts that we have reached only the beginning of the tale: "Vot tut-to i nachinaetsia, mozhno skazat', nit', zaviazka romana" (And here's where, one might say, the thread, the opening of a novel begins; 6: 205). The next-to-the-last page of *Dead Souls* features a similar promise: "There are two large parts ahead—that's not a trifle" (6: 246). The Kopeikin fragment is, however, given a sort of completeness through circularity. It begins with the postmaster's exclamation that Chichikov is "none other than Captain Kopeikin" (6: 199) and ends, "And the chief of that gang was, my good sir, none other than . . ." (6: 205). We can complete the sentence with either *Kopeikin* or *Chichikov*, making the circle complete: Chichikov is revealed to be Kopeikin, who becomes a robber chief, who is revealed to be Chichikov. In the larger narrative, it is the chronological structure that forms a circle, for the story of Chichikov's childhood and early career is told at the end of the novel and carried up to the point at which he conceives the scheme that forms the plot of *Dead Souls*.

Thus the Kopeikin "digression" is actually a miniature mirror of the novel in which it is found.[4] In particular, the endings of the two narratives share a special status: both tales end immediately after a promise that the narrative has just begun. Although the Kopeikin story is forcibly broken off right after the promise that it is only a beginning, the reader does not expect the thread to be taken up again. The story stands by itself, with the enigma of Kopeikin's life in the forest remaining unnarrated, unnarratable. Gogol's reader has traditionally made greater demands on *Dead Souls* itself. Our knowledge of Gogol's biography, of the ten years he spent trying to write the promised sequel to *Dead Souls*, has obscured that work's homology not just with the Kopeikin story but also with other works of Gogol that are presented as incomplete.

The Promise of Closure

We find an almost identical structure at the beginning of Gogol's career. The most sophisticated story in his first collection, *Evenings on a Farm near Dikanka*, is "Ivan Fedorovich Shpon'ka and His Auntie" ("Ivan Fedorovich Shpon'ka i ego tetushka"). The story is incomplete because, as the narrator explains, his wife used the final pages of it as liners for her cake pans, and the tale as printed ends with a promise of continuation: "Meanwhile, a completely new scheme had ripened in Auntie's head, about which you will learn in the next chapter." Yet another promise of completion is included in the narrator's introductory apology. He informs the curious reader that he can hear the end of the story from a certain Stepan Ivanovich in the town of Gadiach, who knows it by heart and will gladly tell it all over again "from beginning to end" (1: 284). The written word, which has taken on corporeality and is thus subject to the hazards of the physical universe (ovens, for example), is fragmentary and insufficient; it must be supplemented by the living oral word, which alone is integral and incorruptible, "from beginning to end."

"Ivan Shpon'ka," the "Story of Captain Kopeikin," and *Dead Souls* all end with promises of continuation. In the case of "Ivan Shpon'ka" and "Captain Kopeikin," the reader who fails to recognize the promise as a statement *in* the work rather than *about* the work will be disappointed on turning the page to find that the tale is ended. In fact, however, open-endedness constitutes a special sort of Gogolian closure: the promise of continuation is the sign that the work is over.[5]

A closer look at the ways in which Gogol's published fictional works end will help us place *Dead Souls* more squarely in context. Despite its special status as Gogol's only large-scale work of fiction, it belongs with other works of the period 1837–42 whose endings leave promises unfulfilled. Gogol's works fall into two broad categories: those with what I shall call conclusive closure, where plot intrigues are resolved and some sort of equilibrium is achieved by the end of the work, and those with promissory closure, which are often presented as fragments of works in progress or as narratives broken off before their planned conclusions and which seem to point into the future with a promise of continuation. The distribution of the two kinds of works is roughly chronological, with conclusively closed works predominating in the period before 1837. Within the category of promissory closure, there are several subcategories, all of which either have been or will be discussed in detail in this chapter: (1) works that end with a promise of continuation (like "Ivan Shpon'ka" and "Captain Kopeikin"); (2) works (like "Captain Kopeikin") structured such that a thematic or temporal circularity compensates for the apparent incompletion of the plot; (3) works that set up a paratactic series of events which could theoretically be added on to indefinitely; (4) works that embody *zaviazka* without *razviazka*; and (5) works that end at a point of maximum rhetorical intensity. Works with promissory closure may belong to one or more of these subcategories; *Dead Souls* belongs to all of them.

In *Evenings on a Farm near Dikan'ka* (1831–32) and *Mirgorod* (1835), continuous coherent stories end with a tying up of all narrative loose ends. ("Ivan Shpon'ka" is a major exception in *Evenings*.) By the end of the story, the central conflict (usually with the Devil) has ended with either the hero's triumph or his death, and the narrator is left to contemplate the reestablishment of equilibrium, of "business as usual." Paradigmatic for this type of ending is the conclusion of "Vii," in which the companions of the hero, Khoma Brut, are shown complacently continuing their habitual pursuits after Khoma's spectacular destruction by the powers of darkness.

Other works that end conclusively can nevertheless be regarded as fragmentary, but their fragmentation is embodied not in the lack of an ending but in internal discontinuity and incongruity. Here belong "Nevskii Avenue" ("Nevskii prospekt," 1835), "Diary of a Madman" ("Zapiski sumasshedshego," 1835, originally "Scraps from the Diary of a Madman"), and "The Nose" ("Nos," 1836). "Nevskii Avenue" combines overwrought melodrama with low comedy in a generic patchwork that finds its most adequate metaphorical representation within the story itself, in a description of the St. Petersburg bohemians:

Sometimes you'll encounter them wearing a fine tailcoat and a stained cloak, an expensive velvet waistcoat and a frockcoat all spattered with paint. In just the same way, you'll sometimes see on one of their unfinished landscapes a nymph sketched in upside down, which the artist, unable to find another place, dashed off on the stained primer of his former work, which he had once painted with delight. (3: 17)

Attempts to reconcile the two halves of "Nevskii Avenue" are usually strained, for the effect of their juxtaposition depends precisely on their utter incongruity.[6] The same incongruity has been a legendary stumbling block for the reader of *Dead Souls*, in which the comic grotesque coexists with lofty rhetorical outbursts once commonly referred to as lyrical digressions.

The disconnected structure of "Diary of a Madman" and "The Nose" might perhaps originate in an attempt to parody the distorted picture of reality offered by French-inspired melodrama. In "St. Petersburg Notes for the Year 1836" ("Peterburgskie zapiski 1836 goda"), Gogol tellingly characterizes this distortion:

If you were to collect all the melodramas that have been presented in our day, you might think you had a cabinet of curiosities, in which all monstrosities and mistakes of nature had been purposely gathered together, or, better, a calendar, in which all strange events had been noted with calendrical coldness, where opposite each date had been posted: today in such-and-such a place there was such-and-such a swindle, and today they cut off the heads of such-and-such robbers and incendiaries. (8: 183)

It is precisely this arbitrary arrangement, this "calendrical coldness," that Gogol adopts to present his array of "mistakes of nature." "The Nose" begins, "On March 25 there occurred in St. Petersburg an unusually strange event" (3: 49); the first entry in the madman's diary is, "October 3. On this day there occurred an unusual adventure" (3: 193). The absence of a logical connection among the three parts of "The Nose" is clouded by the "fog" at the endings of the first two sections: in a world where natural laws have been revoked, the reader has no right to expect consequentiality. In "Diary of a Madman," the disruption of the natural order is motivated not by a mysterious supernatural agency but by the delusions of an insane person. The false order imposed on his delirium by the diary form is laid bare toward the end of the story, when the dates become utter nonsense: "January of the same year, which came after February" (3: 212).

On a larger scale, the internally fragmentary structure of "Nevskii Avenue" and "Diary of a Madman" is echoed in the composition of *Arabesques* (1834–35), the collection in which the two stories originally appeared. This two-volume miscellany, admitted by its author to be "a mixture of everything, a kasha" (8: 749), contains stories and nonfictional essays that range over topics as diverse as architecture and geography, historiography and folk music. While the stories depict the modern world as "a multitude of diverse pieces [mixed together] without meaning or sense" ("Nevskii Avenue"), the essays are linked by a pervasive unifying thread—the theme of art, specifically literature. It is fitting that this unity should be invisible to the cursory glance, for in these sketches Gogol exalts the wholeness that can be achieved only by the true artist and that is based not on external form but on inner thought. Friedrich Schlegel elaborated the Romantic theory of the arabesque, and the homage to him implied in Gogol's title *Arabesques* is borne out in the composition of the work, for the encompassing of art and scholarship in an encyclopedic miscellany is a quintessentially Romantic project. To quote Schlegel's *Dialogue on Poetry*: "The innermost mysteries of all the arts and all the sciences [*Wissenschaften*] are . . . a possession of poetry."[7]

Internally discontinuous works like "The Nose" and "Diary of a Madman" may nevertheless be conclusively closed: at the end of "The Nose," Major Kovalev's nose is back in its place and all's right with the world; in "Diary of a Madman," Poprishchin's intrigues and delusions have found their last resting place in the madhouse. The transition from conclusively closed works to works whose endings point to possible or promised continuation can be illustrated by the 1842 revision of "The Portrait" ("Portret," 1835). Both versions of the story deal with a too-realistic portrait into which the soul of a demonic usurer has passed. Both versions end in a similar way: the son of the man who painted the accursed portrait finds the painting at an auction and delivers a monologue about its origins to the assembled crowd. In the 1835 version, he recalls his father's prophetic dream that the demonic force of the painting will be dissipated if its story is solemnly told at the first new moon fifty years after it was painted. As soon as the artist's son announces that he believes this anniversary to have arrived, he and the crowd redirect their attention to the painting. Before their eyes, the features of the moneylender-Antichrist are transformed into an insignificant landscape. The spell is broken, the curse has lost its force, and the story ends.

In the 1842 version, the young man's narrative sets up a paratactic series of events connected with the moneylender and, later, with his portrait. Each person who borrows money from the usurer meets a tragic fate; their stories are recounted one after the other. After the usurer dies and his demonic force passes into his portrait, the same curse attends ownership of the painting. The artist who acquires the portrait at the beginning of the story and whose appalling history occupies the first half of "The Portrait" is but one more in this series of unfortunate art collectors. As in the 1835 version, the crowd turns to view the portrait at the end of the young man's monologue. In this case, however, it has disappeared: someone has taken advantage of the crowd's absorption in the monologue to steal the fatal painting. The implication is that the thief will succumb to the same curse that afflicted previous owners of the portrait; the paratactic series of events may theoretically continue indefinitely, extending beyond the conclusion of the story as printed.

In *Dead Souls*, as in the 1842 version of "The Portrait," an open-ended paratactic series of events is established. The final chapter of *Dead Souls* reviews Chichikov's life, which consists of cyclical repetitions: self-limitation and self-denial, enrichment through confidence scheme, expansion into luxurious living, exposure of the scheme, defeat and humiliation, self-limitation and self-denial, and so on and on. We realize that the first ten chapters have been the detailed depiction of one of these cycles and that by the end of the novel it is time for yet another cycle to begin.[8]

The revision of "The Portrait," which transformed the conclusively closed story into one that points beyond its own ending, dates from 1840–42, when Gogol rethought and revised many of his works in preparation for the publication of his four-volume *Collected Works* (*Sochineniia Nikolaia Gogolia*, 1842). This period is marked by a special preoccupation with promissory endings and intentional fragments. Gogol revisited not only completed, published works but two unrealized projects as well: a novel of Italian life, a chunk of which he published under the title "Rome (A Fragment)" ("Rim [Otryvok]") in the journal the *Muscovite* (*Moskvitianin*) in 1842, and a play about an ambitious civil servant, *The Order of St. Vladimir* (*Vladimir tret'ei stepeni*), parts of which he published in his *Collected Works* under the heading "Dramatic Fragments and Separate Scenes (1832–37)." Besides the complete one-act play *The Gamblers* (*Igroki*) and the programmatic apologia *After the Play* (*Teatral'nyi raz"ezd posle predstavleniia novoi komedii*), this section includes four scenes salvaged from the manuscript of the abandoned comedy: *Morning of a Man of Affairs* (*Utro delovogo cheloveka*), *The Lawsuit* (*Tiazhba*), *Servants' Quarters* (*Lakeiskaia*), and *Fragment* (*Otryvok*).[9] Although Gogol referred to these scenes as "little scraps" (5: 477), they are not just pages torn out of his notebooks. He carefully reworked them for publication as fragments, and because his attitude toward publication was by no means cavalier, it is fair to approach them as works with their own shape and logic. Gogol changed the names of the characters to obscure the fact that the scenes originally belonged to a single play. Each of the four scenes sets in motion the machinery of a conventional dramatic intrigue: a civil servant's schemes for advancement, a dispute over an inheritance, sexual dalliance in the servant class, a mother's scheme to disrupt her son's love affair so that he can marry an heiress. Just as each plot begins to thicken, however, the scene breaks off, usually in the middle of a speech promising future conspiracy or revenge. The Russian word *razviazka* (denouement) is a calque of the French; it preserves the connotation of un-tying knots, untangling the intricate snarls of entwined destinies. But Russian also has a word for the converse operation, *zaviazka*, the initial tying up of the plot's intrigues. *Zaviazka* is usually trans-lated, inadequately, as "beginning"; instead, one might coin the equivalent *nouement*. At any rate, the dramatic fragments embody *zaviazka* without *razviazka*: they display in the baldest possible form Gogol's disdain for conventional plot structures.[10] Like "Captain Ko-peikin," they end at the moment of *zaviazka*; like "Ivan Shpon'ka," with its Freudian dream of marriage, and *Dead Souls*, with its apoca-lyptic address to Russia, they end at a moment of maximum rhetori-cal intensity.[11]

"Rome," the other fragment of an incomplete project that Gogol offered his public in 1842, also ends at a rhetorical high point, soon after the promise of a *zaviazka*. Although fragmentary in plot, its temporal and thematic structure forms the circle of the *uroboros*, the serpent that bites its own tail.[12] The story's *fabula* is straightforward. A Roman prince travels to Paris to be educated. After several years he returns with a new understanding of and love for his native Italy. At the carnival in Rome he spots a beautiful peasant girl named An-nunziata. To learn who she is, he decides to enlist the services of a low-class character named Peppe, whom he takes outside of town so that they can confer in private. Just as he is about to tell the curious Peppe what he wants of him, the prince is struck dumb by the pan-orama of Rome spread out before him. He then sees Annunziata for the second time. End of story. The *siuzhet*, however, is quite differ-ent. The opening scene centers on the prince's *second* glimpse of An-nunziata, outside Rome in the crowd of revelers returning from the carnival at sunset. Then the narrator tells of the prince's education in France, return to Rome, and first encounter with Annunziata. The story ends with the prince standing in dazed oblivion before the magnificent panorama of Rome. The final words of the story are "My God, what a view! Enveloped by it, the prince forgot himself, the beauty of Annunziata, the mysterious fate of his people, and everything in the world" (3: 259). Thus in chronological terms the first scene of the story immediately follows its final scene, and the temporal circle is closed.

In a study of how lyric poems end, Barbara Herrnstein Smith has characterized conventional closure as a moment when there are "no 'loose ends' to be accounted for, no promises that go begging" (p. 35). This is certainly not true of those works of Gogol with what I have called promissory closure: they are marked precisely by their promises that go begging. Like them, *Dead Souls* is given a closure that looks like an opening. Robert Maguire has said that *Dead Souls* is an encyclopedia of all Gogol's previous works; I would add that the closure of *Dead Souls* is an encyclopedia of promissory endings.[13] The text ends with a promise of continuation; the seeming incompletion of the plot is subtly contradicted by the neat circularity of Chichikov's biography; the next scheme in the paractactic series bribes—real estate scam—smuggling operation—dead-souls scheme is yet to be added; the threads of Chichikov's dilemma have been not untied in a satisfying *razviazka* but abandoned in their entangled state of *zaviazka*; and the final page leaves the narrator in the throes of a rhetorical spasm of such intensity that it threatens to overwhelm the entire preceding narrative. On the one hand, the promise of continuation, the open-ended paractactic series, the lack of *razviazka,* and the rhetorical crescendo without decrescendo all seem to tell us that the work is unfinished, that completion lies in the future. On the other hand, we know that precisely this set of features marks closure for an important category of Gogol's works written during the same period as *Dead Souls.*

Stupendous Fragmentariness

We can gain a deeper understanding of Gogol's interest in fragmentation as both incompletion and discontinuity by returning to the fragment "Rome," in which fragmentation is of thematic as well as formal interest. When the hero of "Rome" achieves his adolescent dream of going to Paris, he is at first exhilarated by the bustling capital. Gogol's Paris is the modern city that subjects the individual to the shock of multiple stimuli and forced, intimate contact with the amorphous crowd. Eventually, the prince recognizes the superficiality of a society in which only the new has value and nothing—not art, scholarship, or friendship—is given time to mature and intensify. Paris embodies a particular malignant fragmentation, in which the individual is powerless to effect reintegration.

With the prince's return to Rome, we learn of another sort of fragmentation that offers the individual a valuable active role. The ambiguous title, "Rome (A Fragment)," suggests that Rome, the city itself, is the fragment.[14] In *Middlemarch*, George Eliot describes the same early-nineteenth-century Rome in which Gogol lived as the "city of visible history, where the past of a whole hemisphere seems moving in funeral procession with strange ancestral images and trophies gathered from afar," a city of "stupendous fragmentariness" (1: 348). It was just this stupendous fragmentariness, as the token of a wholeness embracing centuries, that fascinated Gogol. It was not the ideal homogeneity of the imperial past that he desired to see but the present motley ruin, with its telescoping of historical eras. In a letter to his friend Mar'ia Balabina he writes:

If someone asked me . . . what I would prefer to see before me—ancient Rome in its terrible and brilliant grandeur or present-day Rome with its present ruins—I would choose present-day Rome. No, it has never been so beautiful. It is beautiful because this is its 2,588th year, because in one half of it breathes the pagan era, in the other the Christian era, and the two of them are the two greatest ideas in the world.[15]

The erosion of the material splendor of antiquity sets the mind free to reconstruct it more beautifully and completely.

Despite Gogol's protestations to the critic S. P. Shevyrev that the prince cannot be identified with him, the quality of their appreciation of Rome is essentially the same: [the prince] "found everything equally beautiful: the ancient world, which stirred from under a dark architrave; the powerful Middle Ages, which had left everywhere the traces of artist-giants and the magnificent largesse of the popes; and, finally, the modern era, with its teeming population, which had attached itself to the first two. He liked their marvelous merging into one" (3: 324). The prince is equal to the challenge of reconciling the incongruity of Rome's architecture, just as the reader of "Rome" (and "Nevskii Avenue" and *Dead Souls*) must meet the challenge of reading a text that jumps unceremoniously from the sublime to the grotesque and back again.[16] This is not the demonic kaleidoscope of Paris, which dizzies the spectator into mindless wandering from one stimulus to the next. The unity that the prince discerns in Rome is not an inherent property of the city but is imposed by the perceiver's vantage point; from a superior height, the perceiver embraces wide spatial and temporal diversity at one glance: the prince "could now look over everything calmly, as if from a window of the Vatican" (3: 240).[17]

In relation to literature, this act of unification and reconstruction is ultimately the reader's responsibility. Gogol asks a similar effort of his sisters in a letter from Aachen in 1836. He begins a detailed drawing of the city's cathedral, an example of that architectural form which he considered to be the highest expression of the human striving toward divine unity. But he leaves the drawing unfinished: on the left, five stained-glass windows drawn in careful detail; in the middle, the roughly sketched nave and portal; on the right, merely a rectangle drawn with broken lines. Underneath it he writes, "No time to finish. You can complete the rest in your heads" (11: 54).[18]

Gogol's fascination with the promise of unrealized possibilities in the fragment is, of course, a Romantic preoccupation. I have already mentioned *Arabesques*, a work permeated by the spirit of Schlegel's *Dialogue on Poetry*. It is again Schlegel who offers a gloss on Gogol's approach to the fragment in his "systemless system" of aesthetics, the *Athenaeum Fragments*: "The feeling for projects, which could be called fragments from the future, is only distinguished from the feeling for fragments from the past by its direction, which in the former case is progressive and in the latter, regressive."[19] This sense of the fragment as not only a broken, incomplete artifact but as an anticipated, promised project is reflected both in Gogol's feeling for the ruins of Rome and in the promissory closure of the works of 1837–42.[20]

The Parable of "Dead Souls"

If *Dead Souls* asks us to "complete the rest in our heads," what is the nature of the completion that it requires? As with "Captain Kopeikin," we can look within the text for clues to how to read the entire work. At a crucial moment in the novel, the townspeople cry, "Chto zh za pritcha, v samom dele, chto za pritcha eti mertvye dushi?" (What sort of parable, in fact, what sort of parable are these dead souls? 6: 189). The idiomatic meaning of "Chto za pritcha" is simply "What is it?" But no figurative expression in Gogol can be taken just figuratively; as Dmitri Chizhevsky and Nabokov remind us, when a character says, "Chort ego znaet," very often the Devil really does know what's going on.[21] Here the townspeople have stumbled upon an important insight, for the parable, particularly the New Testament parable, is the type of discourse that is most apposite to both Gogol's *Dead Souls* and Chichikov's "dead souls." Frank Kermode has written that parables "call for completion; the parable-event isn't over until a satisfactory answer or explanation is given; the interpretation completes it" (p. 24). What *Dead Souls* seems to require is precisely that: not an ending but an answer, not continuation but interpretation. When *Dead Souls* appeared, critics who were well disposed toward Gogol were eager to mention the sequel and to insist that judgment be reserved until it appeared. Indeed, the second volume as conceived by both author and readers would eliminate the need for judgment or interpretation altogether, for it would itself be the interpretation of, the solution to, the parable that is part I.

The New Testament parable is cast in the realistic details of its hearers' everyday life; it "provides a reliable index to petit-bourgeois and peasant life in the Roman levant."[22] The realistic milieu, once established, is exaggerated and distorted; normal relationships are paradoxically reversed. For example, we must remember how shocking it was for Jesus' audience to hear a member of the despised Samaritan tribe held up as an exemplary hero. The distortion of the everyday puts the hearers on guard, ready to respond actively to the disturbing message being offered.[23] The parable is meant to influence its hearers, not by giving them a clear message but by forcing them to seek an ever-elusive solution to an unfathomable mystery. In interpreting the riddle, the hearers are inevitably forced to examine their own existence. It is this sequence from the external to the internal that Ernst Fuchs has in mind in his maxim "The truth has us ourselves as its object" (p. 143). There is a moment of accusation involved. Eta Linnemann writes: "The parable is also used readily when a man has to hold another responsible for his deeds and omissions. By setting the action of the other man in the light of the parable, he compels him to pass his own verdict on himself, and in this way can convict him" (p. 20). The polyvalence of the parable is essential; each hearer may find in his or her own heart the sin to which the parable has reference. Where no consensus can be reached on meaning, no limitation can be placed on applicability.

In both Chichikov's "dead souls" and Gogol's *Dead Souls*, the plot is composed of the elements of everyday life. Chichikov's victims are conversant with the sort of transaction he proposes; the haggling, the lists of names, the bureaucratic sanction, are all familiar steps in the process of selling human beings. Chichikov distorts the routine, however, by seeking to buy only *dead* souls. When Nozdrev openly utters the paradox (which has burgeoned in the townspeople's minds like the "leaven of the Pharisees," of which Jesus speaks in Matthew 16: 6), it becomes the object of collective interpretation and eventually leads to self-interpretation. The townspeople cry, "Na kakoi konets, k kakomu delu mozhno *pritknut'* eti mertvye dushi?" (lit. "To what end, to what object, can these dead souls be *attached*?" 6: 190; emphasis added), using the verb from which *pritcha* (parable) is derived to describe the task that lies before them.

The townspeople, like the readers of a Gogolian text, are asked to reconcile seemingly irreconcilable incongruities:

The dead souls, the governor's daughter, and Chichikov got bunched together and mixed up in their heads in an unusually strange way. . . . There's no logic in dead souls, how can you buy dead souls . . . and why has the governor's daughter gotten mixed up here? If he wanted to carry her off, then why buy dead souls for that purpose? If he wanted to buy dead souls, then why carry off the governor's daughter? (6: 189–90)

Each of the two "interpretive communities" of the town, the female party and the male party, deals with the incongruity by ignoring one of its terms: the women concentrate on the abduction of the governor's daughter, the men on the dead souls. Only Nozdrev, with his creative disregard for logic, is able to incorporate both components of the mystery into his interpretation.

The townspeople are compared to a schoolboy whom his mischievous friends have awakened by stuffing a paper filled with snuff—a "hussar"—up his nose. The schoolboy's awakening and momentary confusion is followed by a flash of heightened perception. This perception is at first limited to his immediate surroundings but gradually takes in such a detailed view from the window that he would seem to be endowed with a temporary clairvoyance, only to return to the most immediate and intimate location, his own nose:

> He can't understand where he is, who he is, what has happened to him, and only after a moment does he begin to make out the walls lit up by the slanting rays of the sun, the laughter of his comrades, who have hidden themselves in the corners, and the new morning looking in the window, with the awakened forest resounding with thousands of bird voices, and the illuminated creek, which here and there disappears in twists and turns between the slender reeds and is strewn with bare little boys, who beckon their friends to come swimming, and only then does he finally feel that a hussar is sitting in his nose. (6: 189)

A version of this sequence (unconsciousness–heightened consciousness–self-consciousness) is reflected in the reception of the dead-souls mystery of the townspeople, who are awakened out of their sleep of moral complacency. In the course of their quest for meaning, their vague, buried guilt for past misdeeds becomes actively disturbing, if still strangely ephemeral: "Everyone suddenly found in himself such sins as had never even existed" (6: 193).

Like Chichikov's "dead souls," Gogol's *Dead Souls* presents a surface of normality. The novel seemed to its original audience, and has continued to seem, like a representation of everyday life. The kaleidoscope of names and details, combined with the narrator's assertions about the universality of the character types he describes, gives a surface impression of a faithfully observed world. The distortions and exaggerations in style, character, and plot, however, soon set the reader adrift from the mundane and familiar. One of Gogol's contemporaries expressed the sense of chronological disorientation: "Sometimes you think he is describing some distant past, known to us in legends; but meanwhile a conversation about 1812, [an allusion to] the governor-general, and other passages show that he wanted to depict Russia in its present-day aspect."[24] The narrator anticipates that the ambiguity of his hero will produce in the reader the same reaction that "dead souls" produced in the townspeople: an urgent desire for a final, simple solution, "a conclusive definition by a single feature" ("zakliuchitel'noe opredelenie odnoi chertoiu"; 6: 241). This he refuses to give; instead we are offered another parable, the virtually uninterpretable tale of Kifa Mokievich and Mokii Kifovich, followed by a troika speeding off into the distance, taking our desire for completion with it.

The narrator of *Dead Souls* insists that his readers find themselves in his parable: "Now the current generation sees everything clearly; it is amazed at the errors, laughs at the folly, of its ancestors, not perceiving that this chronicle has been inscribed by heavenly fire, that each letter in it cries out, that from every quarter a piercing finger is pointed at it, at it, at the current generation" (6: 211). Jesus, too, ties the fulfillment of his prophecy to its contemporary audience: "Verily I say unto you, This generation shall not pass away, till all be fulfilled" (Luke 21: 32). In both cases, the effect of the pointed finger is not to isolate the message in time but to render it timeless; each successive generation of readers is intended to include itself among the current generation. For the parable to be turned inward upon its hearers, it must remain enigmatic. There are mysterious hints throughout *Dead Souls* that Chichikov, the inveterate con man, will be redeemed. These hints necessarily provoke the question How could he possibly be redeemed? Because he is not alone in his crimes but is constantly portrayed as a member of a collective, the question becomes How can they be redeemed? and, ultimately, How can we?

The promissory closure of *Dead Souls* protects the status of the text as a parable or riddle that eternally escapes the last word. Such openness is both powerful and dangerous. One of the subtlest scholars of parables, Eta Linnemann, stresses the lack of control that the speaker of the parable has over what the audience makes of it: "A successful parable is an event in a double sense; it creates a new possibility in the situation, and it compels the person addressed to a decision. That is to say . . . it compels the making of a decision; it cannot decide the outcome of it" (pp. 30–31). Like Gogol's *Dead Souls*, Chichikov's *strannyi siuzhet*, or strange plot, reaches its audience in an open and fragmentary form. The incomplete information possessed by the people of the town of N. about Chichikov's life and character forces them into acts of guessing and divination that border on the creative act of telling stories. The questions Who is he? Where did he come from? and To what can we attach these dead souls? generate diverse answers that more than once blossom into narratives.[25] The problem, from Chichikov's point of view, is that the answers his audience generates to complete his parable are not the answers he intended. He is absent from the scene of their interpretive activity (holed up in his room with the flu), and he is utterly shocked when presented with its results by Nozdrev: "The whole time Nozdrev was chattering Chichikov kept rubbing his eyes, trying to decide whether he was hearing all this in a dream. The counterfeiter, the abduction of the governor's daughter, the death of the public prosecutor for which he was supposedly responsible, the arrival of the governor-general—all this gave him a real fright" (6: 214–15). The townspeople's orgy of interpretation has consequences that transcend the plane of the verbal; they threaten Chichikov's very existence, and he is forced to flee.

As Donald Fanger has noted, Gogol's parable produced the same flurry of discussion and argument that Chichikov's parable produced in the provincial town (p. 202). Gogol's reaction, like Chichikov's, was to flee—not from justice but from the grave responsibility for his ambiguous, open message. The task of the sequel to *Dead Souls* is to dispense with dangerous enigma: "There comes a time when one must not speak at all about the lofty and the beautiful without having at the same time shown *as clearly as day* the paths and roads to it for everyone. The latter circumstance was little and weakly developed in the second volume of *Dead Souls*, but it should have been practically the main thing; and that is why it was burned" (8: 298; emphasis added).[26] Throughout the writing of part II Gogol agonizes over his style, praying that he can make it absolutely lucid and intelligible, as is evident in his correspondence:

My language will not be accessible to everyone until I come to know people the way I would like to know them. (13: 284)

I feel that the work will progress, that even the language will be correct and sonorous, and that the style will get stronger. (14: 36)

Before I seriously take up the pen, I want to fill myself with the sound of Russian sounds and speech. I am afraid of sinning against the language. (14: 99)

The chastely pellucid language for which Gogol claims here to be striving is very different from the Baroque excrescence of his previ-

ous works, because it is to serve a very different purpose. Part II is
to be the sermon preached on the text of the part I parable, hence it
must present an accessible, unambiguous, and unmistakable message
to the greatest possible number of people. Part I aspires to the role
of parable, whose incongruities and ambiguities engage the audience
in active interpretation and, eventually, self-knowledge. With part II,
Gogol hopes to relieve the audience of its responsibility for complet-
ing the rest in their heads: the author himself will provide the answer
to the enigma, thus avoiding the dangerously creative acts of interpretation that Chichikov permitted his audience to engage in. Although in the foreword to the second edition of *Dead Souls* (1846)
Gogol invites his readers to participate in the writing of the sequel,
he is planning to exclude them in a more important sense: when this
perfectly finished and perfectly comprehensible work is achieved, it
will no longer need the reader's completion in the way the fragment,
the ruin, and the parable do.

In one way the tragic artistic failure of Gogol's last years is true to
the logic of part I, as becomes clearer if we consider an analogy with
the writing of part II of *Don Quixote*. In the dedication to the second
volume, Cervantes declares that he has written his sequel as a response to the forged continuations of part I: "For much pressure has
been put on me from countless directions to send [Quixote] out, in
order to purge the disgust and nausea caused by another Don Quixote who has been running about the world masquerading as the
second part" (p. 465).[27] In chapter 72 of part II, Quixote and Sancho
Panza actually encounter a character from the false part II and prevail
upon him to sign a document stating "that he did not know Don
Quixote de la Mancha . . . and that it was not he who was written of
in a history entitled *The Second Part of the Exploits of Don Quixote de
la Mancha*, composed by a certain Avellaneda, native of Tordesillas"
(pp. 928–29). This conflation of the real and the fictional, in which
a character is permitted to deny his own past at the request of another, more "authentic" character in order to serve Cervantes' purpose of denying an actual forgery, is a brilliant continuation of the
themes of part I. In an analogous fashion, Gogol's intention to write
part II of *Dead Souls*—unachieved and therefore insubstantial and
fragmentary yet exerting a powerful influence on the imaginations

of author and reader—continues the logic of part I, in which the ghostly serfs "greatly live a life on earth," filling Chichikov's imagination and ultimately destroying his plans.

In a pathetically self-referential discussion of Derzhavin in *Selected Passages from Correspondence with Friends* (*Vybrannye mesta iz perepiski s druz'iami*, 1847), Gogol writes:

> He harmed himself greatly by not burning at least half of his odes. This half of the odes presents a striking phenomenon: no one to this day has so laughed at himself, at the sanctity of his best beliefs and feelings, as did Derzhavin in these unhappy odes. It is just as though he tried here to paint a caricature of himself: everything that in other passages is so beautiful, so free, so permeated by the inner strength of the soul's fire, is cold, soulless, and forced here; and worst of all, here are repeated the same locutions, expressions and even whole phrases, that have such an aquiline sweep in his inspired odes and that are simply ludicrous here, resembling a dwarf donning the armor of a giant, and not even correctly at that. (8: 230)

This passage expresses the feelings of any reader familiar with Gogol's best work when confronted by the sad remnants that have survived of part II; we can only guess at what he felt constrained to burn. Gogol's failure to write the sequel to *Dead Souls* was his last creative act.[28] Through it he ensured that his work would escape the fixity of the last word. Instead, it remains a riddle, a promise, a project, a fragment from the future.

5

The Landscape of *Arabesques*

Нет, нет! я никогда не буду украшать Природы.
Деревня моя должна быть деревнею, пустынею. . . .
Пастушка пойдет искать заблудшейся овцы своей и
проложит мне тропинку. К тому же я люблю прео-
долевать затруднения, люблю продираться сквозь
чащу кустарника и разделять сросшиеся ветви.
—N. M. Karamzin

Dead Souls (1842) is bracketed in Gogol's career by two works, *Arabesques* (1834–35) and *Selected Passages from Correspondence with Friends* (1847), whose themes and structure reflect the tension between Gogol's extra-artistic strivings toward fixity, clarity, and plenitude and his aesthetic preoccupation with mobility, obscurity, and deficiency. Gogol's theory of history appears in *Arabesques* in an intricate, digressive, fragmented form; *Selected Passages* asserts an ideal of order, rectitude, clarity, truth, and unity but reverts to the crooked, obscure structure of *Arabesques* and crosses the boundary between truth and lies with the audacity of Nozdrev.

Detail and Panorama

In Gogol's *Arabesques*, as in Herder's historiography, landscape is destiny. According to Gogol's (and Herder's) historical scheme, the character of a people is deeply affected by the geography of its homeland, and even forms of government are dictated by the lie of the land. The preoccupation with landscape in *Arabesques* is more than just a thematic one, however. Like many works of art, *Arabesques* contains the clue to how it is written and how it should be read. The right way to read *Arabesques* is most vividly expressed as the right way to view a landscape; this is no coincidence, for early Romantic theories of landscape gardening are central not only to *Arabesques* but also to *Dead Souls*, the work for which it in many ways serves as both introduction and gloss.

Gogol's letters about *Arabesques* at the time of its publication are characteristically apologetic. To Pogodin he writes: "I am sending you my omnium-gatherum [*vsiakaia vsiachina*]. Smooth it out and pat it down a bit: there is much that is childish in it, and I have tried to throw it out into the world as soon as possible, so as to throw all the old stuff out of my desk at the same time and to brush myself off and start a new life" (8: 748). The impulse to take Gogol at his word, to regard *Arabesques* as a work whose composition is dictated solely by what manuscripts happened to be lying on his desk one day in 1834, has betrayed itself in the attitudes of critics and editors from the time of its publication. Gogol himself, in his 1842 *Collected Works*, sets the precedent for the destruction of the integrity of *Arabesques* by separating the fictional pieces from the nonfictional ones. This separation is also observed in the fourteen-volume Academy edition, sending Viktor Shklovskii back to the Tikhonravov edition to recapture the original shape of the work.[1] Even the recent Ardis translation of *Arabesques* (1982), advertised on its cover as the "first complete English translation," omits the two fictional fragments "Chapter from a Historical Novel" ("Glava iz istoricheskogo romana") and "The Captive" ("Plennik"). The omission is a serious one, for along with the "Glance at the Composition of the Ukraine" ("Vzgliad na sostavlenie Malorossii"), presented as the first chapter of an entire history of the Ukraine, and the internally fragmentary "Diary of a Madman," published in *Arabesques* as "Klochki iz zapisok sumasshedshego" (Scraps from the Diary of a Madman), the fragments exemplify the discontinuity and incompletion that are the subject of philosophical inquiry elsewhere in the text.[2]

Critics like Shklovskii and Fanger have resisted the urge to ignore the distinctive unity of *Arabesques*. They may find their warrant not only in the external evidence of Gogol's careful assembly of the parts of the work but in the clues to the proper way to read the text that are offered within it. In the essay "On the Middle Ages," Gogol writes:

People have regarded [the history of the Middle Ages] as a pile of dissonant, heterogeneous events, as a crowd of fragmented and senseless movements that have no main thread to combine them into a single whole. In fact, its terrible, unusual complexity cannot help but seem chaotic at first; but look more attentively and deeply, and you will find a connection and a goal and a direction. However, I will not deny that to know how to find all this, you must be gifted with the kind of sensitivity that few historians possess. (8: 16)

I have already cited this passage as proof that Gogol shared Herder's sense of a harmonious order underlying the chaos of temporality, but it is perhaps even more compelling as a guide for the reader of *Arabesques*. Throughout *Arabesques*, whether the subject is history, geography, or art, Gogol reiterates the need not just to apprehend multifarious, individual, partial detail but to use one's intellectual powers and artistic sensitivity to assemble the seemingly fragmentary data of experience into a unified whole.[3] The two mental operations are likened at one point to two ways of perceiving a landscape: "You cannot come to know a city completely by walking through all its streets: for this you must go up to an elevated place from which it would be entirely visible, as if on the palm of your hand [*kak na ladoni*] (8: 30)."[4] Neither the close-up perception of detail (walking through the streets) nor the panoramic overview (standing on a height) is sufficient for a true conception of the whole, although panoramic vision, with its similarity to divine vision, always occupies a more important place in Gogol's world than the perception of fragmented reality.[5] For Gogol, detail without overview is embodied in the demonic fragmentation of nineteenth-century life ("vsia drob' prikhotei i naslazhdenii, nad vydumkami kotorykh lomaet golovu nash XIX vek" [the whole fragmentation of whims and enjoyments over which our nineteenth century racks its brains]; 8: 12). But overview without differentiation leads to monotony and excessive abstraction, as in the panoramic paintings that Gogol opposes to those of K. P. Briullov: "They are like views from a distance; there is only a general expression in them. We feel the terrible situation of the whole crowd, but we do not see a person in whose face there is the whole horror of the destruction he himself has seen" (8: 110). The all-embracing genius of Briullov has been made possible only by the

obsession with parts, with the perfection of the individual subcategories of the painter's art, that prevailed during the nineteenth century. Briullov "strives to capture nature with a giant's embraces and
squeezes it with the passion of a lover. Perhaps he has been greatly
helped in this by the fragmented working-out in parts that the nineteenth century prepared for him. Perhaps if he had appeared earlier,
Briullov would not have achieved that many-sided and at the same
time full and colossal striving" (8: 113). The only way for Briullov to
compose large-scale canvases that have the look of truth is by taking
advantage of the nineteenth century's minute observation of nature:
"They have noticed such secret phenomena as no one ever suspected
before. All the nature that people often see, that surrounds them and
lives with them, all the visible nature, all those trivialities [*vsia eta
meloch'*] that the great artists disdained, have achieved an amazing
truth and perfection" (8: 107). The negative side of this close observation is that it takes the form of "notes, materials, fresh thoughts"
of the kind travelers enter into their notebooks (8: 107); in Gogol's
view, Briullov is destined to make the unified work of art for which
the nineteenth century has made the sketches.

The need to shift back and forth between the perception of detail
and the perception of the whole accounts for the repeated appearance in *Arabesques* of optical lenses, with their power to diminish
and magnify. There is the telescope, through which one must look
at a building from a distance to make sure that its parts are in the
proper proportion (8: 59). There is the convex lens that reflects an
entire landscape in miniature, the image for Pushkin's all-encom-
passing word:

V nem russkaia priroda, russkaia dusha, russkoi iazyk, russkoi kharakter
otrazilis' v takoi zhe chistote, v takoi ochishchennoi krasote, v kakoi otra-
zhaetsia landshaft na vypukloi poverkhnosti opticheskogo stekla. (8: 50)

(In him Russian nature, the Russian soul, the Russian language, the Russian
character, were reflected with the same purity, the same purified beauty, with
which a landscape is reflected on the convex surface of an optical lens.)[6]

The converse of the operation of the telescope and convex mirror,
which present a large whole in a manageably compact and surveyable
form, is the operation of the microscope, which enlarges parts to the

point where new worlds of detail and ornament, invisible to the naked eye, are revealed. In "The Captive," the eyes of a prisoner in a dungeon project the wondrous images of microscopically observed reality onto the utter blackness that surrounds him:

On vsemi chuvstvami vselilsia v temnotu. I togda pred nim razvernulsia sovershenno novyi, strannyi mir. Emu nachali pokazyvat'sia vo mrake svetlye strui—poslednee vospominanie sveta! Eti strui prinimali mnozhestvo raznykh uzorov i tsvetov. . . . Eti raznotsvetnye uzory prinimali ili vid pestroi shali, ili volnistogo mramora, ili, nakonets, tot vid, kotoryi porazhaet nas svoeiu chudnoiu neobyknovennost'iu, kogda rassmatrivaem v mikroskop chast' krylyshka ili nozhki nasekomogo. (3: 306)

(He implanted himself into the darkness with all his senses. And then a completely new, strange world unfolded before him: bright streams appeared to him in the gloom—the last remembrance of light! These streams took on a multitude of various designs and colors. . . . These multicolored designs took on the appearance of a gaudy shawl or undulating marble or, finally, that appearance that strikes us with its marvelous unusualness when we look at a part of the little wing or leg of an insect through a microscope.)

Gogol ends the *Arabesques* version of this fragment immediately after this passage, and with good reason: the proliferating patterns of ornament produced on the prisoner's retina are not just a superfluous growth on the surface of a historical adventure tale. They provide the fragment with its most important reason for being in *Arabesques*, the title of which reminds us that the meandering, capricious line of Arabian ornament, which had such a powerful hold on the imagination of German Romanticism, is central to the plan of Gogol's work. The problem of relating Arabian geometric ornament to certain types of argument and exposition has already been solved by Howard Stern in his book on Walter Benjamin, and his conclusions are relevant to Gogol's *Arabesques*.

The Crooked Line

Stern begins with an astonishingly Gogolian passage in Benjamin, which speaks of the difference between seeing a landscape from a height (in Benjamin's case, an airplane) and coming to know it by walking through it. For Benjamin the two types of knowledge are analogous to reading a text versus copying it. The pedestrian and the copyist construct their panoramic knowledge of the whole through their fragmented encounter with "a strict succession of partial views."[7] The model for Benjamin's road must be, in Stern's words, "a *line* that in some reasonable sense covers an *area*; for if the contrast of pedestrian and aviator is to be meaningful, it must be possible for the pedestrian to acquire knowledge, however fragmented and paradoxical, of the entire terrain" (p. 54). One solution is the Sierpiński line, a figure described by the mathematician Wacław Sierpiński in 1912. The theoretical limit of the recursive procedure that produces the Sierpiński line is a continuous line that completely fills a square (see illustration). In the crudest terms, it is a line so crooked that it transcends its one-dimensionality and begins to cover an area.

The relevance of the line that mediates between one-dimensionality and two-dimensionality to the peculiar nature of Gogol's *Arabesques* is further illuminated by Benjamin's comparison of Arabian architecture and ornament to a particular form of argument that he

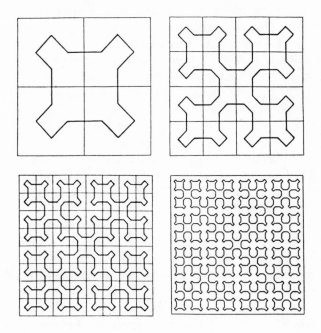

The Sierpiński Line

calls the tractatus. Like an Arabian building, the tractatus gives no clue to its structure from without; one must enter the courtyard to see the articulation of the parts of the building. As Stern writes, "The tractatus does not immediately reveal its structure or contents; one needs to wander around in it to discover its governing principle" (p. 56). Its facade is covered not with pictorial representations but, in Benjamin's words, "with unbroken, proliferating arabesques. In the ornamental density of this presentation the distinction between thematic and excursive expositions is abolished" (p. 82). If a thematic essay is one that covers a certain conceptual area and an excursive or digressive essay is one that ignores thematic coherence and follows its own willful, meandering line, then the tractatus, in which the distinction between these two types of exposition is abolished, must resemble Sierpiński's model, which mediates between line and area. In Stern's words, "Related areas will not necessarily be treated together . . . , but eventually the entire surface will be covered by one meandering line of development" (p. 57).

Benjamin's definition of the tractatus can, without too much difficulty, be applied to Gogol's *Arabesques*. As we wander through the landscape of *Arabesques*, we keep encountering the same objects and ideas—Gothic cathedrals, Greek marbles, the beginnings of the modern era, the education of the young—from different viewpoints and in different contexts, both fictional and nonfictional. It would be theoretically possible to compose a thematically coherent essay on, say, the vocation of the artist, by assembling bits from "On the Teaching of World History," "The Portrait," "A Few Words on Pushkin," "On the Architecture of the Present Day," "Nevskii Avenue," and "The Last Day of Pompeii." When read actively and attentively, the meandering arabesques of Gogol's thought begin to map out areas of thematic coherence.[8]

It is by now clear that there is a congruence between the macrolevels and the microlevels of the text of *Arabesques*. A work whose apparent fragmentation and discontinuity mask an inner unity takes as a major subject the need to combine close examination of individual parts with a panoramic survey of the whole. The same congruence holds with reference to the unusually complex, dense, and capriciously meandering line that appears in Arabian ornament. Such a line is the structural principle for Gogol's work, and it becomes the subject of explicit comment within the text. It appears in its most striking form in the essay on architecture. Gogol calls for the expansion of the architect's repertory of shapes to accommodate complex ornaments, based on the new understanding of nature "in all its secret phenomena":

Neuzheli vsë to, chto vstrechaetsia v prirode, dolzhno byt' nepremenno tol'ko kolonna, kupol i arka! Skol'ko drugikh eshche obrazov nami vovse ne tronuto! Skol'ko priamaia liniia mozhet lomat'sia i izmeniat' napravlenie, skol'ko krivaia vygibat'sia, skol'ko novykh mozhno vvesti ukrashenii, kotorykh eshche ni odin arkhitektor ne vnosil v svoi kodeks! (8: 74)

(Must everything encountered in nature always be just the column, dome, and arch? How many other forms have we not even touched! How a straight line can break and change direction, how a crooked one can bend, how many new decorations can be introduced—none of which a single architect has yet entered into his codex.)[9]

Strangely enough, Gogol's words have recently been echoed by Benoit Mandelbrot, the inventor of a new way of looking at shapes in nature. In his "casebook and manifesto," *The Fractal Geometry of Nature*, Mandelbrot writes: "Clouds are not spheres, mountains are not cones, coastlines are not circles, and bark is not smooth, nor does lightning travel in a straight line. . . . Many patterns of Nature are so irregular and fragmented that, compared with [standard geometry,] Nature exhibits not simply a higher degree but an altogether different level of complexity" (p. 1). Mandelbrot has found a method of modeling and defining the apparently messy shapes of nature, shapes with fractional dimension: lines so crooked that they exceed one dimension and approach two, surfaces so rough that they exceed two dimensions and approach three. Like the text of *Arabesques*, fractal shapes resemble themselves at all levels of generality and on every scale: whether regarded through a microscope or a telescope, the degree of roughness of these seemingly chaotic outlines and shapes remains constant.

Intricacy and Sudden Variation

Gogol's taste for the maximally irregular shapes encountered in nature is shared with, and in part derived from, the theorists of the picturesque as it was elaborated in the late eighteenth and early nine-

teenth centuries in England, particularly in the writings of Sir Uvedale Price. Price was concerned both to define the picturesque in
relation to Edmund Burke's categories of the sublime and the beautiful and to discredit the trend in English gardening exemplified by
the work of Humphrey Repton and Lancelot ("Capability") Brown.
Gogol's works give evidence that he was at least indirectly familiar
with the ideas of Burke, Brown, and Price.[10]

In his *Philosophical Inquiry into the Origin of Our Ideas of the Sublime and Beautiful* (1757), Burke defines the sublime as a quality that
inspires astonishment and horror. Some of the attributes required to
make a landscape sublime are darkness, vastness, and suggestions of
danger. A steep precipice crowned by magnificent oaks, with violent
waves crashing on the rocks at its feet, is quintessentially sublime.
Beauty, in contrast, is characterized by delicacy, smoothness, gentle
curves, and gradual variation. In Burke's summary:

On the whole, the qualities of beauty, as they are merely sensible qualities,
are the following: First, to be comparatively small. Secondly, to be smooth.
Thirdly, to have a variety in the direction of the parts; but, fourthly, to have
those parts not angular, but melted, as it were, into each other. Fifthly, to
be of a delicate frame, without any remarkable appearance of strength.
Sixthly, to have its colors clear and bright, but not very strong and glaring.
(p. 197)

Gogol's awareness of the category of the sublime is reflected in his
association of vastness and extreme height with astonishment:

A building must rise immeasurably high, almost right above the head of the
viewer; he should stand, struck by sudden astonishment, hardly in a condition to encompass its height with his eyes. . . . The word *breadth* must
disappear. Here the sole legislative word is *height*. (8: 62, 65)

Compare Burke:

Extension is either in length, height, or depth. Of these the length strikes
least; a hundred yards of even ground will never work such an effect as a
tower a hundred yards high, or a rock or mountain of that altitude. (p. 147)

As for the category of the beautiful, we need only read Price's description of a woman in whom Burke's idea of beauty has been taken
to its extreme to recognize the egglike smoothness, roundness, and
whiteness of the governor's daughter in *Dead Souls*:

Hardly any mark of eyebrow; the hair, from the lightness of its colour, and from the silky softness of its quality, giving scarce any idea of roughness; the complexion of a pure, and almost transparent whiteness, with hardly a tinge of red; the eyes of the mildest blue, and the expression equally mild,—you would then approach very nearly to insipidity, but still without destroying beauty. (1: 205–6)

The school of landscape gardening exemplified by Capability Brown, realizing the impossibility of creating the sublime by artificial means, concentrated on producing the effect of the beautiful. The straight lines, avenues of trees, and rectangular shapes of the formal garden were replaced by serpentine, gently curving streams and paths winding through immaculately trimmed lawns with rounded, widely spaced clumps of trees. Brown's gardens were meant to seem more artless and natural than the Renaissance Italian garden or the formal plantings of seventeenth-century France. As Price points out, however, a smooth, regular curve is no less unnatural than a straight line and much less imposing (1: 231). The curves, the clumps of trees, and, in particular, the exposure of the manor house on all sides with nothing but grass surrounding it, created a monotony and baldness that was ridiculed by the advocates of the picturesque. In the words of Richard Payne Knight, they "shave the goddess whom they come to dress" (p. 23). In *Dead Souls*, it is clear that Manilov's English garden has been planted by a follower of Brown:

The manor house stood exposed all by itself, on an elevation open to any winds that might take it into their heads to blow; the slope of the hill on which it stood was clothed in clipped turf. On it two or three flower beds with lilacs and yellow acacia bushes were scattered about in the English fashion; here and there, five or six birches in small clumps raised their sparse, small-leaved tops. (6: 22).

Manilov's grounds deviate from Brown's prescriptions only in the gaudy coloring of the summerhouse, which should have been painted the purest white.[11]

In 1794, partly in response to the "shaven goddesses" being perpetrated on the English countryside in the name of Burke's idea of the beautiful, Price published his *Essays on the Picturesque, as Compared with the Sublime and the Beautiful*. Here he defines the picturesque as a third category, distinct from the sublime and the beautiful but at times partaking of both. In his scheme the cardinal qualities of the picturesque are sudden variation, as opposed to the gradual variation characteristic of beauty, and intricacy, a quality of line and shape antithetical to Capability Brown's smooth and regular curves: "Intricacy in landscape might be defined as *that disposition of objects which, by a partial and uncertain concealment, excites and nourishes curiosity*" (1: 22). The effect of intricacy is produced by allowing the naturally complicated outlines and shapes of freely growing vegetation to efface the regular outlines created by human efforts. Price's description of a picturesque scene provides a vivid illustration of what sudden variation and intricacy mean visually:

The ground itself in these lanes, is as much varied in form, tint, and light and shade, as the plants that grow upon it; this, as usual, instead of owing any thing to art, is, on the contrary, occasioned by accident and neglect. . . . [The] hollows are frequently overgrown with wild roses, with honeysuckles, periwincles, and other trailing plants, which with their flowers and pendent branches have quite a different effect when hanging loosely over one of these recesses, opposed to its deep shade, and mixed with the fantastic roots of trees and the varied tints of the soil, from that which they produce when they are trimmed into bushes, or crawl along a shrubbery, where the ground has been worked into one uniform slope. (1: 27–28)

According to the memoirs of P. V. Annenkov, Gogol understood the aesthetic value of intricacy in landscape:

Raz on skazal mne: "Esli by ia byl khudozhnik, ia by izobrel osobennogo roda peizazh. Kakie derev'ia i landshafty teper' pishut! Vsë iasno, razobrano, prochteno masterom, a zritel' po skladam za nim idet. Ia by stsepil derevo s derevom, pereputal vetvi, vybrosil svet, gde nikto ne ozhidaet ego, vot kakie peizazhy nado pisat'!" (p. 283)

(Once he said to me: "If I were a painter, I would choose a special sort of landscape. What trees and landscapes they paint today! Everything is clear and sorted out; the master has read through it, and the spectator follows him haltingly. I would enchain tree with tree, entangle the branches, let light show through where no one expects it, that is the kind of landscape one should paint!")

The emphasis here on taking the spectator by surprise with unexpected combinations of light and shade is fully consonant with Price's conception of the picturesque.[12]

The half-century-long aesthetic revolution that culminated in Price's formulation of the theory of the picturesque is reflected in Russian texts on landscape gardening published in the late eighteenth and early nineteenth centuries. The intricate textures of time-worn vegetation and the curiosity aroused by partial concealment are mentioned in a 1771 translation of William Chambers's influential *Designs of Chinese Buildings* (1757):

In their gardens they also keep the stumps of rotten trees, some of them standing on their roots, others overturned onto the earth, and they pay great attention to their shape, as well as to the color, bark, and moss found on them. They employ various stratagems for arousing surprise. . . . Another of their stratagems consists in hiding a certain part of the ensemble with trees and other intervening objects. This naturally arouses curiosity in the viewer for a closer inspection.[13]

In the journal published by A. N. Bolotov, *Magazine of Economics* (*Ekonomicheskii magazin*), a translation of C. C. L. Hirschfeld's *Theory of the Art of Designing Gardens* (*Theorie der Gartenkunst*, 1779–85) compares the art of gardening to the dramatist's art:

The layout must be such that the connection of all the parts of the garden may be surveyed not upon entering it—the most common and inevitable error of the old symmetrical manner—but only gradually. It is necessary that as in the drama, or as in natural landscapes, the art of the *nouement* [*zaviazka*] be observed and that the places one approaches not be seen in advance; it must be completely impossible to see what kind of scene comes next, and the stroller must always be kept in suspense.[14]

In the same translation, the aesthetic value of sudden variation is expounded:

In the romantic character [of gardens] art may take a very small part, but it is the product almost solely of nature. Nature forms it not only through mountainous terrains, cliffs, caves, grottoes, waterfalls, cataracts, and strange situations and views of these objects but also by unusual linkages and oppositions, by excessive disorder in the layout, and by contrasts achieved through suddenness.[15]

Although Price was not translated into Russian, the aesthetic theories to which he gave the most precise formulation formed the basis of Russian gardening handbooks of the period.

The most skilled exponent in Russian of the aesthetic ideals of the picturesque prior to Gogol, however, is Zhukovskii, whose account in verse of a stroll through Pavlovsk, "Slavianka (An Elegy)" ("Slavianka [Elegiia]," 1815), was praised by Gogol as "tochnaia zhivopis'" (precise picture-painting; 8: 378).[16] In Zhukovskii's accounts of his journeys in Saxony and Switzerland he uses the epithet "zhivopisnyi" (picturesque) so obsessively that it transcends cliché.[17] More important, he applies the epithet not vaguely or all-encompassingly, as many writers do, but precisely, to scenes with intricacy and sudden variation—a choice made the more striking in view of the fact that the mountainous landscape of Switzerland would fit more comfortably into the category of the sublime. The phenomena that impress Zhukovskii in his travels are those enumerated by Price as components of the picturesque: the mottled textures of vegetation and rocks worn and decayed by time; the intricate meandering line of paths laid out in a "natural" manner; and sudden, dramatic contrasts of light and shade, the wild and the domestic, culminating in the ultimate opposition: "It seems as if you are standing at the place where the earth ends and heaven begins."[18]

In "Slavianka," Zhukovskii offers the classic expression of the aesthetic pleasures afforded by a stroll through a Romantic garden, with its constantly changing views: "Chto shag, to novaia v glazakh moikh kartina" (With every step a new scene appears before my eyes; 1: 479). Zhukovskii's drafts for the third, fourth, and sixth stanzas, analyzed from a different point of view by A. S. Ianushkevich (pp. 133–34), illuminate his relation to the picturesque. If one were to isolate the invariants in these sketches, they would have to include the following words and ideas: *izvilistyi* (sinuous), *v'iushchiisia* (winding), *izluchistyi* (meandering), *kudriavyi* (curly), contrast of dark tree against bright trees or bright tree against pale trees, *glukhaia dich'* (dense wilderness), *spletshiesia kusty* (interwoven bushes), *pereplelis'* (intertwined), *splelis'* (interlaced), *zaglokhshii* (overgrown). In other words, through all his reworkings Zhukovskii keeps the cardinal ideas of the picturesque before him: sharp contrast and the intricate outlines produced by nature when given its head.

The word *picturesque*, which came into wide use at the end of the eighteenth century, connotes among other things the idea of copying pictures. Indeed, the gardening practice of the time was heavily influenced by the landscape paintings of Salvator Rosa, Claude Lorrain, and others. But Price introduces a refinement in his definition of the picturesque that is designed to guard against restricting the category to purely visual phenomena. For him the picturesque refers to "the turn of mind common to painters," the kind of thing painters are struck by and take delight in. Thus the qualities of the picturesque may be encountered by all the senses, not just vision. Price concedes that, without this qualification of the term, it would be ludicrous to call a capricious movement by Scarlatti or Haydn picturesque, yet, in his words, "such a movement, from its sudden, unexpected, and abrupt transitions,—from a certain playful wildness of character and appearance of irregularity, is no less analogous to similar scenery in nature, than the concerto or the chorus, to what is grand or beautiful to the eye" (1: 44, 46). Following Price we may seek the picturesque in verbal art, as well as in painting and music.[19]

The aesthetic of intricacy and sudden variation is preached and practiced throughout *Arabesques*. In the essay on architecture, the need for sharp contrast is explicitly linked to the picturesque garden:

True effect is contained in sharp opposition: beauty is never so bright and evident as in contrast. . . . The more monuments there are in a city of different types of architecture, the more interesting it is—the more often it forces one to examine it, to stop with pleasure at every step. How would it be if in an English garden instead of continual, unexpected views a stroller found the very same path or at least one so similar in its surroundings to what had been seen before that it seemed long familiar? (8: 64)[20]

The point of *Arabesques* and of certain works within it is to avoid such monotony at all costs. We have already seen how the intricate, more-than-one-dimensional line abolishes the distinction between thematic and digressive exposition in *Arabesques*; sudden variation is just as powerful an organizing principle. "Nevskii Avenue" is about neither the high-romantic fate of Piskarev nor the low-farcical anecdote of Pirogov but rather the point at which the two meet in jarring, genre-crunching contrast.

Price's emphasis on the curiosity aroused by intricacy and sudden variation, with their "partial and uncertain concealment" and exhilarating confrontations of opposites, finds its counterpart in *Arabesques*. For Gogol, curiosity is the emblem of youth, that "freshness" that causes the narrator of *Dead Souls* to guess the lives of people met on the street. *Arabesques* is a work written by a young man (his preface apologizes in advance for the errors caused by his youthful haste), about youth (both the youth of civilization and the youth of such characters as Chertkov and Piskarev), with a young audience in mind (the schoolboy targets of the lessons on history and geography). In the essay on the Middle Ages, Gogol explicitly links sudden variation with the arousal of curiosity, insisting that the merging of the classical and modern worlds, the chaos in which petrified fragments of Roman law mix with the amorphous beginnings of modern European society, is "more interesting for us and arouse[s] our curiosity more than the immobile time of the universal Roman empire" (8: 15). Intricacy, which obscures smooth and regular outline, is just as important for teaching geography: "Strict analytical systematics cannot be retained in the head of a youth. . . . A child can only retain a system when he does not see it with his eyes, when it is artfully hidden from him" (8: 105).

Elsewhere Gogol seems to realize that the preference for the irregular, for the detour over the straight path, is not restricted to youth. In the middle of the essay on architecture, which ends with the passage (8: 74), cited above, celebrating the infinitely capricious lines found in nature, Gogol chides humanity for its attraction to the crooked road:

Um i vkus cheloveka predstavliaiut strannoe iavlenie: prezhde nezheli dostignet istiny, on stol'ko dast ob"ezdov, stol'ko nadelaet nesoobraznostei, nepravil'nostei, lozhnogo, chto posle sam divitsia svoei nedogadlivosti. (8: 69)

(The human mind and taste present a strange phenomenon: before attaining the truth, a man will make so many detours, will cause so many incongruities, irregularities, so much that is false, that later he himself will be amazed at his slow-wittedness.)

These words bring to mind a famous passage in *Dead Souls* regarding the human preference for obscure concealment over bald, illuminated truth:

Kakie iskrivlennye, glukhie, uzkie, neprokhodimye, zanosiashchie daleko v storonu dorogi izbiralo chelovechestvo, stremias' dostignut' vechnoi istiny, togda kak pered nim ves' byl otkryt priamoi put', podobnyi puti, vedushch-

emu k velikolepnoi khramine, naznachennoi tsariu v chertogi! Vsekh drugikh putei shire i roskoshnee on, ozarennyi solntsem i osveshchennyi vsiu
noch' ogniami; no mimo ego, v glukhoi temnote, tekli liudi. I skol'ko raz,
uzhe navedennye niskhodivshim s nebes smyslom, oni i tut umeli otshatnut'-
sia i sbit'sia v storonu, umeli sredi bela dnia popast' vnov' v neprokhodimye zakholust'ia, umeli napustit' vnov' slepoi tuman drug drugu v ochi. (6:
210–11)

(What crooked, overgrown, narrow, impassable roads, leading them far
astray, have humans chosen in trying to attain eternal truth, while before
them the entire straight path has been open, like a path leading to a magnificent temple intended as a king's mansion! It is wider and more splendid than
all other paths, lit up by the sun and illuminated all night by lamps; but
people have streamed past it in deep darkness. And how many times, already
guided by significance descended from the heavens, have they managed re-
gardless to recoil and go astray, managed in broad daylight to again end up
in the impassable backwoods, managed to again send a blind mist into each
other's eyes.)

The irony of this passage is that the preference for the crooked, obscure, and intricately winding path over the straight, brightly illuminated, and immediately apprehensible one is not just a moral or
cognitive preference but an aesthetic one. Moreover, it is a preference that is both encouraged and satisfied by Gogol in his artistic
practice.[21]

The Garden of History

We have arrived at the goal toward which my crooked path has
been tending—Pliushkin's garden, the apotheosis of the picturesque
and the aesthetic heart of *Dead Souls*. The description of Pliushkin's
overgrown garden beautifully captures the effects of varied texture
and light and freely growing, interlacing branches and vines that for
Price are the hallmarks of the picturesque. The narrator's conclusion
to the scene formulates the source of its power:

Slovom, vsë bylo kak-to pustynno-khorosho, kak ne vydumat' ni prirode, ni
iskusstvu, no kak byvaet tol'ko togda, kogda oni soediniatsia vmeste, kogda
po nagromozhdennomu, chasto bez tolku, trudu cheloveka proidet okon-
chatel'nym reztsom svoim priroda, oblegchit tiazhelye massy, unichtozhit
grubooshchutitel'nuiu pravil'nost' i nishchenskie prorekhi, skvoz' kotorye

progliadyvaet neskrytyi, nagoi plan, i dast chudnuiu teplotu vsemu, chto sozdalos' v khlade razmerennoi chistoty i opriatnosti. (6: 113)

(In a word, everything was somehow desolately beautiful, as neither nature nor art could invent but as happens only when they unite together, when nature passes its final chisel over the often senselessly piled-up work of man, lightens the heavy masses, destroys the crudely perceptible regularity and the beggarly holes through which the uncovered, bare plan peeps, and gives a marvelous warmth to everything that has been created in the coolness of measured purity and neatness.)

P. A. Pletnev was the first to recognize the centrality of this passage to the aesthetic system of *Dead Souls*: "Ego kniga tochno etot sad" (His book is like this garden; p. 493).[22] The narrator asserts that beauty resides not in planning, order, and symmetry but, on the contrary, in disrupted planning and violated symmetry. As we have seen, this assertion can serve as a model for *Dead Souls*, a text itself generated by a disrupted plan—Chichikov's scheme of buying dead serfs. Throughout the text, wholeness, fixity, and order are overcome by fragmentation, mobility, and chance. Ritualized, prescribed discourse (games, bureaucratic procedures, bourgeois social euphemism, referentiality) is subordinated to and violated by disruptive, creative discourse (cheating, con artistry, the linguistic innovation of the Russian peasant, and, most important, lying and divination, which either ignore referentiality or use it as a springboard into untrammeled fabulation); the creative discourse displays the same vegetative force as Pliushkin's neglected garden.[23] Gogol's own plan for *Dead Souls* was itself disrupted, securing for the work its status as an open-ended enigma. If a historiographical scheme can be regarded as a plan projected into the past, we may conclude that in *Arabesques* yet another of Gogol's plans was disrupted, for his historiography is here fractured and twisted into the form of the tractatus, not the "magnificent complete *poema*" (8: 26) that he himself prescribed.

The collaboration between man and nature revealed in Pliushkin's garden is what Price prescribes as the ideal foundation of picturesque landscape gardening. Gardeners should not only study and imitate the effects of accident and neglect but allow room in their schemes for the two to play an active role (3: 35). Unlike other arts, landscape gardening must reserve a special place for accident, according to

Price, because the medium in which it works is living vegetation: "Trees and plants of every kind . . . should have room to spread in various degrees, and in various directions, and then accident will produce unthought-of varieties and beauties, without injuring the general design" (3: 36). It is clear from the description of Pliushkin's garden that when nature is allowed to collaborate with the gardener, the result is not merely a synchronically static composition of light, color, and shadow but a complex record of diachronic change as well. The wildly spreading trees and bushes, crumbling summer-house, and storm-damaged birch tell a story of past growth, decay, and disaster. In effect, the picturesque garden is not just landscape but also history.[24] What is more, Pliushkin's garden holds the record of Chichikov's personal fate. Through a subtle system of verbal echoes, Chichikov's fatal encounter with the governor's daughter is encoded into the garden scene. Her Burkean beauty, the smooth white roundness that stands out against the murky ballroom crowd, is present in the damaged birch tree, if on a larger scale: "Belyi kolossal'nyi stvol berezy . . . podymalsia iz etoi zelenoi gushchi i kruglilsia na vozdukhe, kak pravil'naia mramornaia, sverkaiushchaia kolonna" (The colossal white trunk of a birch . . . rose out of that green thicket and was rounded in the air like a symmetrical marble gleaming column; 6: 112–13). The sun's irradiation of her translucent skin at her first encounter with Chichikov is here repeated on a young maple leaf: "Solntse prevrashchalo ego vdrug v prozrachnyi i ognennyi, chudno siiavshii v etoi gustoi temnote" (The sun suddenly rendered it transparent and fiery, shining marvelously in that thick darkness; 6: 113). Finally and most importantly, the intricate interlacing of the leaves and branches in the garden—"pereputavshiesia i skrestiv-shiesia list'ia i such'ia" (leaves and twigs that entangled and criss-crossed; 6: 113)—reprises the entanglement of Chichikov's fate with that of the governor's daughter, "kogda . . . ikh ekipazhi tak stranno stolknulis', pereputavshis' upriazh'iu" (when . . . their carriages so strangely collided, entangling the harnesses; 6: 166).[25]

To be sure, the type of historiography modeled by the picturesque garden is not a scholarly or a scientific one. Like the "chronicle of the world" (8: 73) that architecture represents or the "living chronicle" of Ukrainian folk songs (8: 91), like *Arabesques* itself, it is a fragmented, partially concealed record that demands a complementary act of imagination on the part of the viewer or reader. Gogol could envision two ways of modeling history: the clear, complete, obvious *poema*, like the panoramic view from a height, and the tortuous, meandering succession of partial views presented to the person walking through a landscape. In *Arabesques* he promises to lead readers to the heights, while forcing them to follow a winding path along the ground. In doing so he is being true to an aphorism he quotes in his review of Pogodin:

Kak zhe mudreno raspoznat', otchego chto proiskhodit, chto k chemu klonitsia! Kak perepletaiutsia prichiny i sledstviia! Povtoriaiu vopros: mozhno li predstavit' istoriiu? Gde forma dlia nee? Istoriiu vpolne mozhno tol'ko chuvstvovat'. (8: 194)

(How difficult it is to identify why something happens, what leads to what! How interwoven are causes and effects! I repeat the question: Is it possible to represent history? Where is the form for it? The entirety of history may only be felt.)

Where is the form for feeling the interwoven strands of history? *Arabesques* and Pliushkin's garden answer: in the intricacy and sudden variation of the picturesque landscape.

6

The Final Tractatus

Народ наш не глуп, что бежит, как от чорта, от
всякой письменной бумаги. Знает, что там притык
всей человеческой путаницы, крючкотворства и
каверзничеств.

—N. V. Gogol

Природа, чтоб пленять и удивлять своими картинами,
употребляет утесы, зелень деревьев и лугов, шум во-
допадов и ключей, сияние неба, бурю и тишину, а
бедный человек, чтоб выразить впечатление, про-
изводимое ею, должен заменить ее разнообразные
предметы однообразными чернильными каракуль-
ками, между которыми, часто бывает, гораздо труд-
нее добраться до смысла, нежели между утесами и
пропастями до прекрасного вида.

—V. A. Zhukovskii

In *Selected Passages from Correspondence with Friends*, Gogol seems at
first glance to be returning to the ideals of Herderian historiography.[1] The following passages are representative in their exaltation of
clarity, order, fixity, law, and the straight path to truth:

There comes a time when one must not speak at all about the lofty and the
beautiful without at the same time showing as clear as day the paths and
roads to it for everyone to use. (8: 298)

We find that the careers are precisely what they are supposed to be [*chto im
sleduet byt'*] when examining each within its lawful boundaries, that every last
one has been, as it were, created from on high in order for us to answer to
all the demands of our governmental way of life; and they were made that way
not because each person, as if vying with everyone else, tried either to expand the limits of his career or even to step out of its limits entirely. (8: 271)

Look how in nature everything takes place in an orderly and wise fashion, under such a harmonious law [*v kakom stroinom zakone*], and how everything reasonably proceeds one from the other. Only we rush about, God knows why. (8: 296)

Even more than on writers, the *Odyssey* will have an effect on those who are still preparing to be writers and who, in high schools and universities, still see their calling before them mistily and obscurely [*tumanno i neiasno*]. It can from the very beginning lead them onto the straight path, saving them from unnecessarily wandering about the crooked alleys in which their predecessors have frequently stumbled upon each other. (8: 241)

The motto of *Selected Passages* could perhaps be found in Gogol's wishful statement about Karamzin: "How ridiculous . . . are those of us who assert that in Russia it is impossible to speak the whole truth. . . . No. Have such a pure, such a well-arranged soul as Karamzin had, and then proclaim your truth: everyone will hear you out, from the tsar down to the lowest beggar in the state" (8: 267).

As with *Arabesques* and *Dead Souls*, however, the structure of *Selected Passages* contradicts its surface rhetoric. This paean to the straight, the clear, the complete, and the true returns to the crooked, fragmentary, elliptical form of Benjamin's tractatus. The title *Selected Passages*, like "Rome (A Fragment)," points to the fact that something is missing. As in *Arabesques*, disparate themes jostle against each other, and the reader can, with an effort, construct areas of thematic coherence out of the seeming chaos. Chopped up and scattered among the rambling extracts are essays on Russian poetry, the Orthodox priesthood, the poor, the word, and so on. Once the tractatus structure of *Selected Passages* is recognized, certain passages that may at first seem paradoxical, even ludicrous, achieve a kind of logic. For example, after listing a number of reasonable artistic exercises that Zhukovskii allegedly had to perform before translating Homer, Gogol seems to make an illogical leap:

Finally, he had to become more deeply a Christian in order to acquire that clear-seeing, deepened view of life that no one may have except a Christian who has already grasped its significance. See how many conditions had to be fulfilled for the translation of the *Odyssey* not to turn into a slavish transmittal but for the *living word* to be heard in it and for all of Russia to accept Homer as its own! But something marvelous emerged. It is not a translation but rather a re-creation, a restoration, a resurrection of Homer [*vossozdanie, vosstanovlenie, voskresen'e Gomera*]. (8: 237)

In other words, to translate the pagan Homer, Zhukovskii had to become a better Christian. As an exercise in objective "truth," this notion leaves a lot to be desired. As a key passage in a tractatus, this description of the "resurrection of Homer" is brilliant, resonating with the recurring themes of the poet, the word, Russia, and the final words of the entire work, "voskresen'e Khristovo" (the resurrection of Christ; 8: 418).

The idea that only a Christian can successfully translate Homer is by no means the only paradox in *Selected Passages*. The work is saturated with blatantly absurd assertions: that poverty is bliss (8: 337), that a wife must order her husband to be her lord and master (8: 341), that the best thing for anyone is a public slap in the face (8: 348). The recipients of Gogol's letters are advised to behave like "iuro-divye" (holy fools), burning money in front of their serfs (8: 322), dividing their money into seven equal piles (8: 338–39), praising only cheap and simple attire (8: 309). The voice speaking in Gogol's letters attains dizzying heights of absurdity in such passages as the following:

To your long letter, which you wrote with such terror, which you asked me to destroy immediately upon reading it and to which you asked me to reply not otherwise than through trustworthy hands and by no means through the mail, I am responding not only not in secret but, as you see, in a printed book, which perhaps half of literate Russia will read. (8: 343)

I see and hear all: your sufferings are great. . . . All of this is difficult, difficult, and I can say nothing more to you than "It is difficult!" But here is your consolation. This is only the beginning; you will receive even more contumely. (8: 367–68)

V. G. Belinskii's review of *Selected Passages* conscientiously catalogues Gogol's paradoxes and absurdities, with pauses to exclaim in exasperation and bewilderment (pp. 222–39).[2] Belinskii, in looking for logic and reason, is missing an important point: Gogol's textual model, the New Testament, operates with similarly disturbing, patently absurd figures of thought and inoperable suggestions for action. The aim is to puzzle, to confound, "that seeing they may see, and not perceive; and hearing they may hear, and not understand; lest at any time they should be converted, and their sins should be forgiven them" (Mark 4: 11–12). But Belinskii's reaction, itself representative of the reaction of "half of literate Russia," demonstrates that whatever the stated aims of this *imitatio Evangeli*, its effect on its audience is anything but as clear as day, a straight path to the truth.[3]

Perhaps most intriguing and disturbing in a work that purports to be concerned with "polnaia pravda" (the whole truth) is Gogol's treatment of Pushkin. Again the explicit message is in favor of clarity, against ambiguity:

Khristianin, namesto togo, chtoby govorit' o tekh mestakh v Pushkine, kotorykh smysl eshche temen i mozhet byt' istolkovan na dve storony, stanet govorit' o tom, chto iasno. (8: 276)

(A Christian, instead of speaking about those places in Pushkin whose meaning is still obscure and can be interpreted in two directions, will speak about that which is clear.)

Near the beginning of *Selected Passages*, however, Gogol makes a statement that, without mentioning Pushkin, betrays a more complicated attitude toward the latter's poetic philosophy: "I am a writer, and the duty of a writer is not just the provision of pleasant diversion to the mind and taste; he will be strictly called to account if his works do not provide anything of utility [*pol'za*] to the soul and if he leaves behind no sermons for people [*v pouchenie liudiam*]" (8: 221). This passage, which clearly contradicts the place of utility and sermons in Pushkin's aesthetic universe, is much more characteristic of Gogol's treatment of Pushkin's works in *Selected Passages* than is the promise to stick to that which is clear.[4] Far from avoiding the ambiguous, Gogol goes so far as to distort known facts in the service of his own outré interpretations. In doing so, he provides a clue to his complex attitude toward clarity and obscurity in language.

Gogol's cavalier approach to the facts of Pushkin's poetic biography struck his contemporaries most powerfully in the case of the 1832 epistle "To N***" ("K N***"), first published posthumously. The unfinished epistle, which begins "S Gomerom dolgo ty besedoval odin" (For a long time you conversed alone with Homer), was generally understood by Pushkin's contemporaries to be addressed to N. I. Gnedich, the translator of the *Iliad*. Gogol, in demonstrating the dubious proposition that one of the major themes of Russian lyric poetry is "love for the tsar," builds his interpretation of the poem on the premise that it is addressed to Nicholas I:

> I will now reveal the secret [of this poem]. . . . Here is its provenience. There was a soiree in the Anichkov Palace, one of those soirees to which, as you know, only the elite of our society were invited. Among them at that time was Pushkin. Everyone had already gathered in the halls; but the sovereign did not emerge for a long time. Sequestered from everyone in another part of the palace and taking advantage of his first moment free of business, he had opened the *Iliad* and imperceptibly became carried away, reading it during the whole time that music was resounding and dances were seething in the halls. He came down to the ball a bit late, carrying on his face the trace of other impressions. The bringing together of these two opposites slipped by unnoticed for everyone, but in Pushkin's soul it left a powerful impression, and its fruit was the following majestic ode. (8: 253–54)

This charming fairy tale, so utterly unbelievable for anyone familiar with the facts of Pushkin's (or Nicholas's) life, failed to convince such informed readers as Belinskii, Pletnev, and S. P. Shevyrev. Shevyrev chastises Gogol for his "mistake" and fumes in a letter to Pletnev: "How could he interpret Pushkin's epistle to Gnedich in such a way! The interpretation is even unseemly, if you carefully read the entire epistle."[5] Shevyrev puts his finger on what, apart from all external evidence, makes Gogol's premise untenable: except for the first line, the entire poem is reduced to absurdity once one attempts to link it to the scene Gogol depicts. The first scholar to devote detailed attention to Gogol's misreading, V. V. Sadovnik, singles out the following lines from Pushkin's epistle as particularly difficult to reconcile with Gogol's palace ballroom scene:

> Ты нас обрел в пустыне под шатром,
> В безумстве суетного пира,
> Поющих буйну песнь и скачущих кругом
> От нас созданного кумира.
>
> (Pushkin, 2: 353)

> You found us in the desert under a tent
> In the madness of a frivolous feast,
> Singing a wild song and hopping around
> The idol that we ourselves had created.

With the indignation of a loyal subject Sadovnik notes,

Poslednee vyrazhenie, esli priderzhivat'sia tolkovaniia Gogolia, dolzhno byt'
otneseno neposredstvenno k avgusteishemu khoziainu prazdnika. Mog li
Pushkin dopustit' samuiu vozmozhnost' podobnogo sblizheniia? (p. 142)

(The latter expression, if one holds to Gogol's interpretation, must be directly applied to the most august host of the celebration. Could Pushkin
have admitted even the possibility of such a comparison?)

It is not enough for Gogol to concoct this flamboyantly wrong-
headed interpretation of Pushkin's epistle; he then asks, "V prave li
byl Pushkin upodobit' [monarkha] drevnemu bogovidtsu Moiseiu?"
(Was Pushkin justified in comparing [the monarch] to the ancient
God-seer Moses? 8: 254). Having satisfactorily answered this imper-
tinent question in the affirmative, Gogol moves on to set up an opposition between the epistle "To N***," in which "Pushkin" falls in
the dust before the majesty of the sovereign, and his "I have erected
a monument to myself not made by [human] hands" ("Ia pamiatnik
sebe vozdvig nerukotvornyi," 1836), in which he asserts that his poetic monument rises above the monument to Alexander I (Gogol
uses Zhukovskii's censored version, which substitutes Napoleon for
Alexander; 8: 255). Thus a text that is rendered false by its mistaken
connection with Nicholas is adduced to correct or temper the impression that Pushkin was excessively proud, an impression created
by a *genuine* poem: "Ne meshaet zametit', chto *eto byl tot poet*, kotoryi byl slishkom gord i nezavisimostiiu svoikh mnenii i svoim lich-
nym dostoinstvom" (It would be good to note that *this was that same
poet* who was too proud both in the independence of his opinions
and in his personal sense of dignity; 8: 255; emphasis added).

The epistle to Gnedich is only the most obvious of the obfusca-
tions that Gogol indulges in throughout *Selected Passages* whenever
Pushkin's name appears. He offers direct quotations of Pushkin,
which sound suspiciously Gogolian in content and style (8: 229,
252–53);[6] he approves of a speech in *The Captain's Daughter* that in
context is the butt of obvious satire (8: 343); and he ends his letter
on Russian lyric poetry with an assertion that is given the lie by
Pushkin's poetry and his life: "It is noteworthy that in all other lands
the writer finds himself rather scorned by society for his personal
character. Here it is just the opposite [*U nas naprotiv*]" (8: 261). Go-

gol even dares to attack other false interpreters of Pushkin: "Neko-
torye stali pechatno ob"iavliat', chto Pushkin byl deist, a ne khristianin; tochno kak budto oni pobyvali v dushe Pushkina" (Some
people have begun to announce in print that Pushkin was a deist and
not a Christian, just as if they had been [able to see into] Pushkin's
soul; 8: 274).

There are a number of possible reasons why Gogol might permit
himself this desecration of the poetic body of his dead idol. First, it
enables him to transform Pushkin into a fictional character, so that
by the time Pushkin is called upon, in "Four Letters to Various
People about *Dead Souls*" ("Chetyre pis'ma k raznym litsam po po-
vodu 'Mertvykh dush'"), to offer an interpretation of a text by Gogol, he has himself become a purely Gogolian creation (8: 292). Second, Pushkin himself has provided Gogol with a kind of carte
blanche in the moral to his poem "The Hero" ("Geroi," 1830), a
poem to which Gogol himself refers (8: 260):

> Тьмы низких истин мне дороже
> Нас возвышающий обман.
>
> (Pushkin, 2: 319)
>
> (Dearer to me than a thousand base truths
> Is a deception that elevates us.)

The multiple ironies generated around the figure of the tsar in this
poetic dialogue are irrelevant to Gogol, who has divested himself of
"pustye rytsarski-evropeiskie poniatiia o pravde" ("empty European
chivalric notions about truth; 8: 342). The elevating deception that
presents Pushkin as a profoundly Christian admirer of autocracy is
no doubt dearer to the Gogol of *Selected Passages* than a thousand
"base" and complicated truths about a poet whose political and reli-
gious views are still being debated.[7]

Deeper and subtler than the propaganda purposes of Gogol's mis-
readings, however, is the fear of the very act of interpretation that
they betray. One may ask how Gogol expected to get away with such
obvious distortions, how he expected to fool "half of literate Russia."
One answer is that he had no such expectation, that his appropriation and misuse of Pushkin's poetic legacy is an object lesson in the
dangers of sending the word out into the world. In the context of a
work that is preoccupied with correcting interpretations of part I of

Dead Souls and forestalling interpretation of part II, the perversion of Pushkin's texts may stand as an ominous demonstration of where one may be led by "istolkovanie na dve storony" (interpretation in two directions; 8: 276).

Selected Passages teems with paradoxes, but when one contemplates the brazenly undeceptive deceit practiced on Pushkin here, a paradox from another Gogolian text rings in the mind:

Khlestakov ne lgun po remeslu: on sam pozabyvaet, chto lzhet, i uzhe sam pochti verit tomu, chto govorit. On razvernulsia, on v dukhe, vidit, chto vsë idet khorosho, ego slushaiut—i po tomu odnomu on govorit plavnee, razviaznee, govorit ot dushi, govorit sovershenno otkrovenno i, govoria lozh', vykazyvaet imenno v nei sebia takim, kak est' . . . Eto voobshche luchshaia i samaia poeticheskaia minuta ego zhizni—pochti rod vdokhnoveniia. (4: 99, 100)

(Khlestakov is not a liar by trade: he himself sometimes forgets that he is lying and almost believes what he is saying. He has become expansive, he is in high spirits, he sees that everything is going well, that people are listening to him—and for that reason alone he speaks more fluently, more freely, he speaks from the heart, he speaks completely frankly, and telling a lie, he displays himself precisely in that lie just as he is . . . . This is in general the best and most poetic moment in his life—almost a type of inspiration.)[8]

Gogol admitted to Zhukovskii after the publication of *Selected Passages* that he had appeared in it "as a Khlestakov": "Pravo, est' vo mne chto-to khlestakovskoe" (It is true, there is something Khlestakovian in me; 13: 243).[9] This Khlestakovian quality is not as simple and obvious as it may seem. It involves not just the foolish bombast and boasting of the false inspector general and the false Orthodox prophet but also the creative flexibility, the boundary crossing, and the paradoxical genuineness of Khlestakov and Nozdrev. In subverting the proclaimed clarity, straightness, and truth of *Selected Passages* through an enigmatic, crooked, and deceptive form and texture, Gogol is showing himself "takim, kak est'" (just as he is).

The narrative strategies of *Dead Souls*, which subvert and twist the order and fixity of Gogol's Herderian historiography, perform the same task with a great deal more artistic success. The narrator of *Dead Souls* is, without realizing it, keenly attuned to the peculiar character of the novel:

Strannye liudi eti gospoda chinovniki, a za nimi i vse prochie zvaniia: ved' ochen' khorosho znali, chto Nozdrev lgun, chto emu nel'zia verit' ni v odnom slove, ni v samoi bezdelitse, a mezhdu tem imenno pribegnuli k nemu. Podi ty, slad' s chelovekom! ne verit v boga, a verit, chto esli pocheshetsia perenos'e, to nepremenno umret; propustit mimo sozdanie poeta, iasnoe, kak den', vsë proniknutoe soglasiem i vysokoiu mudrost'iu prostoty, a brositsia imenno na to, gde kakoi-nibud' udalets naputaet, napletet, izlomaet, vyvorotit prirodu, i emu ono ponravitsia, i on stanet krichat': "Vot ono, vot nastoiashchee znanie tain serdtsa!" (6: 207)

(These civil servants are strange people, and those in all other professions along with them: after all, they knew very well that Nozdrev was a liar, that one could not believe a single word of his, not about the merest trifle, but meanwhile they had recourse to none other than him. Go ahead, try to deal with a human being! He doesn't believe in God, but he does believe that if the bridge of his nose itches, then he is certainly going to die; he'll pay no heed to the creation of a poet, as clear as day, saturated with harmony and the lofty wisdom of simplicity, and will seize on a work in which some daring fellow entangles, intertwines, warps, and twists nature—and he will like it, and start shouting: "There it is, there is real knowledge of the heart's secrets!")

As with any text by Gogol, one must be careful not to accept unquestioningly the surface rhetoric of this passage. These civil servants are not as foolish as they may seem, for although Nozdrev is a liar, he is leading them to the truth about Chichikov and about themselves. And what audience ignores the work of art that is as clear as day, harmonious, and simple—a work that could not possibly have been written by Gogol—and seizes upon a work in which some daring fellow twists and entangles, warps and entwines? The same audience that has given *Dead Souls* an immortal life.

Reference Matter

Notes

BOOK EPIGRAPH: "No entanglement is a chaos unless a world may arise from it" (*Ideen*).

Introduction

EPIGRAPH: "This artfully ordered confusion, this charming symmetry of contradictions, this wonderful eternal alternation of enthusiasm and irony, an alternation that lives even in the smallest members of the whole, seems to me already to be an indirect mythology. . . . Surely the arabesque is the oldest and original form of the human imagination" (*Dialogue on Poetry*).

1. In a brief essay, S. Woodward approaches the problem of disorder in Gogol from a different vantage point, identifying disorder with the female capacity for reproduction. I will argue that, at least in *Dead Souls*, women are associated not with what Woodward calls (pro-)creativity but with sterile fixity and lack of imagination.

Chapter 1

EPIGRAPH: "The novel arose out of a deficiency of history" (notebooks).

1. The first five books of the *Ideen* were available to Gogol in Russian in a free translation published in 1829: *Mysli, otnosiashchiesia k filosoficheskoi istorii chelovechestva, po razumeniiu i nachertaniiu Gerdera*, or *Thoughts on the Philosophy of the History of Mankind, According to Herder's Argument and Outline*. Herder's *Ideen* is cited here according to the English translation, *Outlines of a Philosophy of the History of Man*, by T. Churchill. Listed after the page references to the English edition are the corresponding volume and page numbers in the Bernhard Suphan edition (*Sämtliche Werke*) and, where applicable, the page numbers in the Russian version, *Mysli*. Thus, the source

refers to pp. 2–3 of Herder, *Outlines*, then to vol. 13, pp. 14–15, of Herder, *Sämtliche Werke*, and finally to pp. 3–5 of Herder, *Mysli*. This style and sequence of citations will be used hereafter. In a book that uses *War and Peace* as a model for a far-reaching theory of narrative, Gary Saul Morson has explored Tolstoy's critique of the systematizing and ordering tendency of all historiography (see esp. part II).

2. The source refers to vol. 8, p. 16, of N. V. Gogol, *Polnoe sobranie sochinenii*, hereafter cited in the text or cited simply as Gogol. All citations of Gogol's works are from this edition, and all translations are mine, unless otherwise indicated.

3. White, p. 73.

4. See, e.g., Herder, *Sämtliche Werke*, 13: 147–48; Herder, *Mysli*, pp. 211–12.

5. Müller, p. 274. For a discussion of Gogol's relationship with Zhukovskii, including the latter's own historical researches, see Chapter 3 below.

6. Schlözer, *Predstavlenie*, pp. 35, 36.

7. Cf. the anonymous essay on Herder in the *Moscow Telegraph* (*Moskovskii telegraf*, 1828): "He was the first to utter the great idea that the life of a particular person and the life of the entire human race are subject to identical laws of development" ("Gerder," p. 144).

8. See Schlözer's own self-description, cited by P. Miliukov: "May it be permitted for me to introduce the language of the greatest of natural scientists into the history of all peoples. I cannot see a better method of avoiding the confusion of ancient and medieval history and of explaining the obscure passages than a certain *Systema populorum, in classes et ordines, genera et species redactorum*. The possibility exists. As Linnaeus divides animals according to their teeth, and plants according to their stamens, so the historian should classify peoples according to their languages" (p. 89).

9. Schlözer, *Predstavlenie*, pp. 18, 34.

10. When Gogol cites Schlözer's injunction to the historian to know history "vdol' i poperek" (through and through, lit. "lengthwise and crosswise"; 8: 38), he is referring precisely to this combination of diachrony and synchrony: "Every type of event must be read in a twofold way: once *lengthwise* [*vdol'*], forward and backward, and then *crosswise* [*poperek*], to the side, or in a synchronistic (simultaneous) manner" (Schlözer, *Predstavlenie*, p. 44).

11. Schlözer, "Poniatie o vseobshchei Istorii," *Moskovskii vestnik*, pp. 162–63. Gogol was also indebted to the *Moscow Herald* for his characterization of Schlözer as a "genius of opposition" (genii oppozitsionnyi; 8: 86): "Schlözer introduced opposition into the historicopolitical literature of his age. . . . It was as if he were created for opposition" ("Avgust Liudvig Shletser," p. 317). See also Gogol's characterization of Herder: "As a poet, he is

higher than Schlözer and Müller" (8: 88); and the *Moscow Telegraph*'s: "Herder was not only a poet but a man in the purest sense: citizen, philosopher, and poet" ("Gerder," p. 140).

12. The irony of the project of universal history is that despite (or because of) its grandiose ideal of comprehensiveness, its practitioners tend to leave only fragments behind: Schlözer's plan of universal history "was so extensive that he not only did not erect an edifice according to it but could not even finish the preparatory tasks" ("Avgust Liudvig Shletser," p. 321); the twenty-four volumes of Müller's *Universal History* "are rather remarks on history than a history itself" ("Ioann Miller," p. 392); Herder's "*Ideas on the Philosophy of the History of Mankind* reveal his genius in all its force and include all his forms of contemplation. . . . But the execution could not satisfy such a plan: no type of exposition could sustain it. Herder himself felt this keenly . . . and left it to his contemporaries and posterity to consider all his other works as its continuation and as parts of this great work" ("Gerder," pp. 142–43).

13. Schlözer, *Predstavlenie*, pp. 58–59, 40–41, 102.

14. "Ioann Miller," p. 399.

15. Georgievskii, "Gogolevskie teksty." See vol. 9 of Gogol, *Polnoe sobranie sochinenii*, for Gogol's notes on history. See also the discussion by Iurii Mann in the commentary to N. V. Gogol, *Sobranie sochinenii*, 6: 469–76.

16. The Böttiger referred to is *Vseobshchaia istoriia. Gimnazicheskii kurs. Sochinenie erlangenskogo professora Bettigera. Perevod s nemetskogo* (Moscow, 1832); see Gogol, 10: 459.

17. Cf. Gogol's 1833 letter to M. A. Maksimovich: "My joy, my life! Songs! How I love you! What are all the stale chronicles in which I'm now burrowing compared with these ringing, living chronicles!" (10: 284).

18. Cf., e.g., Schlözer, *Predstavlenie*, pp. 154–55, with Gogol, 8: 131–32.

19. "Man alone is in contradiction with himself and with the earth" (p. 128; 13: 195–96). See also p. 123; 13: 189–201.

20. This is perhaps an expanded paraphrase of the following passage in Herder: "We are children of the eternal, whom we here learn by imitation to know and love, whom everything incites us to know, and whom both our sufferings and enjoyments impel us to imitate. Yet since we know him so obscurely, since we imitate him so feebly and childishly, nay, even perceive the reasons why we cannot know him and imitate him otherwise in our present organization, is it possible for us to attain no other—do our indubitably best capacities admit of no advancement? Then, too, these our noblest faculties are so little adapted to this world: they expand themselves beyond it, since everything here is subservient to the wants of our nature. And still we feel our nobler part incessantly contending against these wants: precisely that which seems the end of man's organization finds its birthplace

indeed upon the earth, but by no means its state of perfection. Has the deity, then, broken the thread, and with all these preparations in the human frame produced at last an immature creature, deceived in the whole of his destination? All things upon earth are fragments: and shall they remain for ever and ever imperfect fragments, and the human race a group of shadows perplexing themselves with vain dreams? Here religion has knit together all the wants and hopes of mankind into *faith* and woven an *immortal* crown for humanity" (pp. 104–5; 13: 164–65). See also p. 125; 13: 191–92. Herder ends with a loose quotation of a poem by Anna Luisa Karsch that conveys a similar idea:

> Da sind Wohnungen, Welten und Räume—
> In voller Jugend glänzen sie
> Da schon Jahrtausende vergangen:
> Der Zeiten Wechsel raubet nie
> Das Licht von ihren Wangen.
>
> Hier aber unter unserm Blick
> Verfällt, vergeht, verschwindet alles:
> Der Erde Pracht, der Erde Glück
> Droht eine Zeit des Falles.
>
> (pp. 130–31; 13: 200)

(Out there are habitations, worlds, and spaces that bloom in unfading youth, even though ages upon ages have rolled over them, and defy the changes of time and season: but everything that appears before our eyes decays and perishes and passes away; and all the pride and happiness of earth are exposed to inevitable destruction.)

These several passages allude to 1 Corinthians 13: 12: "For now we see in a mirror dimly, but then face to face. Now I know in part; then I shall understand fully, even as I have been fully understood."

Chapter 2

EPIGRAPH: "Only the romantic type of poetry . . . is endless, just as it alone is free, and recognizes as its first law that the caprice of the poet tolerates no law over itself" (*Athenaeum Fragments*).

1. For the relation between planning and chance disruption in Tolstoy, see Morson, pp. 84–99, 200–202, 269–71.

2. See Gogol's letter to V. A. Zhukovskii about the initial stages of writing the novel, Nov. 12, 1836 (N.S.): "Vsia Rus' iavitsia v nem!" (All Rus' will appear in it! 11: 73). E. A. Smirnova notes the connection between Gogol's historical models and his presentation of characters as types (*Poema Gogolia*, pp. 22–23). Gogol uses the archaic word Rus' for Russia when he wants a poetic and grandiose tonality.

3. Richard Peace has also discussed the particularity of Gogol's types, which are "generalized in their idiosyncracies and individualised in their typicality" (p. 258; see also pp. 234–38, 251). In a discussion of the type in Balzac, Peter Demetz distinguishes between the traditional, Romantic concept of the type and the new, "scientific" (taxonomical) concept: "These traditional types symbolize supra-human, overpowering forces of existence, while a scientific type (as suggested by the methodological traditions of zoology and comparative anatomy) summarizes recurrent human characteristics in a model reminiscent of many individual lives. Traditional, or romantic, types incarnate ontological energies of fate and failure; the new, or scientific, type is concerned with the representation of the many by the one" (p. 408). The Gogolian type constitutes a third category, which mimics the scientific representation of the many by the one but in fact presents a detailed, specific individual.

4. Cf. the directions given by the narrator of "Ivan Fedorovich Shpon'ka i ego tetushka" ("Ivan Fedorovich Shpon'ka and His Auntie," 1832): "When you see a yard where there's a big pole with a quail sitting on it and a fat peasant woman in a green skirt comes out toward you, that's his yard" (1: 284). See also the "generalized" description of the town in "The Carriage" ("Koliaska," 1836): "In the middle of the square are quite small shops; in them you can always see a bundle of ring-shaped rolls, a peasant woman in a red kerchief, a pood of soap, several pounds of bitter almonds, birdshot for shooting, denim, and two merchant's assistants who *at all times* play quoits near the doors" (3: 177; emphasis added).

5. "Such a sport of nature, however, occurs in various historical paintings brought to us in Russia who knows when, whence, and by whom" (6: 9). Cf. Morson: "The artist tries to imagine just what is lacking in historical sources: the actions of a particular, insignificant person in a given and unrepeatable situation" (p. 145).

6. The phrase "dead souls" also nonplussed the censors, who refused to let it stand alone as the title of the novel "because the soul is immortal" (6: 890). See the fine analysis of the trope "dead soul" by Michael Shapiro and Marianne Shapiro, pp. 179–81.

7. Cf. a passage in one of the drafts regarding Nozdrev's lies: "No tak kak . . . chem glupee i nelepee dich', tem bolee na nee byvaet strelkov, to podobnaia nebylitsa vsegda imela uspekh" (But since . . . the more stupid and absurd the game, the more marksmen go after it, such a cock-and-bull story was always a success; 6: 375).

8. Richard Peace speaks of two unplanned encounters, with Korobochka and Nozdrev, that "ultimately lead to his downfall" (p. 219); Jerzy Faryno counts three but considers the third to involve not the governor's daughter but Pliushkin. As Faryno himself admits, Chichikov's visit to Pliushkin is

fully intentional, even though he heard of Pliushkin only after setting out. The visit lacks the abrupt, "thunderclap" nature of the encounters with Korobochka, Nozdrev, and the governor's daughter. I would also disagree with Faryno's assertion that the difference between Chichikov's planned and chance encounters is eventually canceled out (pp. 611–12).

9. Lotman, "Khudozhestvennoe prostranstvo," p. 290.

10. Cf. the final scene of *Dead Souls*: "Ne tak li i ty, Rus', chto boikaia neobgonimaia *troika*, nesesh'sia? . . . ne molniia li eto, *sbroshennaia s neba*? . . . Ekh, *koni, koni*, chto za *koni . . . letiashchie* po vozdukhu . . . Chudnym zvonom zalivaetsia *kolokol'chik*" (Do you not, O Rus', rush like a bold *troika*, impossible to overtake? . . . Is the troika not lightning, *cast down from the sky*? . . . Ah, *steeds, steeds*, what *steeds . . . flying* through the air. . . . The *little bell* breaks out into a marvelous ringing; 6: 246; emphasis added).

11. See J. B. Woodward, pp. 176–77. William Mills Todd III has thoroughly analyzed Chichikov's social standing in the town of N. from a different perspective in a wide-ranging study of the literary sociology of nineteenth-century Russia (pp. 178–200).

12. Sobakevich's conversation, although it violates the rules of politeness, is just as mechanically predictable as Manilov's, for it merely negates Manilov's statements as relayed by Chichikov (6: 96–97).

13. According to Hesiod's *Theogony*. See Hesiod, p. 145.

14. Cf. the lampoon of Themis in an 1807 epigram by Zhukovskii: "S poviazkoi na glazakh za shalosti Fermida! / Uzh nakazanie! uzh podlinno obida! / Kogda vam khochetsia prokaznitsu uniat', / Tak ruki ei sviazat'" (Themis has a blindfold over her eyes because of her mischief! / What a punishment! What a real insult! / If you really want to stop the mischief maker, / Then tie up her hands; *Sochineniia*, 1: 54). All subsequent references to Zhukovskii's verse are to this edition. See also an 1827 review of a book published that year entitled *Themis, or an Outline of the Rights, Privileges, and Obligations of the Female Sex in Russia* (*Femida, ili nachertanie prav, preimushchestv i obiazannostei zhenskogo pola v Rossii*): "Rassmotrev sostav i raspolozhenie Femidy, ne mozhem dovol'no nadivit'sia ee besporiadku!" (Having inspected *Themis*'s composition and arrangement, we cannot be sufficiently amazed at her disorderliness; p. 215).

15. Detienne and Vernant, *Cunning Intelligence*, p. 5. For more on Hermes and the trickster figure, see Fusso, pp. 232–42. On Chichikov as a *pícaro*, see Guillén, p. 79; and LeBlanc, pp. 224–56.

16. See N. O. Brown, p. 60; Kermode, pp. 1–21; and Kerényi, esp. p. 103. Gogol earlier assigned the border position to Pushkin in a remarkably similar phrase, in "A Few Words About Pushkin" ("Neskol'ko slov o Pushkine"): "It was as though fate purposely hurled him there where the borders of Russia are distinguished by a vivid, majestic distinctiveness—where the

smooth immensity of Russia is broken by mountains that touch the clouds, and is fanned by the breath of the South" (8: 50).

17. Hesiod, p. 377.

18. Detienne and Vernant, *Cunning Intelligence*, pp. 107–8. I have slightly altered the translation according to the original, *Les Ruses de l'intelligence*, p. 105.

19. Lotman, "Khudozhestvennoe prostranstvo," p. 291.

20. Cf. Mann, *Poetika Gogolia*, p. 258. Inna Galperina makes interesting observations on Kochkarev as the "auteur" of a play within the play, the "zhenit'ba" of Podkolesin.

21. See Simon Karlinsky's discussion of the possible meanings of *zakon* here (*Sexual Labyrinth*, p. 304).

22. Peace also discusses Podkolesin's inversion of "the ominous symbolism of carriages" (p. 201). In the witty production of *Getting Married* originated by Anatolii Efros at the Malaia Bronnaia Theater in Moscow, the final two speeches of the play are reversed. As published in the play in 1842, they read as follows. Kochkarev says, "Eto vzdor, eto ne tak. Ia pobegu k nemu, ia vozvrashchu ego!" (Nonsense, it's not true. I'll run to him, I'll bring him back!), and exits. Fekla then says, "Da, podi ty, voroti! Dela-to svatskogo ne znaesh', chto li? Eshche esli by v dveri vybezhal—ino delo, a uzh koli zhenikh da shmygnul v okno—uzh tut, prosto moe pochtenie!" (Yes, go, bring him back. Don't you know your matchmaking business? It'd be one thing if he'd run out the door, but for a bridegroom to pop out the window—all I can say is, my compliments! 5: 61). The shifting of Kochkarev's "I'll bring him back" to the end of the play represents a misunderstanding of the play's economy. (The shift occurs in the production performed in December 1988; Iurii Mann believes it did not occur in the original production.) Gogol intended the final note to be not that of a conventional promise of revenge but that of admiration (*pochtenie*, "respect") for the originality of the denouement devised by Podkolesin.

23. Cf. the echo of this speech in the conversation of the lady who is pleasant in all respects: "[Nozdrev] rodnogo ottsa gotov prodat' ili, eshche luchshe, proigrat' v karty" ([Nozdrev] is ready to sell out his own father, or better yet, lose him at cards; 6: 187). See Peace's discussion of Nozdrev's "hostility of intimacy" (pp. 221–22) and James B. Woodward's chapter on the "paternal theme" in *Dead Souls* (pp. 215–29).

24. In Gogol's discussion of the character of Khlestakov, lying is also associated with a sense of physical well-being: "Vret, potomu chto plotno pozavtrakal i vypil poriadochno vina" (He lies because he's had a hearty breakfast and drunk a fair amount of wine; letter to M. S. Shchepkin, May 10, 1836, 11: 39).

25. Cf. Innokentii Annenskii: "Nozdrev is not at all a liar and perhaps he is not even Nozdrev. He is a kind of irrepressible, insane abundance: the gay

indifference of nature itself" ("Estetika 'Mertvykh Dush,'" p. 52). See also James B. Woodward: Nozdrev's tricks and lies "are exposed by their sheer blatancy as simply another form of provocation, as a challenge to the 'stasis' of rules and regulations" (p. 40). Woodward makes an interesting argument that Nozdrev is given the symbolic aura of a hunter and soldier (pp. 33–51).

26. See P. A. Pletnev's comment on the characterization of Nozdrev: "Vy izumleny budete neistoshchimostiiu ego ottenkov, vsegda novykh, vsegda poeticheskikh, *vsegda istinnykh*" (You will be amazed at the inexhaustibility of his nuances, always new, always poetic, *always true*; p. 490).

27. Cf. J. B. Woodward, pp. 39–40. In an 1807 translation of a fable by Florian, Zhukovskii depicts truth and fable as sisters, who are opposed in much the same terms as Mizhuev and Nozdrev. "Truth" is "neprigozha, kak smert' khudaia, / Litsom ugriumaia, s sutulinoi ot let" (Plain, lean as death, / Gloomy of face, with a back stooped with age; 1: 53). Cf. Gogol's description of Mizhuev: "Eto byl muzhchina vysokogo rosta, litsom khudoshchavyi, ili, chto nazyvaiut, izderzhannyi" (He was a man of tall stature, with a lean or what they call worn-out face; 6: 63). "Fable" is a rich, lively woman in ornate clothes who comes riding up in a splendid troika. Fable proposes a fruitful union between herself and her sister:

> "Izvol'-ka vyslushat' moi sestrinskii sovet:
> Nam dolzhno byt' druzhnei i zhit' ne tak, kak prezhde,
> Zhit' vmeste; a tebe v moei khodit' odezhde.
> S toboi i dlia menia otvorit dver' mudrets,
> So mnoiu i tebia ne vygonit glupets . . ."
> . . . S tekh por
> Vezde sestritsy nerazluchny:
> I Basnia ne glupa, i s Istinoi ne skuchnoi!
>
> (1: 54)

> ("Be so good as to listen to my sisterly advice:
> We should be more friendly and not live as before
> But live together; and you should wear my clothes.
> With you along, even the wise man will open the door to me;
> With me along, even the fool will not drive you out. . ."
> . . . From that time
> The sisters have been inseparable everywhere:
> And Fable is not foolish, and Truth is not boring!

28. Karlinsky, *Sexual Labyrinth*, p. 231.

29. Nozdrev's figurative androgyny is borne out in his name. P. V. Annenkov relates an illuminating anecdote in this regard. At an early reading of *Dead Souls*, a fastidious listener objects to a passage in which Selifan calls Korobochka's little servant girl "nozdria" (nostril), maintaining that the epithet is unseemly: "All the other listeners rose up against this remark, as one

that expressed an excessive delicacy of taste and partly a depraved imagination, but Gogol put an end to the argument, taking the side of the critic and
noting, 'If such an idea occurred to one person, that means it could occur
to many. It must be corrected'" (p. 244). In what could the unseemliness,
tacitly confirmed by Gogol's willingness to change the passage, consist but
in the vaginal symbolism of the nostril, indivisible component of the phallic
nose? Significantly, it is the "nostril girl" who points the way to the tavern
at which Chichikov meets Nozdrev, whose name, while it alludes to the
entire phallic-vaginal nose, expresses only the female component. The male-
female merger extends even to morphology: the feminine noun *nozdri-a* is
given the masculine possessive ending *-ov* instead of the expected *-in*. For a
discussion of androgyny in Gogol, see Fusso, pp. 122–46.

30. For a more detailed discussion of divination, see Chapter 3 below.

31. In his pathbreaking and perceptive analysis of *The Gamblers*, Karlinsky regards Ikharev and his cohorts as creative artists (*Sexual Labyrinth*,
p. 180), but their emphasis on laborious practice and predictable results is
not consonant with Gogol's mythology of creativity. Iurii Mann recognizes
the assimilation of the cheater's craft not to creative art but to "the categories
of 'honest' life, of various professions and occupations" (*Poetika*, p. 259).

Chapter 3

EPIGRAPHS: "It's time for [Zhukovskii] to have his own imagination and
his own enserfed inventions" (Jan. 2, 1822); "Here for the first time you see
all the poetry of the enserfed person" (1839).

1. In a suggestive essay Barbara Heldt has discussed the reluctance to
name as a characteristic of the narrator of *Dead Souls*: "In a world of secrecy
textual disclosure, too, must be secret and indeterminate" (p. 90).

2. See Todd, pp. 184–85. Cf. A. A. Bestuzhev [Marlinskii]'s comment on
French Neoclassical theater: "Chudnoe delo: Frantsuzy, stol' okhochie pos-
meiat'sia i poshalit' vsegda, stol' razvratnye pri Liudovike XV i dalee, . . .
stanovilis' vazhny vkhodia v teatr, stydilis' uslyshat' na stsene pro rumiany, i
slovo *obed* iz"iasniali perifrazami, kak neprilichnost'!" (It's a strange business: the French, always so eager to laugh and play tricks, so debauched
during the reign of Louis XV and after, . . . became solemn when they
entered the theater, were embarrassed to hear about rouge on the stage, and
explained the word *dinner* in periphrasis, as if it were indecent!" (part LIII,
p. 88).

3. Cf. the "pen envy" that Gogol attributes to his friend Mar'ia Balabina
in a letter of Oct. 12, 1836 (N.S.): "Stokrat, stokrat zhelala by ia imet' iskus-
noe pero podobnoe vashemu'" (I'd wish [feminine form of verb] a hundred
times, that I had a skillful pen like yours; II: 70).

4. See Karlinsky, "Portrait of Gogol as a Word Glutton," pp. 178–81.

5. Katherine Lahti analyzes this passage as well as other passages relating to language in *Dead Souls* and develops a sophisticated theory of the opposition between nature and artifact in the novel.

6. Gogol's efforts in *Evenings* were professional enough to warrant a scholarly note by a historian of Ukrainian lexicography (Horets'kyi, pp. 83–90). One can easily understand Andrei Belyi's impression "chto avtor izuchil slovar' Dalia do slovaria Dalia" (that the author studied Dahl's dictionary before Dahl's dictionary existed; p. 9).

7. Here again Gogol's method of analogy is evident. Cf. his fabricated definition of the insect koramora and its "derived" verb *koriachit'sia* with this notebook entry: "*Stroka*—podlaia mukha zheltogo tsveta, kusaiushchaia korov pod khvostom; mukha strochit korovu, a korova strochitsia" (*Stroka*—a lowly fly, yellow in color, which bites cows under the tail; the fly stroches [maddens] the cow, and the cow is bestroched [goes mad from being bitten by a *stroka*]; 7: 326).

8. Karlinsky, "Portrait of Gogol as a Word Glutton," p. 176.

9. For an amusing discussion of Gogol's concern with names and its relation to his own family history, see Gregg.

10. In an earlier draft the muzhiks have already come to life before Chichikov looks at the list. When he rises that morning, the narrator says, "V ume u nego sideli muzhiki" (The muzhiks were sitting in his mind; 6: 442).

11. See Nabokov, p. 102. Vladimir Nabokov has given poetic definition to Gogol's "homunculi," the phantom beings who live an offstage life in his narrative and drama (see pp. 42–54, 80–84, 100–103).

12. E. A. Smirnova has demonstrated that the opening of chapter 6 echoes Zhukovskii's 1820 "Song": "Our joys are taken away" ("Pesnia": "Otymaet nashi radosti"). Smirnova says: "In this passage Gogol creates prose variations on Zhukovskii's theme" (*Poema Gogolia*, p. 37; see also pp. 123–25).

13. Cf. Vengerov's famous article "Gogol Had Absolutely No Knowledge of Real Russian Life" ("Gogol' sovershenno ne znal real'noi russkoi zhizni," 1913): "Gogol never dropped in to see a Russian landowner, never had dinner at any Manilov's house, never saw Sobakevich put away a side of mutton, never spent the night at Korobochka's. . . . Not a one of this kaleidoscope of personages, so typical of Russian life according to the common conception, did Gogol ever see or observe with his own eyes. He invented it all out of whole cloth [*vsë iz sobstvennogo pal'tsa vysosal*], created it all by a process of introspection and artistic combination, for at the basis of his generally Russian typification he placed Ukrainian impressions" (p. 135). Frederick Griffiths and Stanley Rabinowitz have noted the strangeness of the lyric voice's lament for its lost vitality: "With characteristic paradox, the new

bardic voice intrudes to announce itself with an apologia for its silence! . . . His profession of silence contradicts itself in the very act of being spoken. His blocked channels of perception are belied by the existence of the vivid tale that he conveys to us" (pp. 74, 75).

14. Cited in Ianushkevich, p. 141.

15. The literature on Gogol's relationship with Zhukovskii is voluminous. See Ianushkevich, pp. 265–73; Sakharov. In an excellent article, E. A. Smirnova touches on the main topic of this chapter, Zhukovskii's and Gogol's shared concern with the soul, but does not explore the ways in which Gogol transformed Zhukovskii's concept of the soul ("Zhukovskii i Gogol'"). I. E. Mandel'shtam (pp. 22–28) offers a detailed stylistic comparison of the two writers, concluding: "Even a superficial inspection of the early works of Gogol convinces one that the poet [Gogol] did not so much create as write variations on Zhukovskii's themes" (p. 23).

In the 1819 report on the moon, Zhukovskii speaks of his work in history as the deciphering of an ancient text, but with an act of imagination added to the work of decoding: "I tak, byt' mozhet, / Kogda fantaziia pomozhet / Mne podruzhit'sia s starinoi, / Ia razgadaiu spisok moi, / *Byl' nebylitseiu pripravliu*, / I vsepoddànneishe predstavliu / Vam, gosudarynia, v stikhakh" (And so, perhaps, / If imagination will help / Me to make friends with olden times, / I will decipher my manuscript, / *Will spice truth with fable*, / And will present it most humbly / To you, Your Majesty, in verse; 2: 113; emphasis added).

16. Kanunova, 1: 158–60, 403, 421–23. See also the discussion by R. V. Iezuitova: "Zhukovskii's familiarity with Herder's theoretical views . . . allowed him to come to a new understanding of the essence of historicism as a particular aesthetic category" (p. 122).

17. Zhukovskii, *Sochineniia v proze* (hereafter *Proza*), pp. 308–9.

18. Cited in Ianushkevich, p. 170. The description of Zhukovskii's last days by the priest Ioann Bazarov incorporates the myth of Providence into the circumstances of the poet's death. Zhukovskii had invited Bazarov to celebrate communion with him and his family in Baden during the sixth week of Lent but was forced to change the meeting to a later time because of "unexpected circumstances"—the sudden decision of two of his friends to visit. "The good old man [Zhukovskii] . . . did not know that this disposition was from on high, from the wise will of God, who intended for him to taste this last joy of the Christian's earthly faith two days before his passage into eternal life. . . . Thus Radovits and Reitern came to Baden, and according to human ideas, *hindered* Zhukovskii from taking communion in the sixth week, but in the fortunes of Providence they were only tools of the Higher Wisdom" (Zhukovskii, *Proza*, p. 794).

19. Zhukovskii, *Proza*, p. 535.

20. Sometimes the similarity between Gogol's and Zhukovskii's nonfictional writings verges on textual identity (see Smirnova on Gogol's "Boris Godunov," in "Zhukovskii i Gogol'," pp. 244–45). Cf. the following passages from Zhukovskii's "Fragments of a Letter about Switzerland" ("Otryvki iz pis'ma o Shveitsarii," 1833) and Gogol's "On the Middle Ages." Zhukovskii's is quoted first.

One may compare the life of the human race to a choppy sea: storms of passions create momentary waves, which rise and fall and are constantly replaced by others. Each wave seems to be some sort of original creation; and if each of them could think, it might imagine, in its swift existence, that it acts and creates for eternity. But along with all its quickly passing comrades, it belongs to a single common movement; sometimes the movement seems to be a storm: the abyss seethes, then suddenly everything is smooth and pure; and in what was a formless chaos of waters a moment ago the pure sky is calmly reflected. (*Proza*, p. 262)

Everything in [the Middle Ages] was poetry and unaccountability. You will suddenly sense a change when you come into the realm of modern history. The change is all too perceptible, and the condition of your soul will be like the waves of the sea, previously arising in high irregular mounds but then lying down and forming a regular current with their entire immeasurable plain. The actions of man in the Middle Ages seem completely unaccountable. . . . But all of them, combined into a whole, display an amazing wisdom. (8: 24)

21. See Todd, p. 249; Smirnova-Chikina, pp. 190–92.
22. S. P. Shevyrev later commended Zhukovskii for the timelessness of the subject of the ballad. Although a translation from the German, it spoke directly to the feelings of those bereaved by the war with Napoleon: "Along with [Liudmila, other] betrothed maidens sinned by secretly murmuring for their fiancés, carried away by the wars of a new stormy era, which betrayed the hopes of peace. More than one Russian maiden mourned a corpse in the person of her intended"; *Muscovite*, 1853, cited in Mordovchenko, p. 119.
23. See Todd's discussion of the way in which Zhukovskii's essay offers a well-defined image of "society" (pp. 16–18, 21).
24. Zhukovskii, *Estetika*, p. 170.
25. In Zhukovskii's essay "Raphael's 'Madonna'" ("Rafaeleva 'Madonna,'" 1824), in his *Estetika*, pp. 307–11. See Wackenroder and Tieck, *Herzensergießungen eines kunstliebenden Klosterbruders*, pp. 11–15. Appropriately, the myth of Raphael propounded in this book lays great emphasis on Raphael's youth. A young man being shown the portraits of the great artists by the Muse is astounded to learn that Raphael is not a dignified gray-haired man but a youth no older than himself: "Über kleine frohe Spiele scheint er sinnend, / Und das Sinnen wieder scheint ihm Spiel" (He seems to be meditating on small happy games, / And the meditation in turn seems to be a game for him; p. 98). This Raphael, like the temporarily rejuvenated Chi-

chikov, would find the governor's daughter, both madonna and toy, an appropriate companion.

26. See, e.g., Smirnova, *Poema Gogolia*, pp. 103–5.

27. Gray's version is a bit less Manilovian: "Large was his bounty, and his soul sincere, / Heav'n did a recompence as largely send: / He gave to Mis'ry all he had, a tear, / He gain'd from Heav'n ('twas all he wish'd) a friend" (p. 120).

28. Polevoi, no. 19, pp. 369–70. The letters of Zhukovskii's friends at times attain (and even exceed) a Manilovian absurdity: "I love you until death; and several days ago I saw that I love you even at the point of death, and I would have proved this to you if I had died: the executors who were with me had already received instructions to extract my heart after death, dry it out thoroughly, wrap it up, and deliver it to you; I do not tell you this in jest"; V. A. Perovskii to Zhukovskii, Sept. 24, 1828, cited in Veselovskii, pp. 296–97. D. S. Likhachev has shown that Manilovism was characteristic of the "hypocritical bureaucratic milieu of the empire of Nicholas I, and particularly of Nicholas I himself" ("Sotsial'nye korni," p. 298). The realm of Zhukovskii, tutor to the tsar's sons, intersects with the court realm that Likhachev describes.

29. Zhukovskii was the illegitimate son of E. A. Protasova's father, A. I. Bunin. According to G. A. Gukovskii, the story of Zhukovskii's unhappy love was "well known to the wide circle of his friends and acquaintances" (p. 142).

30. Zhukovskii to M. A. Protasova, Nov. 27, 1815, in Zhukovskii, *Izbrannoe*, p. 445.

31. A similarly veiled "incest" is found in *The Inspector General*. For a discussion of incest in Gogol, see Fusso, pp. 146–50.

32. Zhukovskii to A. I. Turgenev, Feb. 1, 1815, in Zhukovskii, *Izbrannoe*, p. 434.

33. Smirnova discusses Gogol's early, unironic response to the poem, which "served as a kind of lodestar for the young Gogol in his aesthetic quests" ("Zhukovskii i Gogol," p. 245). V. N. Toporov has traced the textual sources of "The Inexpressible" in Wackenroder and Tieck.

34. See Shklovskii, "Literary Genre of *Dead Souls*," p. 564.

35. Polevoi, no. 20, pp. 532–33.

36. Zhukovskii, *Estetika*, pp. 175–76.

37. The polemics surrounding Zhukovskii's work have been thoroughly analyzed by Iurii Tynianov (pp. 87–227) and by N. I. Mordovchenko (see index). I rehearse the discussions by Tynianov and Mordovchenko at some length here to bring out the connections between the Zhukovskii polemics and the conception of *Dead Souls*.

38. Karamzin, *Polnoe sobranie stikhotvorenii*, p. 148. Gender plays a major

role in the parody: Gogol's letter writer changes the gender of the speaker from male to female and destroys the meter of the poem in the process. The last line of Karamzin's poem, "On úmer vo slezákh" (He died in tears), is in iambic trimeter like the rest of the work. The last line in the letter writer's poem, "Chto oná umerlá vo slezákh" (That she died in tears), suddenly switches to anapestic trimeter.

39. *Rinaldo Rinaldini* (1798) is by Christian August Vulpius (1762–1827). In a letter to Zhukovskii explaining his involvement in a theft while at the Corps of Pages, E. A. Baratynskii cites *Rinaldo Rinaldini*, along with Schiller's *Die Räuber*, as a work that perverted his moral sense: "At this time those of us who had money would buy books in Stupin's dirty shop, which was immediately beside the corps, and what books! Glorioso, Rinaldo Rinaldini, robbers in all conceivable forests and dungeons! And I, to my misfortune, was one of the most avid readers! . . . The books that I mentioned, and Schiller's *Karl Moor* in particular, heated my imagination; the robber's life seemed to me the most enviable in the world" (October–December 1823, in Barratt, p. 33).

40. F. F. Vigel', *Zapiski*, cited in Mordovchenko, p. 147. As early as 1811, Konstantin Batiushkov wrote, with Zhukovskii in mind, of "fashionable writers" who "spend whole nights on graves and frighten poor humanity with apparitions, spirits, the Last Judgment, and most of all with their style" (cited in Mordovchenko, p. 129). Cf. N. I. Gnedich's 1816 lament: "Oh, dear creator of *Svetlana*, for how many souls will you have to give account? How many young people will you tempt into murder? What a series of murderers and corpses, strangling and drowning victims I foresee! What a series of pale victims of balladic death, and what a death that is!" (*Syn otechestva*, 1816, cited in Mordovchenko, p. 149).

41. *Herald of Europe*, 1820, cited in Mordovchenko, p. 158.

42. Viazemskii to A. I. Turgenev, Sept. 5, 1819, in *Ostaf'evskii arkhiv* 1: 305.

43. Zhukovskii, *Estetika*, p. 49. Cf. A. A. Bestuzhev: "Tumany i vdali uvelichivaiut predmety, daiut im zateilivye obrazy. To zhe samoe i s istoricheskimi istinami skvoz' pyl'nyi tuman Drevnosti" (Mists and distances magnify objects, give them intricate forms. The same is true of historical truths through the dusty mist of antiquity; part LII, p. 414).

44. Zhukovskii, *Proza*, p. 254.

45. Pushkin to N. I. Gnedich, Sept. 27, 1822, in Pushkin, 9: 51.

46. See Levin, pp. 222–46, for an analysis of Zhukovskii's translation practice. (Levin includes an extensive bibliography.)

47. Bestuzhev, *Literaturnye listki*, 1824, cited in Mordovchenko, p. 351.

48. *Syn otechestva*, 1825, cited in Mordovchenko, p. 351.

49. Ibid., cited in Tynianov, p. 111.

50. Viazemskii to A. I. Turgenev, Sept. 5, 1819, in *Ostaf'evskii arkhiv* 1: 305.

51. Kiukhel'beker, *Mnemozina*, 1824–25, cited in Tynianov, p. 193. Bestuzhev plays the same game of turning the lexicon of the Zhukovskii school against it in this characterization of Zhukovskii's epigones: "T'ma bezdarnykh i poludarnykh kradunov pevtsa Minvany [Zhukovskii], sdelalis' vialymi pevtsami *uvialoi* dushi, utomitel'nymi pevtsami *tomnosti*, blizorukimi pevtsami *dali*" (A host of untalented and half-talented robbers of the singer of Minvana [Zhukovskii] have become flaccid [*vialyi*] singers of the *faded* [*uvialyi*] soul, tiresome [*utomitel'nyi*] singers of *languor* [*tomnost'*], nearsighted singers of *distance*; part LIII, p. 102).

52. Cited in Mordovchenko, p. 156.

53. Zhukovskii, "In E. N. Karamzina's Album" ("V al'bom E. N. Karamzinoi," 1818), cited in Mordovchenko, p. 156.

54. Viazemskii to A. I. Turgenev, Dec. 12, 1820, in *Ostaf'evskii arkhiv* 2: 121; Turgenev to Viazemskii, Feb. 16, 1821, in ibid., 2: 163; Viazemskii to Turgenev, Feb. 25, 1821, in ibid., 2: 170.

55. In another letter to Turgenev (Nov. 27, 1820), Viazemskii writes, "He does not need to nourish his soul—it nourishes itself, and if one may fear anything for it, it would not be emaciation but indigestion—but he needs to stir up his mind, vary his impressions, ideas, and feelings" (cited in Veselovskii, p. 308).

56. Viazemskii to Turgenev, Feb. 25, 1821, in *Ostaf'evskii arkhiv* 2: 171.

57. Mordovchenko, p. 135.

58. Konshin, *Russkaia starina*, 1897, cited in Veselovskii, p. 306. See Veselovskii, pp. 303–9.

59. Viazemskii to Zhukovskii, Mar. 15 O.S./N.S., 1821, cited in Veselovskii, p. 309.

60. N. I. Bakhtin, *Herald of Europe*, 1823, cited in Tynianov, p. 113.

61. See Ianushkevich, pp. 158–59.

62. Dmitriev to Turgenev, Mar. 18, 1818, cited in Veselovskii, p. 303.

63. Karlinsky, *Sexual Labyrinth*, pp. 87, 92; Southey, "A Ballad, Shewing How an Old Woman Rode Double, and Who Rode Before Her," in Southey, 2: 149–60.

64. The first version (1802) was Zhukovskii's first published poem and had an enormous success. In 1839, inspired by a visit to England, Zhukovskii composed a second, much more literal translation. Gogol, in the *Textbook on Literature for Russian Youth* (*Uchebnaia kniga slovesnosti dlia russkogo iunoshestva*), on which he worked in the first half of the 1840's, lists the second, more faithful version under examples of the elegy (9: 486). In an unpublished paper, Catherine Ciepiela has subtly analyzed the ways in which Zhukovskii alters the relation between speaker and subject in Gray's elegy.

65. Gray, pp. 110, 113, 114.

66. See also the interest taken by Zhukovskii in the "talented mechanic" F. I. Shvetsov, owned by the Demidov family: "Zhal' ochen', chto ia ne

zapisal mnogikh vyrazhenii Shvetsova" (It's just too bad that I did not write down many of Shvetsov's expressions; Zhukovskii's diary, cited in Kanunova, 1: 482).

67. Contrary to what many critics appear to believe, reactionary political views and religiosity do not preclude an opposition to serfdom, as the following note by Zhukovskii indicates: "It is easy to confuse the idea of freeing the peasants with the idea of love for anarchy and republicanism and to label as Jacobin the person who says, 'Do not sell a person like a horse; one must not sell people'" (cited in Ianushkevich, p. 172).

68. Mikhail Weiskopf has identified textual parallels between the troika scenes in *Dead Souls* and Plato's *Phaedrus* as part of a compelling reading of Gogol's works in the context of Russian neo-Platonism. (Cf. Smirnova, *Poema Gogolia*, pp. 135–36). See also Lahti's discussion of the Russian song and its connection to peasant labor. Victor Erlich offers an excellent discussion of the ending of *Dead Souls* and the extent to which it can be taken seriously (pp. 130–41).

69. Chateaubriand, *Génie du christianisme, ou beautés de la religion chrétienne*, 1839, cited in Ianushkevich, p. 89.

70. Zhukovskii, notebooks, cited in Ianushkevich, p. 89.

71. Ibid., p. 90.

Chapter 4

EPIGRAPHS: "Many works of the ancients have become fragments. Many works of the moderns are fragments from the very beginning" (*Athenaeum Fragments*); "In the eyes of some people who are very intelligent but who have no poetic sensitivity, [Pushkin's works] are slight, understated, ephemeral fragments; in the eyes of people gifted with poetic sensitivity, they are complete *poemas*, well thought out, finished, containing within themselves everything they need" (*Selected Passages from Correspondence with Friends*).

1. For the authoritative edition of the surviving text of the sequel, with variants and relevant excerpts from Gogol's notebooks, see Gogol, vol. 7.

2. For discussions of Gogol's use of *poema*, see, e.g., Fanger, pp. 165–68; Gippius, pp. 135–53; Kazintsev and Kazintseva, pp. 318–24; Iurii Mann, "O zhanre Mertvykh dush"; and Todd, pp. 177–79.

3. The web of sources is even more complex: the same "Night" includes several lines later incorporated into the ode "God" ("Bog," 1784) by Gavrila Derzhavin. An episode in Derzhavin's poem "The Grandee" ("Vel'mozha," 1794), in which a maimed veteran waits on the convenience of a slothful nobleman, is a prototype for the plot of "Captain Kopeikin" (see Mann, *Smelost' izobreteniia*, p. 107).

4. The similarity of the Kopeikin and Chichikov narratives in genre and

structure is briefly noted by Fanger (p. 178). Lotman has proposed that the *siuzhet* (plot) suggested by Pushkin for *Dead Souls* was precisely the "gentleman-robber" plot that became the Kopeikin episode; his hypothesis has been cogently challenged by Iurii Mann (Lotman, "Povest' o kapitane Kopeikine"; Mann, *V poiskakh zhivoi dushi*, pp. 16–18). On the folk sources of the Kopeikin story, see Smirnova-Chikina, p. 87; N. L. Stepanov, pp. 43–44; Voropaev.

5. Simon Franklin has compared the open-endedness of *Dead Souls* with that of Pushkin's *Evgenii Onegin*, with illuminating results. See also Robert Belknap's argument, on structural grounds, for the fictionality of the narrator's promise of a continuation to Dostoevsky's *Brothers Karamazov* (pp. 106–10) and Anne Debeaux's exposition of the fragmentary nature of *Dead Souls*. For a brilliant study of the fragment in Pushkin, see Frenkel.

6. Gogol's disdain for the strict separation of genres and stylistic levels was summed up in an 1834 letter to M. A. Maksimovich regarding a proposed folk-song collection: "In my opinion, there is no need to separate the songs. The more diversity the better. I love to encounter one song next to another one completely opposite in content. . . . Separation is the least important thing [*Razdelenie veshch' posledniaia*]" (10: 306). *Selected Passages from Correspondence with Friends* (*Vybrannye mesta iz perepiski s druz'iami*, 1847) has drawn critical attention more for its thematic hodgepodge of mysticism, literary criticism, and reactionary sociopolitical philosophy than for its form, but let me note that it belongs among Gogol's internally fragmentary works. The selections, ostensibly and often actually excerpted from private letters, sometimes begin with ellipses. The reader is left to conjecture that personal news and private concerns have been excised, leaving only the philosophical and critical core of the letters. A paradigm of this self-censorship is the omission of point six of the opening "Testament"; a footnote explains, "This point contains instructions on family matters" (8: 222). For more on the structure of *Selected Passages*, see Chapter 6 below.

7. Schlegel, 2: 364.

8. One of the many flaws in Gogol's conception of the sequel to *Dead Souls* was his decision to have Chichikov continue the *same* dead-souls scheme in a different town, rather than inventing a new scheme that would, like each of Chichikov's previous schemes, have its own specific metaphorical weight.

9. From the point of view of closure, *The Gamblers* belongs with Gogol's two major plays, *The Inspector General* (1836) and *Getting Married* (1842). In each play, a major character suddenly flees, leaving his victim(s) in stunned surprise or powerless anger. In *The Inspector General*, the false inspector Khlestakov escapes in his troika, leaving the townspeople to face the real inspector. In *Getting Married*, the reluctant suitor Podkolesin jumps out the

window, leaving his bride and her matchmakers empty-handed. *The Gamblers* ends with an impassioned speech by the cardsharp Ikharev, who is duped and abandoned by more skillful con men (see Chapter 2 above). Although these works cannot be considered conclusively closed, because their final scenes of anger and vowed revenge convey anything but a sense of equilibrium, they are still not as future oriented as other promissory works, such as "Ivan Fedorovich Shpon'ka and His Auntie," "Rome (A Fragment)," the dramatic fragments, and *Dead Souls*. In *Dead Souls*, which also ends with an escape, the reader is not left gaping with the townspeople but instead accompanies Chichikov on his flight into apotheosis. "The Overcoat" ("Shinel'," 1842), with its conclusive closure, stands apart from the other works of 1842 as strikingly as the open-ended "Ivan Shpon'ka" does from the other stories in *Evenings*.

10. One of Roland Barthes's self-referential fragments may be applied to Gogol: "Liking to find, to write *beginnings*, he tends to multiply this pleasure: that is why he writes fragments; so many fragments, so many beginnings, so many pleasures (but he doesn't like the ends: the risk of the rhetorical clausule is too great: the fear of not being able to resist the *last word*)" (p. 94). See also the complaint of the repeatedly rejected suitor Zhevakin in *Getting Married*: "Vot uzh nikak v semnadtsatyi raz sluchaetsia so mnoiu, i vsë pochti odinakim obrazom: kazhetsia, vsë khorosho, a kak doidet delo do razviazki—smotrish', i otkazhut" (It seems it's already happened to me seventeen times and always in almost the same way: it seems at first that everything's going well, but as soon as the business reaches a denouement—you look, and they refuse; 5: 48).

11. Iurii Mann has, with characteristic incisiveness, suggested that the dramatic fragments are Gogol's "little comedies," the counterpart to Pushkin's "little tragedies" (commentary to vol. 4 of Gogol, *Sobranie sochinenii*, p. 428). The parallel with Pushkin's beautifully shaped fragments would, I believe, reward further examination.

12. See Louis Pedrotti: "Although it bears the subtitle 'fragment,' the story is structurally whole and may be considered closer to completion than many of Gogol's other works" (pp. 20–21).

13. Maguire, seminar on *Dead Souls*, Yale University, 1984.

14. The title also echoes the title of Zhukovskii's aesthetic manifesto, "Nevyrazimoe (Otryvok)" ("The Inexpressible (A Fragment)"). (See Chapter 3 above.) V. N. Toporov has pointed out that in the published version of the poem Zhukovskii omitted "two magnificent lines" that provide a more conclusive ending to the meditation on the ineffectuality of poetic language: "No vdokhnovenie opiat' zagovorilos', / I muza pylkaia zabyla svoi otchet!" (But inspiration has again begun to rave, / And the ardent Muse has forgotten her calculation!; p. 40n.; cf. Gukovskii, pp. 47–48).

15. Gogol to Balabina, April 1838, 11: 444.

16. The shift in tone in "Rome" was apparently a fortunate one for Gogol's audience at the home of Prince D. V. Golitsyn, as S. T. Aksakov relates. The fashionable crowd, almost lulled to sleep by the solemn periods describing the hero's education, were awakened by the lively comic scenes near the end of the story (pp. 56–58).

17. Gogol's penchant for the panoramic landscape view is another sign of his indebtedness to German Romantic philosophy and literature. Cf. Marshall Brown: "The view from a height over a surrounding landscape is one of the most characteristic situations found in German romantic literature. The landscapes are never realistic; they are marked by an abundance and variety of objects and inhabitants, shapes and contours symbolic of the plenitude of life itself. To see the unity in this multiplicity, the form in this chaos, and to discover the universal human experience are the observer's task, set by the central commanding prospect" (p. 43). See also Maguire, pp. 183–85, 189–90. Zhukovskii's travel notes reveal an almost obsessive desire to climb all manner of towers, cliffs, and belfries (*Proza*, pp. 207–12, 225, 236), a desire echoed in Manilov's plan in *Dead Souls* to build a belvedere from which one could see "even Moscow" (6: 39).

18. The narrator of *Dead Souls* delivers a similar injunction to those curious about Chichikov's falling-out with his smuggling crony: "Kak bylo delo v samom dele, bog ikh vedaet; pust' luchshe chitatel'-okhotnik dosochinit sam" (God knows what really happened; it would be best if the reader would volunteer to finish composing the story himself; 6: 237).

19. Schlegel, 2: 206–7.

20. David Rosand has discussed the dual nature of the fragment in painting and sculpture: "If the fragment as decomposed, disintegrated form assumed a satisfying legitimacy in the esthetic eye, then the fragment as unachieved or becoming form could lay claim to similar status. . . . Implicated here . . . is a corollary deepening involvement of the beholder, who is invited to complete the forms in his mind" (pp. 20, 21). See also Peter Szondi on Friedrich Schlegel: "Das Fragment wird als Projekt aufgefaßt, als 'der subjektive Keim eines werdenden Objekts,' als Vorbereitung der ersehnten Synthese. Im Fragment wird nicht mehr das Nicht-Erreichte, Bruchstück-Gebliebene gesehen, sondern das Antizipierte, das Versprechen" (The fragment is conceived as a project, as 'the subjective germ of an object in the process of becoming,' as the preparation for a desired synthesis. What one sees in the fragment is no longer a thing left unachieved, never to be more than bits and pieces, but rather the thing anticipated, the promise; p. 403).

21. See Chizhevsky, pp. 137–60; Nabokov, pp. 89–91.

22. Funk, p. 153.

23. "The hearer . . . affirms, 'This is the world in which I live,' but his

world is then ruptured by an alien 'logic' which leaves him no choice but to confirm or deny" (ibid., p. 194).

24. Arnol'di, p. 70. This passage was omitted from the article when it was reprinted in 1952 because it failed to harmonize with the image of Gogol as a realist that prevailed in that period. See Brodskii, pp. 472–98.

25. In his profound study of the Gospel of Mark and the interpretation of narrative, Frank Kermode reminds us that it is in acts of divination that the interpreter's true art resides: "We tend to reserve our highest praise for those interpretations that seem most intuitive, most theory-free, seeming to proceed from some untrammeled divinatory impulse, having the gratuity, the fortuity of genius. The possibility of such divinations may explain why Hermes once laid claim to a share in the lyre of Apollo" (p. 4).

26. Gogol burned portions of part II in 1845, as well as immediately before his death in 1852. He refers here to the first burning (7: 400).

27. I wish to thank Gary Saul Morson for bringing to my attention the parallel between Cervantes' and Gogol's sequels.

28. Cf. N. M. Pavlov: "The great artist died a martyr to both his understanding and his misunderstanding of his task—a great artist not when he was writing and rewriting the second *Dead Souls* but every time he burned it" (p. 145).

Chapter 5

EPIGRAPH: "No, no! I shall never adorn nature. My countryside must be countryside, a wilderness. . . . The shepherdess will seek her wandering sheep and lay a path for me. Moreover, I love to overcome difficulties; I love to force my way through a thicket of bushes and part the branches that have grown together" ("The Countryside").

1. Shklovskii, *Povesti o proze* 2: 6.

2. I have been informed by Iurii Mann and Sergei Bocharov, the editors of the new complete works of Gogol now under way at the Gor'kii Institute of World Literature in Moscow, that they plan to publish the entirety of *Arabesques* in a single volume.

3. See Mann, *Poetika*, pp. 267–76. Cf. the essay on Johann Müller in the *Moscow Herald* (1827): "Zhelaiushchii prepodavat' nauku prinuzhden obozret' ee kak v tselom ee ob"eme, tak i v otdel'nykh chastiakh" (Whoever wishes to teach a science must survey it both in its entire range and in its separate parts; "Ioann Miller," p. 279).

4. For a discussion of the source of this image in Schlözer, see Chapter 1 above. See also the discussion of heights in Chapter 4.

5. See, e.g., Stillman, pp. 376–89.

6. Cf. Zhukovskii's letter from Switzerland, describing the view from a

boat on Lake Constance: "Lodka plyla bez dvizheniia, i ia, sidia pod teniiu parusa, videl pered soboiu velikolepnoe zrelishche: u menia pered glazami byla, kak budto v sokrashchenii, vsia Shveitsariia" (The boat sailed smoothly, and I, sitting in the shade of the sail, saw a magnificent sight: it was as though all of Switzerland in miniature appeared before my eyes; *Proza*, p. 240).

7. Stern, p. 52. On the arabesque in German Romanticism, see Polheim.

8. See Laurence Sterne, *Tristram Shandy*, vol. 6, chap. 40, in which the narrator maps the crooked lines of the story he has told and promises to keep henceforth to a straight narrative line, drawn with a ruler. In his "Detailed Report on the Moon" ("Podrobnyi otchet o lune," 1820), Zhukovskii performs on his own poetry the same operation I have proposed for *Arabesques*: he compiles a thematically coherent essay on the moon by assembling fragments from his works in which the moon appears. The other aspects of these disparate works are disregarded, and what emerges is a meditation on the moon from all possible angles; as a result of being singled out, the moon is moved from background to foreground, transformed from decoration into *siuzhet* (2: 119–30).

9. A less sophisticated conception of natural outline appears in V. A. Titov's "A Few Thoughts about Architecture" ("Neskol'ko myslei o Zodchestve," 1827): "All the various and irregular outlines that we encounter in nature are formed from the straight line and the circle" (p. 197).

10. For an excellent introduction to the picturesque, see Christopher Hussey, especially his distinction between Brown and Repton on the one hand and Price and Richard Payne Knight on the other. Although the works of all four are often lumped together under the rubric "picturesque" or "English garden," Hussey reserves the term *picturesque* for the formulations of Price and Knight. Priscilla Roosevelt provides a wealth of information on Russian garden design in the late eighteenth century and elucidates the modifications entailed in transferring the "English garden"—mostly of the Brown and Repton type, which I call here "pre-picturesque"—to Russian soil. A. G. Cross describes the fostering of the pre-picturesque English garden style in Russia by Catherine the Great ("'Great Patroness,'" pp. 69–76). The history of Russian garden design is thoroughly analyzed and attractively illustrated in Vergunov and Gorokhov.

11. Manilov's garden and his plans for it bear similarities to other pre-picturesque Russian gardens, notably Pavlovsk. Both the "khram uedinennogo razmyshleniia" (temple of solitary meditation; 6: 22) and the projected belvedere "[otkuda] mozhno videt' dazhe Moskvu" (from which one could even see Moscow; 6: 39) are echoed in an 1843 guide to Pavlovsk illustrated by Zhukovskii: "Novyi shale. Sostoit iz kamennogo polusvoda s solomennoiu krysheiu, na kotoroi ustroen nebol'shoi bel'veder. Otsiuda mozhno vi-

det' do Tsarskogo Sela. . . . Khram Druzhby. Krugloe zdanie, v drevnem grecheskom vkuse" (New chalet. Consists of a stone half-vault with a thatched roof on which a small belvedere has been constructed. From here one may see as far as Tsarskoe Selo . . . Temple of Friendship. A round building in the ancient Greek taste; *Putevoditel' po sadu i gorodu Pavlosku* [sic], pp. 37–38). Even more striking is the echo of Manilov's plan for building a stone bridge with shops on either side where merchants could sell goods to the peasants (6: 25) in the *unrealized* plan for Prince Bezborodko's park in Moscow (designed in 1797–99 by the pioneering landscape gardener N. A. L'vov): "The owner, who loves to share his amusements, has appointed this part of the garden for public promenades, to which there are approaches from both sides. The main entrance from the street consists of a semicircular plaza surrounded by a covered colonnade, under which in various little shops are sold haberdashery items, candy, fruit, and so forth" (cited in Grimm, p. 122). D. S. Likhachev analyzes the similarities between Manilov's grounds and the estate of Nicholas I ("Sotsial'nye korni," pp. 298–300).

12. See also Annenkov's account of Gogol's enjoyment of scenery: "At the summerhouse of Princess Z. Volkonskaia, which rested against an old Roman aqueduct that served it as a terrace, he would lie on his back . . . and look at the blue sky, at the dead and magnificent Roman *campagna*, for hours at a time. It was the same at Tivoli, in the thick vegetation that surrounds its *cascatelli*; he would sit somewhere in a thicket and fix his sharp-sighted eyes on the dark foliage that falls in clumps down the cliffs, and would remain motionless for whole hours, with inflamed cheeks" (p. 276). Annenkov's memories may be influenced in retrospect by the impact of Gogol's fictional vision of Pliushkin's garden.

13. Russian text: "Oni derzhat takzhe v sadakh svoikh pni gnilykh derev, inye na koreni svoem stoiashchie, drugie zhe na zemle oprokinutye, kraine nabliudaia figuru onykh, ravno kak tsvet, koru i mokh, kotorye na nikh imeiutsia. Razlichnye upotrebliaiut oni khitrosti k vozbuzhdeniiu udivleniia. . . . Drugaia zhe khitrost' ikh sostoit, skryvat' nekotoruiu chast' sostavleniia derev'iami i inymi mezhdu tem predmetami. Sie natural'no vozbuzhdaet v zritele liubopytstvo k blizhaishemu rassmotreniiu onogo" (pp. 15–16).

14. Russian text: "Raspolozhenie dolzhno byt' takovu, chtob sopriazhenie vsekh chastei sada ne moglo byt' pri vshestviia v onoi, a podchas obozrevaemo; obyknovenneishaia i neizbezhimaia pogreshnost' starinnogo simmetricheskogo manera. No nadobno, chtob pri onom kak v dramme, ili kak v samoi landshaftnoi nature nabliudaemo bylo iskusstvo zaviaski, i chtob te mesta, k kotorym podkhodish', ne byli napered usmatrivaemy, i bylob sovsem neprimetno, kakaia stsena sleduet za kotoroiu, a guliaiushchei nakhodilsiab vsegda v ozhidanii" (Hirschfeld, no. 56, p. 58). In an excellent ar-

ticle, Raymond Immerwahr judiciously explores the connections between the garden aesthetic propounded by Hirschfeld and Chambers and the literary aesthetic of Schlegel and Novalis. Immerwahr's entire article is in a sense a gloss on a suggestive observation by Arthur Lovejoy: "In one of its aspects that many-sided thing called Romanticism may not inaccurately be described as a conviction that the world is an *englischer Garten* on a grand scale" (cited in Immerwahr, p. 3).

15. Russian text: "V kharaktere romanticheskom mozhet iskusstvo prinimat' ochen' maloe uchastie, no onoi est' pochti edinym proizvedeniem natury. Ona obrazuet ego ne tol'ko odnimi goristymi mestopolozheniiami, skalami, vertepami, peshcherami, vodopadami, kataraktami i strannymi polozheniiami i vidami sikh predmetov, no i neobychainymi sopriazheniiami i protivopolozhnostiami, nepomernoiu besporiaditseiu v razpolozhenii, i postigaemymi nezapnostiiu kontrastami" (Hirschfeld, no. 54, p. 17). Cf. the 1778 *Essay on the Laying Out of Gardens* (*Opyt o raspolozhenii sadov*): "Oppositions often uncover beauties that, judging from the situation of the place, one might not have imagined. The use of opposition is most effective in the internal layout of groves; various turns in paths, the closing and opening of shrubbery, views of great tall trees, and sudden transitions from one degree of shade to another may impress the greatest ideas on the imagination" ([Mason], p. 24). Cross ("English Garden") has identified the original of this translation as George Mason's *An Essay on Design in Gardening* (London, 1768).

16. Although Pavlovsk itself is a pre-picturesque garden, Zhukovskii's *description* of it adheres to the aesthetics of the picturesque as defined by Price (see below). P. A. Pletnev linked Gogol to Zhukovskii precisely through the picturesque quality of his writing: "Besides Zhukovskii, I cannot remember anyone among our writers who drew with words, attracted by the charm of nature and grasping the art of verbal painting [*slovesnaia zhivopis'*]" (p. 493). For other echoes of English garden theory, see N. M. Karamzin, "The Countryside" ("Derevnia," 1792, in *Zapiski*), "Notes of a Longtime Inhabitant of Moscow" ("Zapiski starogo Moskovskogo zhitelia," 1803), "Journey Around Moscow" ("Puteshestvie vokrug Moskvy," 1803), and others. V. T. Adams compares Gogol's nature descriptions to those of Karamzin (pp. 129–32).

17. In an 1834 letter Gogol reveals not only that he was familiar with Zhukovskii's travel writing in manuscript but that he regarded it as at least a lexical model. In defending to an editor his use of the word *chut'e* (sensitivity; lit. "an animal's sense of smell") in the essay on the Middle Ages, Gogol cites Zhukovskii as a precedent: "I cannot change the word *chut'e* at all. There is no word in our language with an equivalent meaning. Besides, I used it because it has received a sort of civic right: Pushkin used it, and

even Zhukovskii in the Journey through Saxony, in an artistic sense, although this beautiful letter of his has apparently not yet been published. What can we do? We must borrow some virtues even from the quadrupeds" (10: 340–41). The word does not appear in the published version of Zhukovskii's text (Gogol, 10: 485).

18. Zhukovskii, *Proza*, p. 247. See also pp. 226, 245–57. Zhukovskii describes, among other things, a "crag column" that has its counterpart in the "birch column" in Pliushkin's garden:

Zhukovskii	*Gogol*
To vdrug ogromnaia, otdelivshaiasia *kolonna*, na kotoroi, *vmesto kapiteli*, mokh i sosny. (*Proza*, p. 226; emphasis added)	Belyi kolossal'nyi stvol berezy, lishennyi verkhushki, otlomlennoi bureiu ili grozoiu, podymalsia iz etoi zelenoi gushchi i kruglilsia na vozdukhe, kak pravil'naia mramornaia, sverkaiushchaia *kolonna*; kosoi, ostrokonechnyi izlom ego, kotorym on okanchivalsia k verkhu *vmesto kapiteli*, temnel na snezhnoi belizne ego, kak shapka ili chernaia ptitsa. (6: 112–13; emphasis added)
(Now suddenly a huge separate *column*, on which, *instead of a capital*, there are moss and pines.)	(The colossal white trunk of a birch, deprived of its top, broken off by a tempest or storm, rose out of that green thicket and was rounded in the air like a regular, marble, sparkling *column*; its oblique, pointed fracture, with which it ended toward the top *instead of a capital*, showed dark on its snowy whiteness like a cap or a black bird.)

19. Sidney Robinson, who identifies a quality of the picturesque as the "use of less power than is available to compose the parts in an arrangement that does not press for a conclusion" (p. xi), extends the analogy to politics and economics. Robinson views the picturesque as incompatible with fascist systems: "Despotism cannot take any risks; any system working at full bore has no unused plenitude with which to amuse itself or entertain irony" (p. 146).

20. This monotonously recurring landscape has already been described in *Arabesques*, in the "Chapter from a Historical Novel." In an attempt to escape the torments visited upon him by a supernaturally enlivened pine tree, an evil lord packs up his household and moves. But no matter how far

he goes, he keeps ending up in the same place: the same forest, the same buildings, the same retributive pine tree (3: 310–21). The notion of the picturesque garden as a place of continual, unexpected views is beautifully expressed in Zhukovskii's "Slavianka" (see above). Likhachev aptly describes the Romantic garden as the locus of "stremlenie k dvizheniiu, k peremenam vo vremeni, v sezonakh goda, v chasakh dnia, k razlichnogo roda pogranichnym iavleniiam v prirode" (striving toward movement, toward changes in time, in the seasons of the year, in the times of the day, toward various types of borderline phenomena in nature; *Poeziia sadov*, pp. 200–291). Likhachev's study is marred by his failure to draw a clear distinction between the garden practice of Alexander Pope, Horace Walpole, Brown, and Repton and the theories of Price and Knight, putting them all under the rubric "peizazhnyi" (landscape) or "romanticheskii sad" (Romantic garden).

21. In a private communication, Svetlana Evdokimova has pointed out that this passage contradicts not only Gogol's aesthetics but the Gospel, in which the road to truth is not the broad but the narrow one: "Enter ye in at the strait gate: for wide is the gate, and broad is the way, that leadeth to destruction, and many there be which go in thereat. Because strait is the gate, and narrow is the way, which leadeth unto life, and few there be that find it" (Matthew 7: 13–14). Jerzy Faryno has demonstrated that the road followed by Chichikov himself in his travels is a tortuous one (p. 614).

22. The phrase that I have translated as "everything was somehow desolately beautiful" ("vsë bylo kak-to pustynno-khorosho") appears in a manuscript that was "dictated and carefully examined by Gogol" in the summer of 1841 (6: 897). In the 1842 *Dead Souls* (and in most editions of Gogol other than the Academy edition) it is replaced by the phrase "everything was beautiful" ("vsë bylo khorosho"). Following Pletnev, Andrei Siniavskii adumbrates the homology between Gogol's landscape descriptions and his prose, in his chapter entitled "The Geography of Prose": "Gogol's style seeks direct comparisons in landscape in order to attest to itself in a materially perceptible form" (p. 342). Siniavskii's meditation leads him not to the picturesque but to the Baroque (pp. 347–51). For more on Gogol and the Baroque, see G. Shapiro; and Smirnova, *Poema Gogolia*, pp. 61–68, 76–78. Gogol's moral to the description of Pliushkin's garden is textually close to a passage in A. I. Galich's influential *Essay on the Science of the Fine Arts* (*Opyt nauki iziashchnogo*, 1825): "No ideia krasoty . . . istoshchaetsia stol' zhe malo proizvedeniiami iskusstva, kak i proizvedeniiami natury. Ibo esli v pervom sluchae vidim odni bezzhizenennye prizraki, to vo vtorom vovse ne nakhodim libo svobodnoi idei, libo prilichnoi formy. Pochemu iziashchnoe . . . raskryvaetsia v polnom bleske togda, kogda priroda vstrechaetsia s iskusstvom i daet prekrasnym ego prizrakam prekrasnuiu zhizn' i dushu" (But the idea of

beauty . . . is just as little exhausted by works of art as by works of nature. For if in the first case we see only lifeless phantoms, in the second we find neither a free idea nor a fitting form—which is why the beautiful . . . unfolds in its full radiance only when nature meets with art and gives its beautiful phantoms a beautiful life and soul; 2: 231).

23. An alternative perspective is offered by Griffiths and Rabinowitz, who read Pliushkin's garden as "the promiscuous erosion even of the categories of art and nature, man and what is not man": "The long surrounding description of the decay and disorder of 'this extinct place' parodies the encomium of the perfecting hand of time and moss among the ruins of 'Rome.' . . . Art and nature join together not to perfect one another but to cancel each other out and produce a warmth that is the warmth of rot" (pp. 77, 78). (Cf. Peace, p. 259; Shapiro and Shapiro, pp. 204–6; Smirnova, *Poema Gogolia*, pp. 67–68; J. B. Woodward, pp. 110–13.) This reading, while it accounts well for the placement of the garden on Pliushkin's estate, disregards both the aesthetics of the picturesque garden and the tonality of the passage itself. Unlike the disgustingly dusty interior of Pliushkin's home, the garden is presented unironically as an oasis of beauty and freshness. Rather than being contaminated by the ugliness of Pliushkin's blurring of categories, the garden scene, like his possession of a biography, sets Pliushkin apart as a character for whom there is hope of transcendence.

24. Bakhtin valued in Goethe precisely his ability to read landscape as history. See the discussion in Morson and Emerson, pp. 415–17. In his plan for Prince Bezborodko's park, L'vov satirizes the "symmetrical" gardener's taste for topiary bushes trimmed into whimsical shapes by describing the monsters they become when neglected. He presents a mock advertisement for some slightly damaged specimens: "Adam and Eve made of yew; Adam has been a bit damaged by the fall of the tree of good and evil, which was knocked over by a big storm. Eve and the serpent in very good condition. Noah's ark made of holly; in rather poor condition on the sides because of lack of water. Tower of Babylon; not yet finished. Saint George made of boxwood; his arm not yet long enough, but he will be able to kill the dragon by April of next year. An old lady-in-waiting made of a tree eaten with wormholes. A pig made of clipped shrubbery, transformed into a porcupine by being left out in the rain for a week" (cited in Grimm, p. 111).

25. Cf. Todd: "The very manner of [the governor's daughter's] introduction into *Dead Souls* realizes the metaphor of plot complication, as her carriage passes Chichikov's, and their harnesses become entangled" (p. 196). The echoes between the scene of Pliushkin's garden and scenes involving the governor's daughter (and other fatal women) can be seen most clearly by presenting the evidence in columns.

Pliushkin's garden	*Governor's daughter (and other women)*
Stvol berezy, lishennyi verkhushki, otlomlennoi bureiu ili grozoiu. (6: 112)	[Uvidev gubernatorskuiu dochku, Chichikov] ostanovilsia vdrug, budto oglushennyi udarom. (6: 166)
(The trunk of a birch deprived of its top, broken off by a tempest or a storm.)	([Upon seeing the governor's daughter, Chichikov] stopped suddenly, as though deafened by a thunderclap.)
Belyi kolossal'nyi stvol berezy . . . podymalsia iz etoi zelenoi gushchi. (6: 112–13)	Ona tol'ko odna belela i vykhodila prozrachnoiu i svetloiu iz mutnoi i neprozrachnoi tolpy. (6: 169)
(The colossal white trunk of a birch . . . rose out of that green thicket.)	(Only she alone showed white and emerged transparent and bright out of the murky and opaque crowd.)
Na snezhnoi belizne ego. (6: 113)	Oval litsa . . . belel kakoiu-to prozrachnoiu beliznoiu. (6: 90)
(On its snowy whiteness).	(The oval of her face . . . showed white with a sort of transparent whiteness.)
I kruglilsia na vozdukhe. (6: 113)	Khoroshen'kii oval litsa ee kruglilsia. (6: 90) S ocharovatel'no kruglivshimsia ovalom litsa. (6: 166)
(And was rounded in the air.)	(The pretty oval of her face was rounded.) (With the enchantingly rounded oval of her face.)
Tsepkie kruch'ia. (6: 113)	[Blesk zhenshchin] zatsepit za serdtse. (6: 164)
(The tenacious little hooks.)	([The glitter of women] will hook on [same root as *tenacious*] to your heart.)
Uglublenie, ziiavshee, kak temnaia past'. (6: 113)	Propast', propalo (passim).
(A hollow, yawning like a dark maw [*past'*].)	(Abyss [*propast'*], disappeared [*propalo*; associated with the fatal danger of women].)
Pereputavshiesia i skrestivshiesia list'ia i such'ia. (6: 113)	Ikh ekipazhi tak stranno stolknulis', pereputavshis' upriazh'iu. (6: 166)
(Leaves and twigs that entangled and crisscrossed.)	(Their carriages so strangely collided, entangling the harnesses.)

Molodaia vetv' klena, potianuvshaia sboku svoi zelenye lapy-listy, pod odin iz kotorykh zabravshis', bog vest' kakim obrazom, solntse prevrashchalo ego vdrug v prozrachnyi i ognennyi, chudno siiavshii v etoi gustoi tem-note. (6: 113)

(The young branch of a maple, which stretched out its green leaf-paws, un-der one of which the sun, having got-ten there God knows how, suddenly rendered it transparent and fiery, mar-velously shining in that thick darkness.)

Khoroshen'kii oval litsa ee kruglilsia, kak svezhen'koe iaichko, i, podobno emu, belel kakoiu-to prozrachnoiu be-liznoiu, kogda, svezhee, . . . ono . . . propuskaet skvoz' sebia luchi siiaiu-shchego solntsa; ee tonen'kie ushki takzhe skvozili, rdeia pronikavshim ikh teplym svetom. (6: 90)

(The pretty oval of her face was rounded like a nice fresh little egg, and like an egg, it showed white with a sort of transparent whiteness; when [it] . . . lets the rays of the shining sun pass through it; her nice delicate little ears could also be seen through, glowing with the warm light that penetrated them.)

The intentionality of these correspondences is suggested by the fact that the phrases "kruglilsia na vozdukhe" (was rounded in the air), "kak temnaia past'" (like a dark maw), "pereputavshiesia" (entangled), and "molodaia" (young) belong to late revisions of the garden scene.

Chapter 6

EPIGRAPHS: "Our common people are not stupid when they run, as from the Devil, from any sort of written page. They know that all human muddle, chicanery [lit. "hook making"] and dirty tricks have adhered to it" (*Selected Passages from Correspondence with Friends*); "Nature, in order to cap-tivate and amaze with its scenes, uses cliffs, the greenery of trees and meadows, the noise of waterfalls and streams, the radiance of the sky, storm and calm; but poor man, in order to express the impression produced by nature, must replace its multiform objects with uniform ink scribbles, through which it is often much harder to get to meaning than it is to get through cliffs and abysses to a beautiful view" ("Journey Through Saxon Switzer-land" ["Puteshestvie po Saksonskoi Shveitsarii," 1824]).

1. Cf. Todd, who sees in *Selected Passages* "a static world of fixed positions and boundaries" (p. 203). *Selected Passages* has been studied more seriously in recent years than in the past. See, e.g., Griffiths and Rabinowitz, pp. 105–17; Sobel; Zholkovsky. My discussion is intended not as a comprehen-sive analysis of this complex work but as a means of better understanding the tension between Gogol's explicit extraliterary assertions and his aesthetic practice.

2. *A propos* of the *Odyssey*: "*Note*. Whether the translator needs to know Greek and whether Zhukovskii knows this language—on this point, an earthly matter and therefore insignificant, the author is silent" (p. 232).

3. See Kermode's discussion of the word *lest* in the passage from Mark (pp. 23–47). In a passage deleted by the censor from his article on Romanticism, Bestuzhev recognizes the Gospel as an artistic model, "a type of Romanticism" (Kotliarevskii, pp. 342–44). For an analysis of the echoes of the Gospel in *Dead Souls*, see Fusso, pp. 219–31.

4. See Pushkin's treatment of "utility" in "The Poet and the Crowd" ("Poet i tolpa," 1828).

5. Shevyrev to Pletnev, Mar. 20, 1847, cited in Bel'chikov, p. 10.

6. See Sadovnik, who finds a distinct Gogolian fingerprint in the phrase "durak-baraban i neukliuzhii tulumbas" (the foolish snare drum and the clumsy bass drum; pp. 146–47).

7. Zhukovskii was undoubtedly pursuing the same "Hero" strategy in his 1849 essay on Goethe's *Faust*, the entire second half of which is based on a mistranslation. In view of Zhukovskii's excellent knowledge of German, one can only assume a deliberate obfuscation, perhaps under Gogolian influence (*Estetika*, pp. 351–55; see Veselovskii, pp. 358–59).

8. Cf. in *Selected Passages* the paradoxical statement that Zhukovskii's translation is a type of originality: "Perevodia, proizvodil on perevodami takoe deistvie, kak samobytnyi i samotsvetnyi poet" (In translating he produced through his translations the same effect as an original and genuine poet; 8: 377). See also the idea that Pogodin, in telling the truth, appears to be lying (8: 232).

9. Gogol to Zhukovskii, Mar. 6, 1847.

Works Cited

Adams, V. T. "Prirodoopisaniia u N. V. Gogolia." *Uchenye zapiski Tartuskogo gosudarstvennogo universiteta* 119 (1962): 77–132.

Aksakov, S. T. *Istoriia moego znakomstva s Gogolem.* Edited by E. P. Naselenko and E. A. Smirnova. Moscow: Akademiia Nauk SSSR, 1960.

Annenkov, P. V. "N. V. Gogol' v Rime letom 1841 goda." In *Gogol' v vospominaniiakh sovremennikov*, edited by N. L. Brodskii. Moscow: Khudozhestvennaia literatura, 1952.

Annenskii, Innokentii. "Estetika 'Mertvykh Dush' i ee nasled'e." *Apollon* 8 (1911): 50–58.

Arnol'di, L. I. "Moe znakomstvo s Gogolem." *Russkii vestnik* 37 (1862): 59–95.

"Avgust Liudvig Shletser [Soch. Gerena]." *Moskovskii vestnik*, 1822, part 4, pp. 315–33.

Barratt, G. R., ed. *Selected Letters of Evgenij Baratynskij.* The Hague: Mouton, 1973.

Barthes, Roland. *Roland Barthes by Roland Barthes.* Translated by Richard Howard. New York: Hill and Wang, 1977.

Bel'chikov, N. F. *Pushkin i Gnedich.* Letchworth, Eng.: Prideaux Press, 1977 [1924].

Belinskii, V. G. *Sobranie sochinenii v deviati tomakh*, vol. 8. Edited by N. K. Gei. Moscow: Khudozhestvennaia literatura, 1982.

Belknap, Robert. *The Structure of "The Brothers Karamazov."* The Hague: Mouton, 1967.

Belyi, Andrei. *Masterstvo Gogolia: Issledovanie.* Ann Arbor, Mich.: Ardis, 1982 [1934].

Benjamin, Walter. *Reflections: Essays, Aphorisms, Autobiographical Writings.* Translated by Edmund Jephcott. New York: Harcourt Brace Jovanovich, 1978.

Bestuzhev, A. A. [Marlinskii]. "O romanakh i romantizme." (Review of

N. Polevoi, *Kliatva pri grobe Gospodnem. Russkaia byl' XV veka.*) *Moskovskii telegraf,* 1833, part LII, pp. 399–420, 541–55; part LIII, pp. 85–107, 216–44.

Brodskii, N. L., ed. *Gogol' v vospominaniiakh sovremennikov.* Moscow: Khudozhestvennaia literatura, 1952.

Brown, Marshall. *The Shape of German Romanticism.* Ithaca, N.Y.: Cornell University Press, 1979.

Brown, Norman O. *Hermes the Thief: The Evolution of a Myth.* Madison: University of Wisconsin Press, 1947.

Burke, Edmund. *Works,* vol. 1. Boston: Little, Brown, 1871.

Byron [George Gordon], Lord. *Poetical Works.* 6 vols. London: John Murray, 1879.

Cervantes Saavedra, Miguel de. *The Adventures of Don Quixote.* Translated by J. M. Cohen. Harmondsworth, Eng.: Penguin, 1950.

[Chambers, William]. *O kitaishikh sadakh. Perevod iz knigi sochinennoi gospodinom Chambersom soderzhashchei v sebe opisanie Kitaiskikh stroenii, domashnikh ikh uborov, odeianii, makhin i instrumentov.* St. Petersburg: N.p., 1771.

Chizhevsky, Dmitri. "On Gogol's 'The Overcoat.'" In *Dostoevsky and Gogol: Texts and Criticism,* edited by Priscilla Meyer and Stephen Rudy. Ann Arbor, Mich.: Ardis, 1979.

Ciepiela, Catherine. "Elegy in a Russian Churchyard: Zhukovsky's Translation of Gray's Elegy." Unpublished MS.

Cross, A. G. "The English Garden and Russia: An Anonymous Identified." *Study Group on Eighteenth-Century Russia Newsletter* 2 (1974): 25–29.

———. "'The Great Patroness of the North': Catherine II's Role in Fostering Anglo-Russian Cultural Contacts." *Oxford Slavonic Papers,* n.s., 18 (1985): 67–82.

Debeaux, Anne. "Les Ames mortes ou le roman inachevé." *Europe* 648 (1983): 170–76.

Demetz, Peter. "Balzac and the Zoologists: A Concept of the Type." In *The Disciplines of Criticism,* edited by Peter Demetz, Thomas Greene, and Lowry Nelson, Jr. New Haven, Conn.: Yale University Press, 1968.

Detienne, Marcel, and Jean-Pierre Vernant. *Cunning Intelligence in Greek Culture and Society.* Translated by Janet Lloyd. Sussex, Eng.: Harvester Press, 1978.

———. *Les Ruses de l'intelligence: La mètis des Grecs.* Paris: Flammarion, 1974.

Eliot, George. *Middlemarch.* 4 vols. Edinburgh: William Blackwood, 1873.

Erlich, Victor. *Gogol.* New Haven, Conn.: Yale University Press, 1969.

Fanger, Donald. *The Creation of Nikolai Gogol.* Cambridge, Mass.: Harvard University Press, Belknap Press, 1979.

Faryno, Jerzy [Ezhi Farino]. "Struktura poezdki Chichikova." *Russian Literature* 7 (1979): 611–24.

Femida, ili nachertanie prav, preimushchestv i obiazannostei zhenskogo pola v Rossii. (Review.) *Moskovskii vestnik,* 1827, part 6, pp. 215–18.

Franklin, Simon. "Novels Without End: Notes on *Eugene Onegin* and *Dead Souls.*" *Modern Language Review* 79 (1984): 372–83.

Frenkel, Monika Dudli [Greenleaf]. "'V malen'koi ramke': Fragmentary Structures in Pushkin's Poetry and Prose." Ph.D. diss., Yale University, 1984.

Fuchs, Ernst. "The New Testament and the Hermeneutical Problem." In *New Frontiers in Theology II: The New Hermeneutic,* edited by James M. Robinson and J. B. Cobb, Jr. New York: Harper and Row, 1964.

Funk, Robert W. *Language, Hermeneutic, and Word of God: The Problem of Language in the New Testament and Contemporary Theology.* New York: Harper and Row, 1966.

Fusso, Susanne. "Čičikov on Gogol: The Structure of Oppositions in *Dead Souls.*" Ph.D. diss., Yale University, 1984.

Galich, A. I. "Opyt nauki iziashchnogo." In *Russkie esteticheskie traktaty pervoi treti deviatnadtsatogo veka,* edited by Z. A. Kamenskii, vol. 2. Moscow: Iskusstvo, 1974.

Galperina, Inna. "Critical Relativism: Gogol's *Marriage,* A Multifaceted Play or Playing in a Play." *Russian Literature* 28 (1990): 155–74.

Georgievskii, G. P. "Gogolevskie teksty." In his *Pamiati V. A. Zhukovskogo i N. V. Gogolia,* vol. 3. St. Petersburg: Imperatorskaia Akademiia Nauk, 1909.

"Gerder." *Moskovskii telegraf,* 1828, part 20, pp. 138–50.

Gippius, Vasilii. *Gogol'.* Leningrad: Mysl', 1924.

Gogol, Nikolai Vasil'evich. *Arabesques.* Translated by Alexander Tulloch. Ann Arbor, Mich.: Ardis, 1982.

———. *Polnoe sobranie sochinenii.* 14 vols. Moscow: Akademiia Nauk SSSR, 1937–52.

———. *Sobranie sochinenii.* Edited by S. I. Mashinskii and M. B. Khrapchenko. 7 vols. Moscow: Khudozhestvennaia literatura, 1977.

Gray, Thomas. *Poems.* London: J. Dodsley, 1770.

Gregg, Richard. "*A la recherche du nez perdu*: An Inquiry into the Genealogical and Onomastic Origins of 'The Nose.'" *Russian Review* 40 (1981): 365–77.

Griffiths, Frederick T., and Stanley J. Rabinowitz. *Novel Epics: Gogol, Dostoevsky, and National Narrative.* Evanston, Ill.: Northwestern University Press, 1990.

Grimm, G. G. "Proekt Parka Bezborodko v Moskve (Materialy k izucheniiu tvorchestva N. A. L'vova)." *AN SSSR. Soobshcheniia Instituta istorii iskusstv* 4–5 (1954): 107–35.

Guillén, Claudio. *Literature as System: Essays toward the Theory of Literary History.* Princeton, N.J.: Princeton University Press, 1971.

Gukovskii, G. A. *Pushkin i russkie romantiki*. Moscow: Khudozhestvennaia literatura, 1965.

Heldt, Barbara. "*Dead Souls*: Without Naming Names." In *Nikolay Gogol: Text and Context*, edited by Jane Grayson and Faith Wigzell. New York: St. Martin's Press, 1989.

Herder, Johann Gottfried. *Mysli, otnosiashchiesia k filosoficheskoi istorii chelovechestva, po razumeniiu i nachertaniiu Gerdera*. St. Petersburg: N. Grech, 1829.

————. *Outlines of a Philosophy of the History of Man*. Translated by T. Churchill. New York: Bergman, 1966 [1800].

————. *Sämtliche Werke*. Edited by Bernhard Suphan. Berlin: Weidmann, 1877–1913.

Hesiod. *The Homeric Hymns and Homerica* (in Greek and English). Translated by Hugh G. Evelyn-White. London: W. Heinemann, 1920.

[Hirschfeld, C. C. L.] "Nekotorie obshchie primechaniia o sadakh." *Ekonomicheskoi magazin, ili sobranie vsiakikh ekonomicheskikh izvestii* . . . , 1787, part 31, no. 53, pp. 3–12; no. 54, pp. 17–25; no. 56, pp. 56–59; no. 57, pp. 65–75.

Horets'kyi, P. I. "Ukraiins'ka leksyka 'Vecheriv na khutori bilia Dikan'ky' M. V. Hoholia i ukraiins'ka leksykohrafiia pershykh desiatyrits XIX st." *Leksykohrafichnyi biuleten'* 6 (1958): 83–90.

Hussey, Christopher. *The Picturesque: Studies in a Point of View*. London: Frank Cass, 1967.

Ianushkevich, A. S. *Etapy i problemy tvorcheskoi evoliutsii V. A. Zhukovskogo*. Tomsk: Tomskii universitet, 1985.

Iezuitova, R. V. *Zhukovskii i ego vremia*. Leningrad: Nauka, 1989.

Immerwahr, Raymond. "The First Romantic Aesthetics." *Modern Language Quarterly* 21 (1960): 3–26.

"Ioann Miller." *Moskovskii vestnik*, 1827, part 2, pp. 267–82, 389–404.

Kanunova, F. Z., ed. *Biblioteka V. A. Zhukovskogo v Tomske*. 2 vols. Tomsk: Tomskii universitet, 1978–84.

Karamzin, Nikolai. *Polnoe sobranie stikhotvorenii*. Edited by Iurii M. Lotman. Moscow: Sovetskii pisatel', 1966.

————. *Zapiski starogo moskovskogo zhitelia. Izbrannaia proza*. Edited by V. B. Murav'ev. Moscow: Moskovskii rabochii, 1986.

Karlinsky, Simon. "Portrait of Gogol as a Word Glutton, with Rabelais, Sterne and Gertrude Stein as Background Figures." *California Slavic Studies* 5 (1970): 169–86.

————. *The Sexual Labyrinth of Nikolai Gogol*. Cambridge, Mass.: Harvard University Press, 1976.

Kazintsev, A. I., and N. A. Kazintseva. "Avtor dvukh poem." In *Gogol': Istoriia i sovremennost'*, edited by V. V. Kozhinov, E. I. Osetrov, and P. G. Palamarchuk. Moscow: Sovetskaia Rossiia, 1985.

Kerényi, Karl. *Hermes der Seelenführer: Das Mythologem vom männlichen Lebensursprung.* Zurich: Rhein-verlag, 1944.

Kermode, Frank. *The Genesis of Secrecy: On the Interpretation of Narrative.* Cambridge, Mass.: Harvard University Press, 1979.

Knight, Richard Payne. *The Landscape: A Didactic Poem.* London: W. Bulmer, 1795.

Kotliarevskii, N. *Dekabristy: kn. A. Odoevskii i A. Bestuzhev.* St. Petersburg: M. M. Stasiulevich, 1907.

Lahti, Katherine. "Artificiality and Nature in Gogol's *Dead Souls*." In *Essays on Gogol: Logos and the Russian Word,* edited by Susanne Fusso and Priscilla Meyer. Evanston, Ill.: Northwestern University Press, 1992.

LeBlanc, Ronald D. *The Russianization of Gil Blas: A Study in Literary Appropriation.* Columbus, Ohio: Slavica, 1986.

Levin, Iu. D. "O russkom poeticheskom perevode v epokhu romantizma." In *Rannie romanticheskie veianiia. Iz istorii mezhdunarodnykh sviazei russkoi literatury,* edited by M. P. Alekseev. Leningrad: Nauka, 1972.

Likhachev, D. S. *Poeziia sadov: K semantike sadovo-parkovykh stilei.* Leningrad: Nauka, 1982.

———. "Sotsial'nye korni tipa Manilova." In *Problemy teorii i istorii literatury,* edited by V. I. Kuleshov, R. M. Samarin, and A. G. Sokolov. Moscow: Moskovskii universitet, 1971.

Linnemann, Eta. *Parables of Jesus: Introduction and Exposition.* Translated by John Sturdy. London: SPCK, 1975.

Lotman, Iurii M. "Khudozhestvennoe prostranstvo v proze Gogolia." In his *V shkole poeticheskogo slova.* Moscow: Prosveshchenie, 1988.

———. "O Khlestakove." In his *V shkole poeticheskogo slova.* Moscow: Prosveshchenie, 1988.

———. "Povest' o kapitane Kopeikine (rekonstruktsiia zamysla i ideino-kompozitsionnaia funktsiia)." *Uchenye zapiski Tartuskogo gosudarstvennogo universiteta* 467 (1979): 39–42.

Maguire, Robert A. "Gogol's 'Confession' as a Fictional Structure." *Ulbandus Review* 2 (1982): 175–90.

Mandelbrot, Benoit B. *The Fractal Geometry of Nature.* San Francisco: W. H. Freeman, 1977.

Mandel'shtam, I. E. *O kharaktere gogolevskogo stilia.* Helsingfors, Finland: Huvudstadsbladet, 1902.

Mann, Iurii V. "O zhanre Mertvykh dush." *Izvestiia Akademii Nauk SSSR, Seriia literatury i iazyka* 31 (1972): 12–16.

———. *Poetika Gogolia.* 2nd ed. Moscow: Khudozhestvennaia literatura, 1988.

———. *Smelost' izobreteniia: Cherty khudozhestvennogo mira Gogolia.* Moscow: Detskaia literatura, 1985.

————. *V poiskakh zhivoi dushi; "Mertvye dushi": Pisatel'—kritika—chitatel'*. Moscow: Kniga, 1984.

[Mason, George.] *Opyt o raspolozhenii sadov. Perevedeno s aglinskogo* [sic] *iazyka*. St. Petersburg: I. K. Shnor, 1778.

Miliukov, P. *Glavnie techeniia russkoi istoricheskoi mysli*. 3rd ed. St. Petersburg: M. V. Aver'ianov, 1913.

Mordovchenko, N. I. *Russkaia kritika pervoi chetverti XIX veka*. Moscow: Akademiia Nauk SSSR, 1959.

Morson, Gary Saul. *Hidden in Plain View: Narrative and Creative Potentials in "War and Peace."* Stanford, Calif.: Stanford University Press, 1987.

Morson, Gary Saul, and Caryl Emerson. *Mikhail Bakhtin: Creation of a Prosaics*. Stanford, Calif.: Stanford University Press, 1990.

[Müller, Johann.] "Neskol'ko pisem Ioanna Millera, istorika Shveitsarii, k Karlu Bonstettenu, drugu ego." *Vestnik Evropy*, August 1810, no. 16, pp. 263–85.

Nabokov, Vladimir. *Nikolai Gogol*. Norfolk, Conn.: New Directions, 1944.

Novalis [Friedrich von Hardenberg]. *Novalis Schriften: Die Werke Friedrich von Hardenbergs*. Edited by Paul Kluckhohn and Richard Samuel. 4 vols. Stuttgart: W. Kohlhammer, 1960.

Ostaf'evskii arkhiv kniazei Viazemskikh. Edited by S. D. Sheremet'ev and V. I. Saitov. 5 vols. St. Petersburg: M. M. Stasiulevich, 1899–1913.

Pavlov, N. M. "Gogol' i slavianofily." *Russkii arkhiv*, 1890, no. 1, pp. 139–52.

Peace, Richard. *The Enigma of Gogol: An Examination of the Writings of N. V. Gogol and Their Place in the Russian Literary Tradition*. Cambridge, Eng.: Cambridge University Press, 1981.

Pedrotti, Louis. "The Architecture of Love in Gogol's 'Rome.'" *California Slavic Studies* 6 (1971): 17–27.

Pletnev, P. A. *Sochineniia i perepiska*, vol. 3. Edited by Ia. Grot. St. Petersburg: Imperatorskaia Akademiia Nauk, 1885.

Pogodin, M. P. "Nechto o nauke." In *Severnye tsvety na 1832 god*. Edited by L. G. Frizman. Moscow: Nauka, 1980.

Polevoi, N. "O sochineniiakh Zhukovskogo." *Moskovskii telegraf*, 1832, no. 19, pp. 354–81; no. 20, pp. 524–48.

Polheim, Karl Konrad. *Die Arabeske: Ansichten und Ideen aus Friedrich Schlegels Poetik*. Munich: Ferdinand Schöningh, 1966.

Price, Uvedale. *Essays on the Picturesque, as Compared with the Sublime and the Beautiful; and on the Use of Studying Pictures for the Purpose of Improving Real Landscape*. 3 vols. London: J. Mawman, 1810 [1794].

Pushkin, Aleksandr Sergeevich. *Sobranie sochinenii*. 10 vols. Edited by D. D. Blagoi, S. M. Bondi, V. V. Vinogradov, and Iu. G. Oksman. Moscow: Khudozhestvennaia literatura, 1959–62.

Putevoditel' po sadu i gorodu Pavlosku [sic], *sostavlennyi P. Shtorkhom. S dve-*

nadtsat'iu vidami, risovannymi s natury V. A. Zhukovskim. . . . St. Petersburg: I. Seleznev, 1843.

Robinson, Sidney K. *Inquiry into the Picturesque.* Chicago: University of
Chicago Press, 1991.

Roosevelt, Priscilla R. "Tatiana's Garden: Noble Sensibilities and Estate
Park Design in the Romantic Era." *Slavic Review* 49 (1990): 335–49.

Rosand, David. "Composition/Decomposition/Recomposition: Notes on
the Fragmentary and the Artistic Process." In *Fragments: Incompletion
and Discontinuity,* edited by Lawrence D. Kritzman. New York: New
York Literary Forum, 1981.

Sadovnik, V. F. "Zametki o Pushkine." *Russkii arkhiv,* 1904, no. 2, pp.
135–63.

Sakharov, V. I. "Zhukovskii v tvorcheskoi biografii Gogolia." In *Zhukovskii
i literatura kontsa XVIII–XIX veka,* edited by V. Iu. Troitskii. Moscow:
Nauka, 1988.

Schlegel, Friedrich. *Friedrich Schlegel, 1794–1802: Seine prosaischen Jugend-
schriften,* edited by J. Minor. 2 vols. Vienna: Carl Konegen, 1882.

Schlözer, August Ludwig von [Shletser]. "Poniatie o vseobshchei Istorii."
Moskovskii vestnik, 1827, part 5, pp. 157–75.

———. *Predstavlenie vseobshchei istorii, sochinennoe Avgustom Liudvigom Shle-
tserom, professorom v Gettinge, perevod s Nemetskogo.* . . . St. Petersburg:
Sviateishii Pravitel'stvuiushchii Sinod, 1809.

Senkovskii, O. I. "Rukopisnaia redaktsiia stat'i o 'Mertvykh dushakh' (s pri-
mechaniiami N. Mordovchenko)." In *N. V. Gogol': Materialy i issledova-
niia,* edited by V. V. Gippius. 2 vols. Ann Arbor, Mich.: Michigan Slavic
Reprint, 1975 [1936].

Shapiro, Gavriel. "Nikolai Gogol' and the Baroque Heritage." *Slavic Review*
45 (1986): 95–104.

Shapiro, Michael, and Marianne Shapiro. *Figuration in Verbal Art.* Princeton, N.J.: Princeton University Press, 1988.

Shklovskii, Viktor [Victor Shklovsky]. "The Literary Genre of *Dead Souls.*"
In N. V. Gogol, *Dead Souls,* edited by George Gibian. New York: Nor-
ton, 1985.

———. *Povesti o proze.* 2 vols. Moscow: Khudozhestvennaia literatura, 1966.

Siniavskii, Andrei [Abram Terts]. *V teni Gogolia.* London: Collins, 1975.

Smirnova, E. A. *Poema Gogolia "Mertvye dushi."* Leningrad: Nauka, 1987.

———. "Zhukovskii i Gogol' (K voprosu o tvorcheskoi preemstvennosti)."
In *Zhukovskii i russkaia kul'tura,* edited by D. S. Likhachev, R. V. Iezuitova, and F. Z. Kanunova. Leningrad: Nauka, 1987.

Smirnova-Chikina, E. S. *Poema N. V. Gogolia "Mertvye dushi": Kommentarii.*
2nd ed. Leningrad: Prosveshchenie, 1974.

Smith, Barbara Herrnstein. *Poetic Closure: A Study of How Poems End*. Chicago: University of Chicago Press, 1968.

Sobel, Ruth. *Gogol's Forgotten Book: Selected Passages and Its Contemporary Readers*. Washington, D.C.: University Press of America, 1981.

Southey, Robert. *Poems*. 2 vols. 2nd ed. Bristol: N. Biggs, 1797–99.

Stepanov, N. L. "Gogolevskaia 'Povest' o kapitane Kopeikine' i ee istochniki." *Izvestiia Akademii Nauk SSSR, Seriia literatury i iazyka* 18 (1959): 43–44.

Stern, Howard. *Gegenbild, Reihenfolge, Sprung: An Essay on Related Figures of Argument in Walter Benjamin*. Bern: Peter Lang, 1982.

Sterne, Laurence. *The Life and Opinions of Tristram Shandy, Gentleman*. Edited by Graham Petrie. Harmondsworth, Eng.: Penguin, 1967.

Stillman, Leon. "The 'All-Seeing Eye' in Gogol." In *Gogol from the Twentieth Century: Eleven Essays*, edited by Robert A. Maguire. Princeton, N.J.: Princeton University Press, 1974.

Szondi, Peter. "Friedrich Schlegel und die romantische Ironie. Mit einem Anhang über Ludwig Tieck." *Euphorion* 47 (1954): 397–411.

Titov, V. A. "Neskol'ko myslei o Zodchestve." *Moskovskii vestnik*, 1827, part 1, pp. 189–200.

Todd, William Mills, III. *Fiction and Society in the Age of Pushkin: Ideology, Institutions, and Narrative*. Cambridge, Mass.: Harvard University Press, 1986.

Toporov, V. N. "Iz issledovanii v oblasti poetiki Zhukovskogo. II. Ob istochnikakh stikhotvoreniia Zhukovskogo 'Nevyrazimoe.'" *Slavica Hierosolymitana* 1 (1977): 39–50.

Tynianov, Iurii. "Arkhaisty i Pushkin." In his *Arkhaisty i novatory*. Ann Arbor, Mich.: Ardis, 1985 [1929].

Vengerov, S. A. *Sobranie sochinenii*, vol. 2. St. Petersburg: Prometei, 1913.

Vergunov, A. P., and V. A. Gorokhov. *Russkie sady i parki*. Moscow: Nauka, 1988.

Veselovskii, A. N. *V. A. Zhukovskii: Poeziia chuvstva i "Serdechnogo voobrazheniia."* St. Petersburg: Imperatorskaia Akademiia Nauk, 1904.

Voropaev, V. A. "Zametki o fol'klornom istochnike gogolevskoi 'Povesti o kapitane Kopeikine.'" *Filologicheskie nauki* 6 (1982): 35–41.

Wackenroder, Wilhelm Heinrich, and Ludwig Tieck. *Herzensergießungen eines kunstliebenden Klosterbruders*. In Wackenroder, *Werke und Briefe*. Berlin: Lambert Schneider, 1938.

Weiskopf, Mikhail. "The Bird Troika and the Chariot of the Soul: Plato and Gogol." In *Essays on Gogol: Logos and the Russian Word*, edited by Susanne Fusso and Priscilla Meyer. Evanston, Ill.: Northwestern University Press, 1992.

White, Hayden. *Metahistory: The Historical Imagination in Nineteenth-Century Europe.* Baltimore, Md.: Johns Hopkins University Press, 1973.

Woodward, James B. *Gogol's "Dead Souls."* Princeton, N.J.: Princeton University Press, 1978.

Woodward, S. "Pro-Creative Disorder in Gogolian Fiction." *Russian Literature* 26 (1989): 297–304.

Young, Edward. *The Complaint; or, Night Thoughts.* Hartford, Eng.: S. Andrus, 1845.

Zholkovsky, Alexander. "Rereading Gogol's Miswritten Book (Notes on *Selected Passages from Correspondence with Friends*)." In *Essays on Gogol: Logos and the Russian Word,* edited by Susanne Fusso and Priscilla Meyer. Evanston, Ill.: Northwestern University Press, 1992.

Zhukovskii, Vasilii Andreevich. *Estetika i kritika.* Edited by F. Z. Kanunova. Moscow: Iskusstvo, 1985.

———. *Izbrannoe.* Edited by I. M. Semenko. Moscow: Pravda, 1986.

———. *Sochineniia.* 6 vols. Edited by P. A. Efremov. St. Petersburg: I. I. Glazunov, 1878.

———. *Sochineniia v proze.* 6th ed. St. Petersburg: Imperatorskaia Akademiia Nauk, 1869.

Index

Library of Congress Cataloging-in-Publication Data

Fusso, Susanne.
   Designing Dead souls : an anatomy of disorder in Gogol / Susanne Fusso.
      p.   cm.
   Includes bibliographical references and index.
   ISBN 0-8047-2049-5 (cloth : acid-free paper)
    1. Gogol, Nikolai Vasil'evich, 1809–1852. Mertvye Dushi.
  I. Title.
PG3332.M43F87   1993
891.73′3—dc20   92-21749
                                                      CIP